ALL THE RIVERS COME TOGETHER

Tracing Family

Glenn Martin lives in Sydney, although he lived in the bush on the far north coast of New South Wales for two decades. He has been a school teacher, a manager of community services organisations, and a commentator on management, business ethics, employment law, and training and development. He has been the editor of publications for management and training professionals and an instructional designer for online learning. He is the author of over twenty books.

ALL THE RIVERS COME TOGETHER

Tracing Family

Glenn Martin

G.P. Martin Publishing

All the Rivers Come Together: Tracing Family
By Glenn Martin

Published 2022 by G.P. Martin Publishing
Website: www.glennmartin.com.au
Contact: info@glennmartin.com.au

Copyright © Glenn Martin 2022
All rights reserved. No part of this publication may be reproduced or transmitted in any form or by any process without the prior written permission of the publisher, except for the inclusion of brief quotations for a review.
Glenn Martin asserts his moral rights as the author of this book.

Book layout and cover design by the author
Typeset in Sitka 11 pt
Printed by Lulu.com

Front cover image by the author. Background – Scottish baptism records from 1780. Image of the author: photo by John O'Connor.

ISBN: 978 0 6488433 4 4 (pbk.)

A catalogue record for this book is available from the National Library of Australia

Maintaining life by earning a living and continuing life by giving birth to the next generation fulfil the fundamental pattern of life. Therefore, the family is still the first form of society.

Hua-Ching Ni

The true drama of human life is the process by which we become individuals, with character, voice, and a worldview.

Carlo Strenger

Couples tie the knot, children come, summers and winters pass, children themselves weave strands. The parents become grey, and watch grandchildren at play. In thirty summers more they will lie entwined with the roots, but their souls will flutter above like birds' wings among the branches.

Glenn Martin

Table of Contents

Introduction 1
    Finding oneself among the ancestors 3
    A glimpse of myself? 8
    Being held in memory 9
    The other family history books 11
    The structure of this book 12
    The end matter 15

Section 1: Self and parents 16
    Introductory notes 17
    "I'll be dead before I'm fifty." 19
    Uncle George: death at the Observatory 21
    Olive Coates's life in four documents 33
    The connection between two brothers 35
    The heirloom tapestries 39

Section 2: Grandparents 44
    Introductory notes 45
    Notes from Orange 46
    Photo of my mother as a baby 55
    A perplexing family photo from 1928 57

Section 3: Great grandparents, paternal (1) 60
    Introductory notes 61
    The artisan ethic 62
    Thomas Martin: a reflection on his wife's death 64
    A map: Martin and Dower ancestors in Cornwall 66

Section 4: Great grandparents, paternal (2) 71
    Introductory notes 72
    Ellen Lewis's children 74
    Upon the death of Edwin Eaglestone, 1916 75
    Morning tea and death certificates..81
    Visiting Sarah Lappan's grave 87
    Margaret Lewis at her mother's grave at Rookwood 92
    Truths about searching for family history 94

Section 5: Great grandparents, maternal (1) 98
    Introductory notes 99
    James Archer: new country and old country 100
    James Archer on the death of his sister Ellen, 1909 102
    The estate of William Archer..104

Section 6: Great grandparents, maternal (2)......................... 112
    Introductory notes 113
    George Briggs Mackie and his brothers 114
    The last one to stay 116
    Alice and Alice – two cousins..120

Section 7: Great great grandparents, paternal (1)................. 132
    Introductory notes 133
    The Pascoe family: Cornish miners in South Australia 134
    William and Elizabeth Dower: a mining family.................138
    The death of mining in the Cornish families 144
    Thomas Pascoe: pioneer farmer in South Australia 148
    The long journey to fulfilment: Thomas Martin................ 153

Section 8: Great great grandparents, paternal (2) 159
    Introductory notes 160
    The two loves of Charles Eaglestone................................... 161

Notes on the Eaglestone family by Rev. Thomas Dand 170
Edward Lewis at Point Puer 175
Edward Lewis: grounds for intercession 183
Sarah Crosby, a desperate spinster 187
A day at the cemetery 195

Section 9: Great great grandparents, maternal (1) 201
Introductory notes 202
Tidying up the record 203
Ellen Welch: unmarried female assisted migrant 206
The romance 209
Emigrants from Ireland: John Neil and Alice Wetherell 215
Addendum to John Neil's story 223
The early life and crimes of William Archer 226

Section 10: Great great grandparents, maternal (2) 231
Introductory notes 232
Alexander Mackie in the workshop, 1872 233
The girl at the wedding 244
Thomas and Frances Bulling come to Victoria 250
Afterword 262

END MATTER 263
Family history (poem) 264
Family tree chart – five generations 265
Profiles of direct ancestors: five generations 266
Other books by Glenn Martin 281

Introduction

Starting from the hard edge, you could argue that we have no need of ancestors. They simply served the purpose of getting us here. There isn't anything that we don't do better than they did. The focus ought to be on the future. If we do well, our children will exceed us. Don't look back.

And in response, someone might plead: "But we are them!" We ought not ignore them, because we come from them, and unless we evolve ourselves consciously, we will simply replicate the worst of what they were, not the best. It is a necessary quest to find the grounds of respect for the ancestors.

Okay, some humility is called for. We know that hubris will lead to our collapse. But it would be good to avoid sentimentality about the past. Life was not better in a hovel.

And yet here we are, having ransacked the world but painted it pretty.

So, if we do collapse, will it be our fault, or the fault of the ancestors?

Why do I delve into family history, that is, my family's history? In the context of this problematic world, it may seem like an irrelevance, a mere pastime, a distraction. Well, because "we are them"! The more of our own past we can see, the broader our perspective on the future can be, which is to say, the broader our perspective can be on the actions that we take now.

Yet there is a personal perspective too. It helps to know your own past – it helps to explain your attitudes, feelings and beliefs.

Some people are in pursuit of a suspected dark story: that uncle, that grandmother, and what they did or what happened to them. I admit to having uncovered secrets, not just unknown things, but things that were deliberately kept secret. And likewise, there have been wonderful surprises. These were not the drivers of my questing, but I have experienced moments of great surprise, sadness, wonder and pride. Yes, when it's family, you can allow yourself pride.

Growing up, this past was like a locked door in my family. There were a few stories, from my parents, but there were no grandparents and only a few broad-brush stories in play – there was a hotel, there was a house painter who had his own business, and maybe all the ancestors came out to Australia from England and Scotland originally. There was said to be a romance between an English lad and a Scottish lass.

I wondered if I could find out if any of these stories were true, or what the truth was. I started tentatively and with modest aims. Does that explain my still beavering away at this work? Perhaps it doesn't. Now I know almost all the direct ancestors back six, and sometimes more, generations. I know where they came from in Britain and Ireland, and what occupations they led.

Does this knowledge influence my life? Does it affect how I see myself?

Yes, I believe it does, immensely. Every time I uncover an ancestor and significant pieces of the story of their life, I understand myself anew. All of that is another mountain stream that flows into the river of me: "All the rivers come together". It changes me as surely as I eat a bowl of soup and that becomes part of me. It is a richer, more complete understanding.

I am not arguing for determinism, or for living within the received confines of tradition. We each have to live our own life. "The true drama of human life is the process by which we become individuals." However, the tree grows from its seed, and in that seed is all of me or you, everything, every possibility. And it goes back to a multitude of sources through DNA – two people, and four, and eight, then sixteen, then thirty-two, and on and on.

Those lives were lived under different conditions – different societies, country-sides, tools and technology, morés, religion. All of those people made decisions and lived out the consequences. They were good, brave, steadfast, foolish, unfortunate, fortunate, and invariably imperfect.

They lived in families, or at the very least, they grew up in families. And what did those families think they were doing – surviving, conquering, serving, ruling, enjoying, improving? Or failing? The family is a vehicle for maintaining life, a safe place in a world that can be harsh and indifferent. A family is the roof over your head, and if it is not that, then it is a sad thing, and the world is that much harder and so, invariably, are you.

Behind the family history quest is the ideal of what a family is. Perhaps the search is a search for evidence of that, or for evidence of different kinds of families to help you make sense of the one you were in, or are in. We bring our idea of what a family is – maybe it's a bond between two people who wrestle with all the tensions of life, and who bring up children, seeking a sensible balance between sternness and indulgence, and hopefully providing sufficient warmth and guidance.

It's not as if we can read books and get a clear idea from that about what a family is, or can be, or should be. It's not a matter of having a theory that we can articulate clearly, with the right abstract words and concepts that interrelate dynamically. It's more a matter of having "stored exemplars" from our experience: knowing people, incidents and episodes that reflect on our conception of family. Which is to say, we learn to be human by living, and we learn what is involved in trying to lead an admirable life in these contexts. What we learn from family history is an extrapolation of this humble matter of observing the families around us.

Finding oneself among the ancestors

One of the key themes of family history these days is finding a person among your ancestors with whom you can relate closely. It might be someone who paints, and you like to paint, or a musician, and you are the musician in your immediate family, or a politician, and you discover a politician in the family tree you didn't know about. Now you can say to people, "I know where I get it from."

This is the theme of the television series, "Who do you think you are?" I do not dispute the allure of this theme. However, the problem is that we have many ancestors – the number doubles with each generation – and it would be surprising if we did not acquire characteristics from several of them. Genetically, we contain traces of all of them.

Accordingly, unless every single one of your ancestors is Irish, it would not ever be true to say you have just discovered you are Irish. For example, among my great great grandparents (we each have sixteen of them), there are three Irish people: one married couple, and another who married an Englishman. Of the other thirteen, four came from Cornwall, six came from the rest of England, and three came from Scotland.

Amidst all the excitement that people express about having discovered their identity, I am bound to be confused. Am I Irish? Am I English? Am I Cornish? Am I Scottish? And I know that for many people, their ancestry is far more complicated than mine is. But when we pursue the facts, it becomes an even more precise matter. Of the three Irish people in my family tree, one was born in Waterford, while the married couple came from Armagh – very different places.

Perhaps I am quibbling, but I don't think so. Why? Because I think that the families of all the people in the fifth generation in my family tree (the great great grandparents) had actually lived in the one spot, give or take twenty miles, for hundreds, if not thousands, of years. You can see an indication of differences in the three Irish people in my family tree: Sarah, from Waterford, was Roman Catholic, from birth until death: she is buried in the old Roman Catholic section at Rookwood.

John and Alice from County Armagh were married in a registry office in Armagh before coming to Australia. Alice was buried as a Presbyterian at Devonshire Street Cemetery (now Central Railway Station) and John was buried at Waverley Cemetery as Church of England. I don't think these two Irish folk were much like Sarah of Waterford.

So, who am I? Who do I think I am? And, is it a concept that evaporates into absurdity? Perhaps I could get my entire body tattooed with a jigsaw puzzle – this bit is for the Martins from Cornwall; next to it is the bit for the Dowers of Cornwall. Over here is Thomas Bulling who was born in Surrey, but he married Frances Maria Jones who was born in Hertfordshire. Mind you, the marriage was in London, and it was 1854; people were getting mobile, further indicated by the fact that Mr and Mrs Bulling emigrated to Melbourne.

The Scots might want to put in their claim for a part of me. They get 18.75%. But, if I am struggling to find some common thread among my ancestors, perhaps it can be found in this: they all knew disenchantment, or they would not have emigrated. What's more, the remarkable thing about my ancestors is that they all emigrated (all sixteen of them) within twenty-three years of each other, the one package of time, between 1838 and 1860. Admittedly three of them journeyed involuntarily – they were convicts. But cosmically you could argue that they did choose, and indeed, they made a life of it in Australia.

Finding oneself is a matter of integrating all of the stories that come from your ancestors. I have many stories. I don't mean stories in the sense that I made them up, I mean stories in the sense that every story is a constellation of facts that convey meaning. I could say I don't yet know what the meaning is, but I think it is something that grows rather than something that solidifies into an object called an 'identity'.

I think that the compass for the exploration of one's family history lies in the perspective one brings. For me it is about four treasures: competency, morality, beauty, and love. I belong to no religion. After the Great Emigration, the ancestors shook out their beliefs in this sun-smitten land and decided to hold the catechisms more loosely. I have relinquished memberships altogether and in the end I have had to cobble together a new synthesis of what is worthwhile in life.

When I look at the ancestors, I can make sense of them in terms of these four qualities: competency, morality, beauty, and love. As artisans they valued being competent – being skilled and able to build, craft, and accomplish projects, and master processes. In parallel, there always seemed to be a commitment to morality, personally held, and perhaps or perhaps not aligned to a religion. I think there was also an unquestioned appreciation of beauty, even when life conditions were difficult or squalid. This has been evident in many ways. And love also is easily inferred by their actions. And these four treasures make for an admirable life, so if one can find them in the past of one's family, one ought to be content.

The stories I have are not of grand public figures or leaders, not the rich or the prominent, but stories about what you would call ordinary people who in some ways were wonderful.

My mother said to me, "I think you are a fourth-generation Australian". She wasn't wrong, and in fact, given that all my ancestors migrated to Australia in a 23-year period, she was remarkably correct. But I think it may take many years, that is, generations, for descendants to settle down in a new place. This is to be understood, if their predecessors had been settled in one place for hundreds of years or more. It feels that way to me. I have been uprooted, in my bones; I have had to rethink everything. The birds that sing now are different from the birds that sang for my great great grandparents.

I have also had to overlay the disruptions in my 'big family' with social and technological change. Things would have been disruptive anyway, and perhaps it is in fact easier to address it when you have the obvious dislocation of bodies across continents, from one end of the world to the other. From an end of the world that saw itself as the centre (Britain), to another that saw itself as the utmost outskirts (the Australian colonies). The physical dislocation makes it easier to countenance the comprehensive mental fracture.

I suppose one entrance into the maze of the family is marriage. One person has a history, of place and biological predecessors, but when one gets married, one teams up with a person of different antecedents. The two become one. And then the children place their stamp on this combining of pasts. It becomes, not just something novel, but something irrevocable. And then there is DNA: the little children bear something of father and mother, and grandfathers and grandmothers, and even Auntie Betsy and Uncle George.

We bring it with us. Is it baggage or a multitude of memories, or even, perhaps mostly, things we don't even know? I think that Helen Archer, born Helen Welch in 1822, gave birth to a child before she came to Australia, and gave that child up to a Roman Catholic orphanage in Glasgow. I think I am the only one who knows this. I don't think she told this story to anyone. And it was only the fluke event of the first United Kingdom Census in 1841 that occurred four weeks before she got onto a ship as a single female domestic servant to go to Australia, that is the reason I know this.

What does it mean that I know this – even without proof that would convince a courtroom (or perhaps it would)? I think about Helen carrying this knowledge all her life, secretly, going to the grave with it, even hoping that the knowledge would die with her. Of course, 'people these days' would treat it all differently, and there would be acceptance and inclusion and forgiveness (if that were deemed necessary), but I am not so sure. I don't have that benign a perception of people in general. That is the danger of family history: it can dig up graves that were all settled.

It's hard to unsettle buried bones. Helen had got used to the image she had created of herself and her position in society. Other people believed that that was the totality. Am I just eroding it, undermining it or worse, fracturing it? Because everyone still has an investment in the created picture. They would be aghast. It is hard to be a family historian.

I didn't set out to be an iconoclast. I have no interest in destroying statues or even illusions. It's just hard when fond ideas prove to be gossamer, blown in the wind. What does one do? Sometimes I have to say what is true, even at the risk of disenchanting folks. I am trying to be diplomatic, tactful. And if all of this was not an issue? I would be rethinking myself, and having respect for what the ancestors endured, endurance seeming to be the only way forward.

What is the same? I think this: that we are surrounded by people who have conceptions about their family, and significant parts of it may be false, but we are subject to the pressure of it. It's as if we have walked into a room full of sleeping dogs and it's hard not to trip over one or more of them. A chorus of critics is sitting in a small stand of tiered seats ready to cry "Alarm!" or "Foul!" as if you were the type of person who is ever-ready to kick sleeping dogs just to wake them up and distress them. You probably like the howls of distressed dogs.

I could let the matter rest. I have choices. The choices spring at me: to accept, reject, attack, avoid or submit to prevailing norms. But none of this matters, because generally the story only arises because there was a question, there was something that did not make sense. There was a gap, or an action without any apparent motive. That is why the stories surface, but then there is no going back.

This is the substance of life. I didn't go looking to be Irish, or English, or Cornish, or Scottish. I am any of them, I am all of them together. I have been looking for people who are some part of me. What was I hoping for? I went looking for the four treasures: competency, morality, beauty and love. Would I find them, would I see them in the throng of people who are my predecessors? Or would they be pedestrian, or wholly tragic, misbegotten, venal, lucky or unlucky?

At the end, I would hope to know them and to understand them better, in some measure. I know my links are tenuous, a whole life that may only be evident in half a dozen documents. For the great great grandparents I have pointed towards, even the people who remembered them have died, the words and images they sustained have faded from our worldly realm. I peep over a high fence. Nevertheless, the intermittent glimpses are remarkable. I promise you that.

So, I have staked out my ground. I am not looking for lost treasure or glory, I am looking for qualities that I admire. How did they face the difficulties of life? How did they blossom or persevere? What is cautionary in their history? And does it satisfy, to learn these odd fragments?

A glimpse of myself?

I hand-drew an Ancestors Chart: two A3 pages taped together: six generations, sixty-two ancestors and me. Now I can think about the question: who am I? Does anything among these people explain me? It is overwhelmingly about artisans: miners, painters, carpenters, stonemasons, a publican, two mining managers.

I have been a schoolteacher and a writer. But, when I was seventeen I had to choose a career, and I chose Engineering instead of Arts. Now I know my father's great grandfather was a Cornish miner who was the manager of a goldmine in Victoria, so I wonder about my choice. Was it in my blood?

But then there is circumstance: my mother's great grandfather (Scottish) was a carpenter working in a goldmine at Collingwood (yes, ridiculous!) when he got killed. His youngest son (my great grandfather) grew up and fled Melbourne and became a house painter in Sydney. My father too was a house painter.

But me? It is still hard to see me on the A3 pages. Then, I was researching Edward Lewis, another of my father's great grandfathers. He was a convict, an ex-child pickpocket in London. After his convict days he became a policeman, and I found depositions he prepared for two court cases. They were cogent reports, and signed with the most beautiful signature, as if he wrote regularly and confidently. My own father's signature was wobbly, an indication that he seldom had occasion to write. This is all I have, just the germ of a connection with an ancestor through the pen.

Being held in memory

Can it make a difference to know your past, to know your ancestors?

Perhaps it means nothing. The fact that so many people explore their ancestry may just be a sign that we live at a time of civilisation where people have the means and the time to delve into it. The past has simply become a pastime. The Romans had their pastimes, and the Victorians. Perhaps it's just a case of idleness giving birth to curiosity, and of course, it's possible that the forebears turn out to be interesting.

Then there are people who have broken links to their past, and it's easy to see that they might feel a special need to mend this break and re-establish their connection to their line. The children who were sent to Australia during the twentieth century with the story (mostly untrue) that they were orphans. The Aboriginal children who were taken from their families and communities over a painfully long period of time, well into my own lifetime, and given a white child's version of opportunity instead of their own life and kin.

For them the past is not a pastime, it is an ache that needs to be nursed. And here we see that knowing your past, your family of origin, is about being held in memory. It seems that those children, where their connection to their own parents and ancestral predecessors has been so clearly and dramatically broken, yearn for it to be mended, and where it can't be mended, at least to know, to be able to hold it in their memory.

For perhaps this is the basis of our relationship to our past – perhaps, regardless of any practical things our parents do or do not do for us, the essential thing they do is to know us, and even just to know of us. And in that sense, they hold us in their memory. We are part of their knowing, a knowing which is so deep it cannot be forgotten.

In the extreme case, even where the parent has abandoned the child, or has been torn away unwillingly, the knowledge is still there, it always remains. Fifty years into the future, the son meets the mother and the mother says, "I always knew this would happen one day". Or the child who last saw her mother when she was four says, "You never forget your mother's face". And even if, in fact, she has forgotten it, because time can be worn thin, there is still a place in her mind for that picture.

In turn, as we grow up, there is a reversal, and we find it is we who are holding the memory of our parents, and all who came before them. We are, we have become, the holders of the past.

But we also live without this knowledge. We live in the present, the insistent present. It is full, it requires our attention. It is the stuff of risk, opportunity, pleasure and pain, loss and gain. We live in a time when things, and even lifestyles, become old-fashioned very quickly. Furniture, clothes and aspirations become accumulations that need to be disposed of on a regular basis. So, what is the point of our predecessors? That's just where we came from. We have even coined a phrase for it: we have 'moved on'. To hang onto the past is to indulge in nostalgia and sentimentality.

In this way we are hurling ourselves into the future, continually buying the new before we have even finished paying for the current version of whatever it is.

Yes, the ideas of nostalgia and sentimentality are valid criticisms. We can recognise instances where we would describe a habit or an attitude in this way. Using the electric kettle you bought thirty years ago because you've always had it may be misdirected attachment. But the all-pervading quest for the new is questionable. It is merely glib rhetoric.

Something as non-exchangeable as a family cannot fall into the category of disposable or irrelevant. Our lives may be a continual succession of shirts and shoes, houses, cars, and even friends, but some things, and some sorts of things, stick. They are not fashion, or even function, but the defining architecture of our lives.

Our freedom is not to deny or ignore our past. Rather, it is to come to see ourselves as unique and powerful and creative, whatever we choose to be on Shakespeare's stage of life. However, the family is the first context in which our life makes sense. I was the first child in my extended family to go to university. Francis and Elizabeth Pascoe were the first people in my family tree to pack up their whole family and take them overseas to Australia, arriving in Adelaide on 3 August 1848.

The past does not need to confine us, but we are defined in relation to it. We can become something other than all the people in our past have ever been, but we always stand in relation to it.

When you have charted the scope and the detail of your family's history, you have set the context for your own life and everything that you have done and everything that has happened in your life has that perspective. It is richer and more complete. As Susan Griffin said, "The history of our family is part of us, and when we hear any secret revealed, our lives are made suddenly clearer to us."[1]

The other family history books

I have written a number of books on family history:
- *A Modest Quest* was about the quest itself, how it started, how it proceeded, the difficulties I faced, and the knowledge that started to open up about my parents' forebears. Most of what I found had not been known to me, and voyaging on, I felt that some things I was finding were not known to anyone still alive.
- *They Went To Australia* was a 'gathering together' book on a particular theme. I got interested in the question about which of my ancestors were the ones who came to Australia, and in what circumstances. I had enough

---

[1] Susan Griffin, *A Chorus of Stones*, Anchor, New York, 1992.

information to tackle it – there were eleven voyages over twenty-three years consisting of single people, couples and entire family groups. I brought it all together as a family-friendly presentation, initially in hard-back. It was visual, and contained a short narrative about each person, couple or family.

- *The Search for Edward Lewis* focused on just two people: Edward Lewis, and Sarah Crosby, the woman he married. I had enough broad context for the 'big family' by now, and I wanted to dive into questions that were more problematic. Edward and Sarah had both been convicts, but there were lots of things I didn't know about Edward. It took me twelve months and over 400 pages to find and tell their tale.
- *No Gold in Melbourne* was another particular story, about a young Scotsman who got a job as a carpenter working in a goldmine in Collingwood in Melbourne in 1863. He was killed, leaving a wife and five children behind. I wondered what the long-term effects on the family were, for example, what the sons did when they grew up, and I explored that.

Even one of my other books has a strong thread of family history: *The Quilt Approach – A Tasmanian Patchwork*. I was in Tasmania looking for traces of Edward and Sarah – which I did find in a general sense. Also, I was curious about a branch of the Archer family that my mother told me we were related to – they were prominent colonialists – and I did visit two Archer properties, both now protected by the National Trust, and met someone from the current generation.

The structure of this book

There are over forty stories in this book. They come from right across my family tree, and from my own lifetime back to the great great grandparents' generation of the early 1800s. I thought it would make sense to divide the stories into groups, but there were many different ways of doing that. Eventually, I decided on ten sections. The divisions are to some extent arbitrary, but it is some kind of order.

Each section contains three to six stories. The sections are as follows.

Section 1: Self and parents

Self: 1950 onwards. Parents: Sydney James Martin (1913-1967), Alma Helen Archer (1923-2017)

Stories: My intent was not to be comprehensive (that's a job for someone else, in a future generation), but to highlight some people and events I thought were significant in the light of the family's history.

Section 2: Grandparents

Father's side: William Thomas Martin (1883-1955), Elizabeth Eaglestone (1882-1957)

Mother's side: Thomas Richard Archer (1886-1936) and Margaret Florence Mackie (1887-1941)

Stories: Again, my aim was not to be comprehensive, but to offer a view into the lives of my grandparents on both my father's side and my mother's side.

Section 3: Great grandparents, paternal (1)

Thomas Martin (1856-1945) and Philippa Dower (1857-1931)

Stories: The great grandparents were the ones who came to Australia, so the stories in sections 3 to 6 contain the perspective that traverses the distance from homes in the British Isles to new homes in Australia. The Martin family came from Cornwall and went to South Australia, and mining was the common occupation.

Section 4: Great grandparents, paternal (2)

Edwin Eaglestone (1858-1916) and Ellen Elizabeth Lewis (1857-1937)

Stories: The Eaglestone family were stonemasons from England, but Ellen Lewis was born of convicts, and it was that difficult period when colonial society was trying to paint over its unpalatable past.

Section 5: Great grandparents, maternal (1)

James Archer (1857-1917) and Alice Neil (1862-1903)

Stories: There was a convict on my mother's side, too, an Archer, and his children were attempting to build up a new life in Australia. Alice, in contrast, had come from northern Irish blood.

Section 6: Great grandparents, maternal (2)

George Briggs Mackie (1863-1926) and Frances Emily Bulling (1865-1934)

Stories: George's father died when George was six months old. His grandparents had brought the whole family from Scotland to Melbourne. And Frances was English. Among a host of siblings and cousins, George had to work out how he was going to live.

Section 7: Great great grandparents, paternal (1)

Thomas Martins (1834-1904) and Mary Ann Williams (1832-1860)

William Dower (1825-1907) and Elizabeth Pascoe (1826-1920)

Stories: The Martin and Dower families were both Cornish, and initially went to South Australia. For miners, the lure of gold was strong, but it would be pursued in a Cornish manner. The dates here tell you that Mary Ann died young. (Martins in Cornwall became Martin in Australia.)

Section 8: Great great grandparents, paternal (2)

Charles Eaglestone (1819-1911) and Hannah Palmer (1830-1890)

Edward Lewis (1829-1897) and Sarah Crosby (1833-1897)

Stories: The lives of the Eaglestone and Lewis families were very different, but for structural reasons they ended up in Section 8 together! But you could say that the lives of both couples contained love and sadness, and I think the former prevailed. Charles Eaglestone was a stonemason from Oxfordshire; Edward and Sarah met as convicts in Hobart Town.

Section 9: Great great grandparents, maternal (1)

William Archer (1813-1894) and Ellen Welch (1822-1912)

John Neill (1825-1891) and Alice Wetherell (1821-1867)

Stories: William had his own story as a convict; Ellen had her own story as an assisted migrant. William and Ellen had an adventurous life together. John and Alice Neil were also assisted migrants, from the north of Ireland, and they made their life in Sydney.

Section 10: Great great grandparents, maternal (2)
Robert Mackie (1832-1863) and Catherine Hood (1832-1900)
Thomas Bulling (1834-1909) and Frances Maria Jones (1832-1890)

Stories: Robert and Catherine met as Scots in Melbourne; Robert was the one who got killed. Thomas and Frances migrated to Melbourne after getting married in London. In the circumstances they encountered, both families established themselves in the colony.

The end matter

At the end of this book there are several items:
- A poem
- A family tree chart of five generations
- A set of profiles for the ancestors in this book
- Other books by Glenn Martin.

Section 1: Self and parents

Self: 1950 onwards.

Parents: Sydney James Martin (1913-1967), Alma Helen Archer (1923-2017)

Introductory notes

The stories in this section are about events affecting my parents and their brothers and sisters. They illustrate some of the odd things that can occur in the life of an ordinary family, such as my mother thinking she would die before she was fifty. This was an odd but heavy burden for a person to carry. I thought she must have had her reasons for the belief, but the reasons only became clear after I began to study family history and put facts together. I never subscribed to her belief, but I still asked myself occasionally: "Should I believe it? Should I worry about it?" It was never a thing that was completely settled for me, even though I grew up in what everyone believed was the age of science, where "old wives' tales" were still a live subject for scorn.

Uncle George's death was something I knew about as a youngster; it was no secret, but it was inexplicable, so I had to put it to one side. When I developed an interest in family history (when I was over sixty), it was quite a wonder to realise I could access the records of the inquest. By this time, all of George's siblings were dead, including my father. It's still a sad story, and as with many stories I uncovered in the Martin family, there was a sense of honour, or honourableness, at the back of it. It seemed to me that he had "done the right thing" by his father, and had hoped to marry, a little later in life, in a traditionally romantic way. It was not to be.

Olive Coates was my father's first wife. Her story is sad for a completely different reason. Hers was a seemingly fated life, marrying, at a young age, a man who was a bigamist. Soon afterwards she married my father, but then she died in her early thirties of acute heart failure. I refuse to reject a connection between the bigamous marriage and her early demise. I think it also casts light on the sadness in my father's life – things that happened for no apparent reason, that were too big to understand, but one must find a way to go on. In the end, he didn't go on; he died of a heart attack at fifty-three.

My father had three brothers. The next eldest to him was William Thomas (he had the same name as his father). My father died at fifty-three, as said, but William Thomas died the very next day. Of course, you can say that was a coincidence, but I think that many people who consider themselves to be of a scientific persuasion are surrounded by a multitude of 'coincidences' that they steadfastly refuse to examine. Just look at it, that's what I say; it's worth having a look at it.

The last piece in this section is about the heirlooms my mother made to pass onto her children and grandchildren. We live in strange times. Some people would consider an heirloom to be a fortuitous chattel, with little or no intrinsic meaning beyond its market value. Some people would attach social pre-eminence to an heirloom: "This is the sword of Sir Henry Dashwood which was given to him personally by the King of the realm." Or suchlike. Accordingly, heirlooms acquire an air of pretension and elitism.

My mother made tapestries which she passed onto her descendants when she died. I think that for her, making the tapestries was a bold act, a defiance of social convention. They represented the idea that one did not have to be a Lord Dashwood to have heirlooms. You could actually invent them yourself if you had the skill. They would mean that you had created something beautiful, worthwhile and lasting – out of nothing.

The stories from this, most recent, period of the family may seem eclectic and incomplete. They are, deliberately so. The tales of this generation are for a later generation to mull over. I am too close to it, and I will not make the judgements about what is significant in that context.

"I'll be dead before I'm fifty."

Next month it will be two years since my mother died. She was ninety-three. The funny thing about it is that she used to believe she would die before she turned fifty. She told us this when we were growing up – there were three of us kids. It is quite disturbing, if you think about it, to have your mother tell you she is going to die. We went to school, we had contact with other kids, so we knew our mother's belief was quite out of the ordinary.

I asked her why she believed this.

"The people in my family just do," she said. "They die before they're fifty."

"Well, like, who?" I said.

"Well, both my parents, for a start," she replied, "and my sister Frances got breast cancer when she was close to fifty, and she nearly died."

This raised a difficult question for us kids. Were we going to die by the time we were fifty? It was like a pronouncement of impending doom.

Of course, there was the other half of the story, dad's family, but there was no joy there. Both of his parents were dead before we were born, or so we had been told. They must have died young too. In fact, we never had any grandparents in our lives. We were told that all of them had died before we were born.

So, what was it like when mum was coming up to fifty? I was still living at home. She was unhappy and she seemed anxious. It was noticeable. She was obviously worried that she was going to die soon. And dad had died when I was sixteen. He had only lasted to fifty-three, which is not much more than fifty. He had a heart attack and left us, in one afternoon. It was a shock and I was numb about it for years.

And yet, the year of mum turning fifty passed, and mum did not die. It was 1973, and the one who was in trouble was not mum, but me. Early in the year, I was on my motor bike and I was hit by a car. My lower right leg was smashed, and I spent most of the year recovering, and mum was there to support me.

It took a year or two, but mum gradually shed the belief she was going to die, and decided that, since she was still alive, she should start living. A few years later she married again, and had twenty years with George before he died. But she kept her determination to live on.

I rang her every Sunday night for years. Then one Sunday night she said, "Victor didn't send me a Christmas card last year. I think he must have died."

Victor was her brother, six years older than her. He was not very communicative, but he always sent her a Christmas card. Mum said it again a few weeks later, and I decided to look for his death on the internet. It had to be possible. And I found him. He had died only one week earlier. I printed out the funeral notice and posted it to her (old-style mail). The next Sunday night she said, "I'm the last one left now." She had outlived all her siblings.

Mum had a fall and broke her femur. I drove up to Lismore Base Hospital, where she had been admitted, and I got there just as she came out of the operating theatre. She was on the trolley with the nurses around her, and she was very groggy, but conscious. She saw me, recognised me, and she looked up at me and said, "You know, I've had a good life." She lived a few months longer before she died, and we put those words on the plaque at the cemetery: "I've had a good life."

So, mum didn't die before she was fifty. She was ninety-three, far outliving the myth. So, I ask, how many instances does it take to create a myth? And the answer is, only two, if they happen to be your own parents.

May 2019; author aged sixty-nine.

Uncle George: death at the Observatory

In August 1961, one of my father's brothers died. The cause of his death was a fractured skull and injury to the brain: that was what was on the death certificate (years later, when I got interested and obtained it). I was eleven when it happened, and I have no memory of hearing about this event at the time. In my teen years I was curious about who all my mother's and father's siblings were, and mum then told me the story about Uncle George, although some of the details she offered were hazy.

Mum said it could have been that he shot himself, or he could have jumped off a building somewhere in Sydney. Either way, it seemed clear that he had committed suicide. He was an older man, that is, well over thirty, and he and a lady had become engaged, but she had broken the engagement off, and he was broken-hearted.

After I heard this story again, later on, other facts seemed to materialise. The Sydney Observatory seemed to be involved, so the idea that he had shot himself waned, and the idea that he had jumped off the Observatory building supplanted it. It is funny how this different story leaked in. It must have come from someone else in the family – a cousin, an uncle or an aunt, or perhaps my mother later remembered it differently.

Relationships in my extended family were not tight. In fact, there were very few people among mum and dad's siblings that we had much to do with while growing up, although mum did keep in touch with her two sisters, and less so with two brothers. As far as my dad was concerned (his name was Sydney, or Sid), there were six siblings and I only knew about two of them while I was growing up, and George was not one of those.

Jumping off the Observatory building to end one's life seemed like an odd thing to do, considering that it is not a tall building. I never visited the Observatory until recently, after I had started doing family history, but you see it on the left when you are driving north out of the city over the Harbour Bridge. It is a squat building which doesn't invite the thought that you would put it on your list of possible places to commit suicide.

I went to The Gap recently, which is the cliff at Watson Bay on the South Head of Sydney Harbour which has attracted many people as the place to end their lives. My visit was not intentional; I was visiting a friend nearby and I had half an hour to pass beforehand. I was attracted first by the lighthouse, a beautiful building designed by the talented convict Francis Greenway, but then I walked along the clifftop and found myself at the spot which is called The Gap.

I knew about The Gap when I was growing up. Everyone knew about The Gap, and occasionally we would read in the newspaper that someone else had killed him or herself there. In that sense we all shared in the sorrow.

So, when I found myself on the spot, I saw the near things, like the fence, which was tall enough for me to just peep over the top, and I saw the signs inviting people in distress to call Lifeline, and I saw a bunch of artificial flowers tied to the fence. But then I saw the edge of the cliff, and the sea beyond, and the sea was moving and sighing; the different blues of the water were shifting around moodily but impassively.

The edge of the cliff was so clean, the rock making a stark edge of it, and you cannot see below, where you would land if you jumped. It was out of sight. Once you threw yourself into the air, you would be gone in a second to the world behind you. There would only be the distant sound of the waves hitting the rocks that would remain to connect you to your former life. There would only be the brief soft sound of your body hitting the rocks, and then nothing.

Accordingly, I wondered all the more about Uncle George, and what had happened that day in August 1961 at the Sydney Observatory.

I perused his death certificate again. He is my father's brother, two years younger than my father. George was born in 1915 at Sans Souci in Sydney. The family seemed to have moved around quite a bit, in the same inner south area of Sydney, judging by the addresses on the birth certificates of the various children.

The death certificate does not tell you how George died. It simply gives you the direct cause of death: "Fractured skull and injury to the brain". The only clue as to untoward circumstances is that a Coronial Inquest was held into his death, conducted by J.L. Craddock. The death certificate gives George's marital status as "Bachelor". His age? Forty-five years. The informant for the certificate was "N. Martin". This was Norman Martin, who was the eldest child, seven years older than George.

I made my first visit to the Observatory. I walked right down Kent Street towards the Harbour Bridge, where all the buildings are old, mostly two-storey tenement buildings built before 1900. I walked along Argyle Street and then up Watson Street. There is a sandstone cliff above you on the right, with a tall steel fence on top, vertical railings and pickets along the top of it. When you turn towards the Observatory, you walk up through a park dominated by giant Moreton Bay fig trees.

On the day I was there, several school groups were in the park, a prelude to their educational trip into the Observatory. There were other people sitting on the grass, looking at the view of the harbour, the boats, and the bridge. It is the kind of place that is an interlude, a place to rest, to take respite and enjoy the beauty. People walk their dogs, or they bring a picnic blanket and food in containers.

The Observatory itself is lovely, an exquisite building of sandstone blocks with small rooms inside designed for scientific purposes, fathoming the stars and their meaning. The artefacts are mostly pre-1900 brass and glass instruments, beautiful in themselves. The building has a squat tower, where only staff can go, but if you were determined, you could probably get by and get up to the top. But again, the top is not far from the ground. You would be most likely to get hurt if you fell; you would probably break bones, but you would still be alive. It would turn out to be an embarrassment rather than a final act.

When I had finished looking around, I went up to the reception desk and asked my question of the two young ladies holding the post. I said that my question did not concern astronomy, and nor did it concern the history of the Observatory, except in a narrow sense. I was interested in whether there might be any record of an event that occurred in August 1961, when a man committed suicide by jumping off the building.

I am sure they had not been asked this question before. I explained that I was studying my family's history, and that this man was my father's brother. Understandably, they did not know anything of the sort, but they did undertake to make enquiries. They were keen to uncover a mystery, and indeed, that is part of the ethos of the place, although the mysteries are generally more distant.

I heard back from them a few days later. They emailed me to say they had searched, but they had not found anything. It was good of them to look. But I realised now that I needed to follow up on what was available anyway. The next step was to obtain the report of the Coroner's inquest. It was held by State Archives out at Kingswood, west of Sydney.

This is what I discovered in the report of the Coroner. Uncle George did not jump off the top of the Observatory building, but he did sustain his injuries in the vicinity. He was found on the roadway in Watson Street about 8:15 on the morning of Friday 11th August with blood streaming from his head, his nose and his mouth. An ambulance was called, and the police. He was taken to Sydney Hospital, where doctors made efforts to save him, but his injuries were too great, and he passed away about 2:20 the following afternoon.

The policeman who attended the incident, Sergeant Lorenz, went up to the park above Watson Street and looked along the steel, spiked fence and found some threads of clothing at one point on the spikes. Uncle George's trousers were torn, and the threads matched. Uncle George also sustained a compound fracture of the femur.

I spoke to a person whose work included dealing with people who were suicidal. She said that people who are about to commit suicide often have second thoughts at the last moment, and try to back away from what they are doing. Sometimes it is too late; they have already set things in motion and there is no going back.

In the movie "Begin Again", appropriately, at the beginning, a girl stands on the subway station platform, contemplating jumping in front of the train to end her life. As it turns out, she doesn't. Instead, she writes a song about it, and this is the beginning of her "beginning again". In the words of the song, she asks herself, "Are you ready to take a step you can't take back?"

I wonder about what happened in that moment when George climbed the fence. At The Gap, you take a step and you are gone. Or you take a leap, and you certainly can't take it back. It is so clean. But George climbs a fence, and it is not so very far to the bottom, to the road below. It is no more than thirty feet. And he tears his trousers, suggesting that he fumbled and perhaps lost his grip, and his balance. And who is to say that in that moment he was not having second thoughts? So he falls, awkwardly, and breaks his femur as well as his skull.

The report of the inquest includes statements from Norm Martin and from a work colleague of George's, Clinton William Trevitt. They are both telling in what they state. Clinton was an assistant chemist for the same employer, Washington Soul Pattinson. He and George had both worked there for the past seven years. George was a storeman. Clinton says:

> He was engaged to be married to a female employee of our firm and this girl died about 12 months ago. Since her death I have noticed a vast difference in the deceased. He became moody and suffered fits of depression during which he refused to talk to anybody. Three days prior to his death he resigned his position for no reason other than the fact he felt he was being persecuted. This was not correct as he was highly regarded by the firm. Although he did not mention that he intended to take his life, I was not surprised when I was told he had done so.

Norm corroborated the evidence about the girl. He said:

> Some 12 months before his death the girl to whom he was engaged died. Since then I noticed deceased suffered from fits of depression. He didn't speak much to me on that score, but I learned from the other members of the family that he was most upset about the death of his fiancée.

(I find it sad that family and friends are reduced to talking about "the deceased" in a legal environment, when the deceased is their brother, or work mate, or simply "George".)

One of the members of the family would have been Thelma, a younger sister, five years younger than my father. Thelma was entered in the hospital records as the next of kin. And the girl did not break off the engagement, as mum had thought; she had died.

I asked my sister what she knew of George's death. She knew more than I did. (She is older than me.) She remembered that dad had to go to help identify George's body at the hospital, and that he came home with a suitcase of George's clothes, which mum sorted through and gave to one of the charities. Perhaps she mended the trousers, for she was a dressmaker.

Norm's statement says that he was the one who identified the body of George, but I don't doubt that my father was there too.

I have also spoken to a member of the family who grew up in contact with George. She is a second cousin of mine, and George used to visit her grandmother (on the Martin side of her family) – George's aunty by marriage. She remembered that Georgie used to come to visit Nanna Martin, as drunk as a skunk, and he would yell out, "Here I come. Are you home, Mrs Martin?" and all the kids would laugh, as you could hear him coming for miles.

This second cousin knew that Georgie was unmarried and he lived with his father. What she knew of his death was this version: George committed suicide after the woman he wanted to marry died. He jumped off the Observatory Tower in Sydney.

Can we say for certain that George committed suicide? We can say, at the least, that he had suicidal thoughts. It's hard to find another explanation for him climbing over the fence at the top of the small cliff above Watson Street. He wasn't, for example, a youth on a dare from his mates. But was he drunk? The policeman who attended the scene did not mention so, and nor did the report from the hospital, so that seems to be ruled out.

I think through the last week of his life. He resigned from his job three days before he jumped or fell from the fence. The eleventh of August 1961 was a Friday, so he must have gone to work on Monday and put in his resignation with immediate effect. On Tuesday, Wednesday and Thursday he wanders around the city in a state of despair, stewing in the emptiness of his predicament, and increasingly heavy with the fatigue of not sleeping. He is a man who was thwarted just when he thought that his life was going to turn for the better. He has borne it in silence for twelve months. The sadness does not change. It will not change.

Did the Observatory have some significance to him? Was it a place where he had gone with the lady from work? Had he proposed to her there? But I don't think that was it. His first intention is likely to have been to jump off the Sydney Harbour Bridge. Maybe he found that it was too difficult to get access up onto the bridge. Hence, he found himself in the vicinity of the Observatory.

And suddenly there is a link between The Gap and the scene of George's death – Watson Street and Watson Bay. George walks away from the Sydney Harbour Bridge, giving up on the possibility of getting access to the dramatically high arch of the thing. He finds himself walking up Watson Street and, looking at the street sign he sees the word, 'Watson' and immediately thinks of Watson Bay and The Gap. But he is here, not there; he must make do. This must be the moment, otherwise he will face a growing mountain of miserable years drinking himself into oblivion. Perhaps there is some residual honour in leaving this way instead.

There are different ways you can end your life, and each of them is symbolic. You can shoot yourself, and that is directly violent. It suggests self-hate. You can slash your wrists, and let your life drain away. You can poison yourself, and that seems to say, 'Life has become poisonous to me'. And you can jump off a height, and that suggests that there is no one who will catch you, with the inference that no one (God or human) cares.

At The Gap, there was a man who lived over the road from the spot for three decades, and he became famous for saving people from jumping. If he saw someone in apparent distress, he would go and talk to them, often beginning with the words, "Can I help you in some way?", and then he would invite them back to his home for a cup of tea. In a way, he was catching them before they fell.

In the movie, "Saving Mister Banks", there is a point where the wife of Mister Banks gives up hope and walks out into the night to end her life. The daughter is about nine, and she follows her mother. The mother wades into a swift-moving stream, and the daughter follows her. The daughter succeeds in pulling her back and the episode ends well. The audience knows it is not the physical strength of the daughter that prevailed, but the fact that the daughter was, in her actions, saying to her mother, "I love you; I help you". It is her spirit that calls her mother back. (The daughter grew up and went on to write the "Mary Poppins" stories.)

Nobody caught George as he fell. No one could save him. In Norm's testimony to the inquest, he said he had seen him the Saturday before, the Saturday prior to that and at various times. From what Norm said about himself and other members of the family being aware of a problem after George's fiancée died, we can ask, could anyone have done more to help him?

We like to think, in our own day, that we are more aware of the thoughts that may lead to suicide among our fellow humans, and that we are generally better at intervening and saving them from that point of self-annihilation. There are posters on the fence at The Gap advertising the services of Lifeline. Barriers to prevent suicide have been erected on the Sydney Harbour Bridge. But ultimately, we know that suicide cannot always be headed off. And George's circumstances, as they dominated his mind, were not reversible. He had met a girl who had loved him back and they had committed to be betrothed. He had hoped to spend the rest of his life with her, and now she was dead.

He was in his forties and he was unlikely to meet any other lady who would want to marry him. He would not talk to anyone in his family about it. What was there to say? They knew the background; George had lived with his father, William Thomas Martin. All the other siblings were married. There was no mother, and perhaps George did not even know where she had gone. Perhaps he did not even remember that she had disappeared when he was just five.

Thelma, his younger sister, the one who was named as his next of kin at the hospital, was told that her mother had died. Frances, who was only a baby at the time, was told that when she was born her mother got a blood clot and the end result was that her mother was left in a vegetable state and had to be institutionalised.

At that time, most of the six children had been farmed out to relatives – grandparents, aunts and uncles – and were brought up by them. My father Sid was sent to live with Uncle Paul and Aunty Maud. All the children grew up and got married and started their own families, except for George; he ended up living with his father, just the two of them, as the father got older. The father died in 1955, aged seventy-two. He was buried in Woronora Cemetery, in the grave of his own parents.

The truth was, George's mother was still alive, even then in 1955, but she was a long way away. She had had a breakdown after the last child, Frances, was born, and she ended up in a mental institution, and never came out. She spent ten years at Callan Park in Sydney, and then was sent out to Orange, to the new Bloomfield Hospital. She died in 1957.

The family member with whom the hospital made contact to break the news about the death was George, because he was the one who had been living with his father. He got in contact with Norm, as the oldest child, and Norm attended the funeral at Orange alone. In writing back to the hospital, George said, "The last time I seen my mother was when I was about six years of age".

Perhaps, between them, George and Norm had borne the burden of knowledge alone. Perhaps that was the way of things, to be silent, and to harbour nobly the dark truths.

There must have been some arrangement among all of William Thomas's children about his estate, because his will gave all of the estate to George. There was no real estate but there was a sum of money, two hundred pounds, and ten shares in an engineering company which were worth two pounds each. My mother told us one other thing about the death of George. She told us that sorting out George's affairs was a bit messy, because he owned a block of land up in the Blue Mountains. The rates on it had not been paid for several years. In the end, the block of land was given to the Council in settlement of the rates debt.

George must have used the two hundred pounds he received upon his father's death to buy the block of land. It must have been a dream, wrapped up in the idea of marrying a lady and moving up to live in the crisp air of the mountains in the company of the lady. And then the lady had appeared, so close to him, at work, and it seemed so right, a gift in return for the years of companionship he had rendered to his father. But then the lady had died, such an awful thing, and the dream was turned upside down.

George died on Saturday, the day following his fall. The funeral was held on Wednesday, the sixteenth of August, at the Crematorium at Rookwood. His plaque is in one of the memorial walls at Rookwood. It says, "In memory of our beloved brother". The service was conducted by the Reverend J.R. Le Huray of the Church of England. It is, in fact, only about twenty metres away from where my father's plaque is situated, another man who died young, in 1967, aged only fifty-three. He had a heart attack.

In the end, the Coroner did not use the word "suicide" in his report. The page of the report is curious. What was originally typed is the phrase: he "died from fractured skull and injury to the brain accidentally received by him", but then the word "accidentally" has been ruled out and initialled by the Coroner, and the rest of the sentence reads "...when he jumped from the fence at Observatory Park to the ground in Watson Street, Millers Point whilst in a mentally depressed state of mind."

So, the Coroner uses the essential word "jumped". He asserts that George's act was intentional. Sergeant Lorenz was a little more circumspect. His statement reads: "There was a large tear in the trouser leg of the deceased indicating to me that he had climbed the fence from the park and had either fallen or jumped to the footpath below."

Sergeant Lorenz would have seen the angles that the limbs made on the ground and made his own guess as to what had gone on in the mind of George at the top of the fence moments before he landed on the roadway. The awkwardness suggested that last-moment ambivalence had intervened. The leg had failed to swing itself over the fence neatly, the trouser leg snagged on one of the iron spikes, and that last instant where he might confirm his decision or reconsider it was suddenly gone.

There were no witnesses to what happened, but there was one person who was close – the gardener, Clarence Alexander Bower. Clarence told the inquest that he was working in Observatory Hill Park at about 8:15 am when he saw a man walking through the park and over towards the fence, then he disappeared from view. The land on the hill curves over, so you would lose sight of a man as he neared the fence if you were working some distance away. Clarence did comment to the Coroner that as the man walked past, he turned and looked at him a number of times. There was no one else in the park at the time.

Confucius says, as he often said the thing that was apt, imagine a horse and wagon coming apart. It is like that. At the time, bloody tears flow. He is observing that for some people, things get stuck. They are too much, and the person never finds their way out. The horse of their desire, and the wagon of their circumstances, separate. It is the saddest of things.

But for us, we are here now, not for any real reason that we can thank ourselves for. We have been along passageways, and we have come through. It is axiomatic that we will go on living.

It is symbolic that George died at the Observatory. He had removed himself from the conditions of his life, and the things you would associate with a normal life – work, home and family. The Observatory was not locked into the normal grind of politics, commerce, lust and corruption. The people who worked in the Observatory buildings inhabited a separate world. Their work was a constant, unperturbed endeavour, the pursuit of the science of astronomy. The science was not even of this world, and the only interface with the polity was the comfort of the annual budgetary allocation of funds.

In modern times, weddings occur here. The atmosphere is regarded as ambient, or felicitous. An afternoon wedding is sure to involve white satin wedding gowns and high heels, and often, a white Rolls Royce.

There is a statue in the park of Hans Christian Anderson, the great Danish writer of stories that we say are for children, although we know they are for the child still left in the adult, still hoping.

Uncle George had been the dutiful one, a younger son who had lived with his father who was alone. His mother had been taken into an institution when he was just five. Who knows what he remembered of that? He must have known terror in those young days. But his father kept the home and managed what of his children he could. The others were farmed out to other relatives. One does not hear of the judgements and provisions of governmental agencies in those days. And this is not even to say that the people at the hospital at Orange were unkind. Even the designers of the hospital had the best of intentions.

When you are up high in the Observatory building, up in the dome where the telescope scans the skies, you can turn the instrument down towards the earth, and see humans come into focus. It is disconcerting, especially as the people appear upside down. But the telescope was not pointing down on that day, and Uncle George did not come into focus. It was a new moon as well, so there was nothing to be seen of that. If you had pointed the telescope at the fence, there would have been nothing to see except for a very brief moment at around 8:15 am.

My father died young, while I was still a youth. I don't know what he knew, I don't know what he thought, I don't know what he felt. He was a quiet man. I guess that he had the capacity to bear things. And then again, perhaps not. Keep your horse and wagon intact.

Image: Sydney Observatory

Olive Coates's life in four documents

Olive Coates was my father's first wife; our mother was the second. Olive had died young. Dad and Olive had two children together. After her death, Olive's sister, Doris, looked after them. She and her husband Wally could not have children of their own. The children grew up with them, and dad married mum.

Something extraordinary had happened in Olive's life. Her story can be told using just four documents.

Document 1: The marriage certificate from when my father married Olive Coates. The wedding took place at St Fiacre's Roman Catholic Church, Leichhardt. My father was a bachelor, just twenty-one years old. The church was a bit unusual, given that my father's family were Methodist. Olive was young as well, twenty-four, but she had been married before; she was a "Divorced Petitioner".

I knew Catholics did not entertain divorce, particularly in 1935. I had to find Olive's first marriage. It was in 1933, just two years earlier.

Document 2: The marriage certificate for Olive's first marriage. The wedding took place at St Fiacre's, the same church. Her betrothed's name was Jamieson Du Barry. What kind of a name is that? Even at first glance, I thought it was a preposterous name. Later, from a newspaper, I learned that this had been a double wedding, with Olive's sister, Doris.

Two months after the wedding, Olive discovered he was a bigamist, and he had in fact been married twice before. Du Barry was not his real family name; nor was Jamieson his real given name. His real name was Horace Waller, a migrant from Yorkshire, who had come out to Australia by himself.

Document 3: The third document could be one of the police or court records about this scandalous man, or the newspaper reports about his trial and sentence to one year's hard labour. The newspaper reports are most illustrative of the nature of Horace's conduct and the social context in which it occurred. The Sydney publication at the time with the greatest penchant for the salacious was the *Truth*. Not content with one headline, it had three: "Cad wrecks three joyous lives", "Bigamist gaoled for a year" and "Plausible scoundrel". It described Waller as "bumptious and vain".

Document 4: Olive's death certificate. She died in 1943 of acute heart failure. So what? It was ten years later. But what happened to the other two women Horace married? The second one, Marjorie, got married again and lived a long life. She was a country girl invested with resilience. But Lily, the first wife, died of heart failure soon after Horace was exposed, even before the trial took place. She was just twenty-one. One imagines her being pursued by journalists looking for a sensational story, particularly if the unfortunate brides were young and pretty, and Lily being mortified.

I think Olive was initially feisty, but her name was kept out of the newspapers too, one assumes, by protective parents. She recovered her balance, met my father and went straight back to the same church to get married properly. But I think, over the years, the experience ate away at her, her innocence and trust having been bitterly compromised by a smooth talker, a superficial charmer. It was an experience she would never live down. A broken heart, acute heart failure, at thirty-two.

The connection between two brothers

Families are, for the most part, ordinary. People are born, they grow up, they meet someone and marry. They have children who grow up, pursue a career, or move somewhere else; and they meet someone and marry. Sometimes they fight and move apart. Sometimes they meet someone else and want something different. Then they marry and have children who grow up, along with the children who were born to someone else, and they get jobs or come to fame or they meet someone.

Occasionally, something stands out. It's unexpected, it wasn't predictable on the basis of the meeting, growing, moving and getting jobs and puttering along. I could argue that for my father's family. I suppose any part of it could be called surprising, given that I knew so little about it. I knew he had some brothers. I knew he had a sister, because she married one of my mother's brothers. I suppose that is not surprising, given that when people are busy meeting, they often run into the sister or brother of the person they are meeting, and then they meet and end up marrying.

I knew my father had an older brother, because our family lived with him up until when I was four. His name was Norm. He had a daughter and no wife; she had gone. And I guess, when I was young, I could see how he and my father looked similar, the same black, tightly curled hair that you couldn't comb. But we never grew up being friends with our cousin. Once we left, moving to a new suburb, we were gone.

Norm married another woman and they moved up to the Central Coast. My father died and later on my mother met and married another man, and they moved up to the Central Coast and my mother met Norm there. That was unexpected. They all had lunch at the bowling club. I suppose they swapped yarns about us children over lunch. All of us children had grown up and left home and got jobs or had early-life crises and met and married someone.

Children would start all over again, without any of the jobs, houses, careers and crises being resolved. They would all just muddle along. The children would also have to muddle. Perhaps moving would solve some of the problems.

My father died when I was sixteen (it was March 1967). It wasn't a long, drawn-out event; it happened one afternoon. He got pains in the chest, mum called the doctor, who came on a house visit on a Saturday, and dad had a heart attack right after the doctor said he would be alright but he should rest. And that was that. No amount of pumping on his chest or doing mouth-to-mouth resuscitation made any difference. I suppose people die in a multitude of ways and at different ages. He was fifty-three.

In the midst of all the drama, messages going here and there from a house that had no phone, children waiting in loungerooms and adults having disconsolate conversations and making more tea, we heard that dad's brother had died the next day. What brother? Not Norm, the older one with whom we had lived, obviously. Another one. He died of cancer. Everybody thought it was strange that two brothers had died within a day of each other.

He was dad's next oldest brother, William Thomas (Bill, I suppose), two years older than dad. I still wasn't quite clear on how many brothers there were; that was a discovery that came much later, when I determined that there were five brothers, although one had died as a baby. There was one younger than dad, George, but he had died six years earlier, by intent. He had met someone, believing that that would lead to marriage, but she had died inopportunely, and he had suffered. He jumped or fell from a stone wall onto a roadway, and within a day had succumbed to his injuries.

My father knew about this; he had been to pick up the clothes his brother would no longer need. It was all that was left. The clothes were parcelled up for charity. The recipients would not know. But the brother who died of cancer? What of him? Had my father had a close connection to him?

They would have grown up together, two years apart. Maybe there was something strong between them. Then I remember that this was not so. Their mother had had a breakdown when my father was seven. The family had been broken up, and my father had been sent to the home of an uncle and aunt. What happened to Bill, the older brother? And what happened to Norm, the oldest one, the one we had lived with? He was twelve; I think he stayed with his father.

Suddenly there is no harmonious rippling through the generations, living, loving, meeting, marrying, pondering one's career. There is a shambles. The younger brother who jumped off the wall had been living with his father. But wasn't he farmed out to aunts and uncles like my father, in 1921? Or did he come back later in adolescence? Did he have a bad time with the foster parents? Did they die? We know that can happen.

There were also two younger sisters; one was just a baby when the breakdown happened. Many years later, I found out that the baby had been taken to a grandmother, her mother's mother, and raised by her. The next sister went to an aunt and uncle and was raised by them. We can't assume that grandparents are being lauded as visitors who are kindly and who bring sweets and presents; sometimes they are busy being de facto parents.

Bill, the brother that died the day after my father, had had throat cancer. That's not really a surprise; so many people smoked after the second world war. I know that my dad smoked when he was young; I suppose his brothers did too. It's surprising that not more family members died this way.

Did any of that family come to my father's funeral? Did any of our family go to Bill's funeral? I know that mum did not go; there was enough grief going on. Then there is the question: would anyone have known anyone else? At this point I think, what a mess! And, on the occasion, would anyone have said anything about their mother and father? They were both dead now (in 1967), but the mother had died in an institution. Norm, the oldest brother, knew: he had gone to her funeral, the only family member.

I guess that what my father and Bill had in common was the knowledge of the breakdown of their mother, and the break-up of the family, and shared ignorance about what and why. There is a relief in death. They both shared in that relief, less than twenty-four hours apart.

I know people hasten to assert: but they did have a happy life, as if to assure themselves against their own personal doubts and feelings of vacuity. And there is truth in that: there is joy in just being alive, whatever the circumstances. But sometimes the circumstances may be felt as both heavy and relentless, with no way out, just as the mother seems to have experienced her thirty-seven years of incarceration.

There was one other connection between my father and Bill, the older brother who died the day after him. It was indirect. The name of Bill's wife was the same name that my wife (of the time) gave to our second daughter. It was an uncommon name, both for their generation and for ours. I did not learn this until many years later. There were no connections between any of the people, no shared stories, no documents where the name could have been read and unwittingly registered in memory. It is not a name that belonged to anyone's forebears. You could say that the confluence of the two names was just a coincidence. Sometimes the rivers run together.

I think about whether my father was separated from his brothers when he went to live with the uncle and aunt, but I have no evidence about this. To the contrary, I think their father had an engineering factory, and both brothers may have been employed in it as young men. Bill's occupation was given as "mill hand" on his death certificate; my father's occupation was given as "storeman" on his first marriage certificate.

Maybe there was a fight between my father and his brother Bill. My father got married when he was twenty-one, to a Roman Catholic girl. My father's family was Methodist, being descendants of Cornish ancestors. Marrying a Roman Catholic might have been an affront to the family. Maybe the two brothers were close, but this put up a wall between them. Maybe the synchronicity of their deaths was a kind of rapprochement.

Mere speculation.

The heirloom tapestries

There is a notion that an heirloom is a precious thing for a family to have. It is a gift from one's forebears. It may carry the meaning of events or people in the past, things that are worth remembering and preserving. An heirloom may also be precious in itself. In any case, the current possessors are fortunate to have it, and they carry the responsibility of taking care of it and then choosing a descendant who will be the steward of it next.

My mother and father got married post-World War Two, when there was still rationing. We lived in the house of my father's oldest brother until I was four. Then mum and dad bought a block of land at Greenacre, in what was then the outskirts of Sydney, a place of scrubby bush. It had a temporary dwelling on it: a one-room fibro building with a lean-to on the side for the bathroom and laundry. We lived in that for five years, mum and dad and us three children, until they were able to get a house built.

The idea of heirlooms was rather remote. We had the rudiments of living – beds, a table and chairs, a little old electric stove, a bath, an ice chest, and a copper out in the yard that you lit a fire under. Concrete tubs in the laundry, a wringer for the clothes, a Hills Hoist in the yard. Chest of drawers, a cupboard for clothes. It would not take long to complete the list of things we owned. There were no heirlooms.

Later in life, mum was able to think of heirlooms. She and dad had built life up from scratch. Too soon, mum had been through the shock of dad dying young, but she had survived and kept the family intact. She gradually acquired small things that she liked – pieces of crockery, a mirror – small things; no fine pieces of furniture, and no precious jewels. And nothing with memory.

Yet, mum had the idea of heirlooms, things that could be passed on, that would be valued, and that would signal that the family itself was a thing of value. Since most of her life was spent creating a home, and her skills were in dressmaking, it made sense that her idea of an heirloom was something that would convey a sense of pride in the home.

Mum then turned her mind to the question of fairness. An heirloom usually comes into the possession of one child, so the others get left out, not even through malice, just by default. The effect is often the same – the other children feel as if they have been left out. She was not going to have this. One suspects that she had observed this dynamic at work in her childhood. She never told any sad stories of this sort, it just seemed that it was a wisdom she had learned, and she was determined not to commit such a mistake herself.

There was also the question of time. In later life, mum had got married again, so she did not have to worry about being the sole bread-winner. She still did dressmaking, but she could gradually turn her time towards other pursuits. She learned cake decorating (one of the ephemeral arts), which she also turned into income by decorating cakes for neighbours' weddings and birthdays. She took up croquet and became a coach and a captain of a team.

And she learned how to make needlepoint tapestries (I have been informed that this is what they are called). She had done knitting and embroidery since she was young, taught by her older sister. She had knitted squares for patchwork quilts. Now she began to purchase patterns and outlines printed onto canvas, and coloured threads to sew onto the canvas to make the picture. The subjects that mum chose were pictures rather than geometric patterns, for example, a peacock on a branch, a cluster of flowers, a swan on a pond, butterflies.

I have been told that this type of work was originally called "Berlin work". It went back to Germany in the early nineteenth century. It was a way that a wider circle of people could create tapestries (modest in size) without having a loom. Printing the outline of the picture or pattern on a canvas enabled amateur embroiderers to create their own works.

The idea spread to Britain, and was popularised through London's Great Exhibition of 1851. The advent of women's magazines also helped, as patterns were published in, or made available through them. The Wikipedia article on Berlin work states that, in the nineteenth century, for the first time in history a significant number of women had leisure time to devote to needlework.

My mother would have been amused by the idea of leisure time, having spent her early married years dressmaking, cleaning, washing clothes for the family by hand, ironing, cooking, and shopping. But there she was in mid-life and with time to learn and enjoy making tapestries (as I will call them).

There was also the idea that this sort of leisure activity had in earlier times been solely the province of middle-class women. I think my mother did not think of herself as middle class; that would have required an attitude of pretension that she had no wish to acquire. She simply seemed grateful that life was now a little easier.

Mum made small tapestries in the beginning, and acquired proficiency. I think that this was when she formulated the idea that these could be passed onto children and grandchildren. Diffidently, she began to refer to them as heirlooms. The pieces became larger.

There were wider scenes: a horse and foal in a meadow; a yacht in a boisterous wind; a snow-covered pastoral scene; a chalet in the alps; a quintessentially English two-storey country cottage surrounded by trees and spring flowers; and a wonderfully bright scene full of flowers and birds, a view across water to a city, and a girl in the foreground with her pinafore blown around by the breeze, holding a parasol.

Over a period of twenty years, she made at least seventeen tapestries. They were displayed on the walls of her home, in every room. On the back of each was a name. She got her husband to type the names onto labels, and stuck them on.

She told me she was specifying the tapestries in her will, and told me I was to distribute them according to the names on the back. They were for us three children, all her eight grandchildren, and her foster-daughter. There would be no fights about who got the heirloom! After her death, I delivered some of them from Sydney, some were picked up, and some went by post to England.

The pieces ranged from small: 170 x 440 mm was the smallest, to larger: 520 x 390 mm. The largest was 820 x 550 mm, hung in her loungeroom. It took her almost a year to complete that one. Every one of them was professionally framed and covered with non-reflective glass, which must have cost her a lot.

The Wikipedia article on Berlin work says that the subjects of the patterns/templates in the nineteenth century included geometric, floral, and pictorial scenes. In England, "sentimental Victorian tastes" dominated. There were also biblical motifs and quotations, and homely messages ("Home Sweet Home"). In retrospect, my mother's choices are just as interesting for what they avoided as much as for what she chose.

Her pictures were primarily England-inspired, with some European influence. There was just one tapestry of an Australian scene, indicated by the gum tree in the foreground, the cattle and creek – and the starker Australian colours.

The subject choices may have been in part determined by the morés of the traditional tapestry world, but I also think my mother had that yearning for England that frequently abides in the bosoms of colonials, even in the third and fourth generations. Her first Australian ancestor, William Archer, was a convict (not that she knew this), but in mid-life he took the family back to England for a few years; then they decided to return to Australia (just as the ex-convict Mary Reibey had done in the 1820s, before she became a businesswoman and one of the founders of the Bank of New South Wales).

The tapestry I have is large, 820 x 550 mm. I call it "Mill and Stream". It adorns a wall in my loungeroom. It is pastoral English (William Archer came from Harpenden in Hertfordshire). It features a pond and millhouse. At the left, a woman is kneeling at the edge of the pond; she seems to be washing clothes. There are ducks on the water, and a boat is moored at the pond's edge. It is in a valley; in the background are fields, hills and stands of trees, and clouds in the sky. The light of the sky reflects off the water.

The millhouse is to the right of the picture. It has a large wooden water-wheel and the wheel is obviously moving – the water is flying off it. It is on the smaller of two adjoining buildings. The second building is much taller. The walls are pale stone, with small vertical windows. The roofs are of reddish-brown tiles. There are two chimneys. When is it situated? My guess: eighteenth century, and used for milling flour.

The scene is bucolic; there is a benign peacefulness about it. For my mother, I think the picture represented a vibrant, stable way of life in nature, and her love of that ideal. I note there is work in it: the woman is washing, the water-wheel is moving, but the ducks are just being ducks, the trees are just being trees, and it is beautiful. I think there is a loving irony in my mother having the woman at the edge of the pond, washing clothes by hand.

When did my mother make the tapestry? Somewhere around 1995.

A person who is more informed than I am about the world of needlepoint embroidery told me that many of the subjects were based on paintings. This particular picture is adapted from a painting by a French painter, François Boucher, called *Le Moulin* (The Mill), 1751, which is now held in the Louvre.

Tapestry by Nell Crowe

(born Alma Helen Archer, 1923; married Sydney James Martin, 1947; married George Crowe 1977; died 2019) Mill and stream, 820 x 550 mm

Section 2: Grandparents

Father's side: William Thomas Martin (1883-1955), Elizabeth Eaglestone (1882-1957)

Mother's side: Thomas Richard Archer (1886-1936) and Margaret Florence Mackie (1887-1941)

Introductory notes

"Notes from Orange" was written at the end of a long quest. It was immensely sad. Elizabeth was my father's mother, and the mental breakdown she had in 1920 was the reason dad was sent, at the age of seven, to his Uncle Paul and Aunty Maud to live. Of course, the mind races to find a solution, or someone to blame. Why did she come unstuck? Was it post-natal depression? Was it the way life was at that time for women generally?

Was it something to do with her own past? She was the granddaughter of two convicts sent to Van Diemen's Land. I read somewhere that there may be signs of their distress that show up in later generations. Do I believe that? Or was it to do with the immediate circumstances of her life, or her relationship with William Thomas Martin?

And would we really deal with it better these days? We have "more effective drugs". Unfortunately, this often means no more than reducing a person to a lethargic melange.

So, this story is an offering. One hopes that sinking oneself into the story, one exercises compassion, and that offers peace to the hungry souls and angry ghosts, and ties up the threads of sadness that have come down to us from her experience.

The other two stories in this section are about photographs, two of them from the 1920s. They were in my mother's oldest photographic album. One is lovely, and it shows my mother as a baby, sitting on her older sister's lap. The other is puzzling, showing three adults in a living room. Are they posed, or does the photo exhibit a resistance to posing for a photo?

Notes from Orange

Elizabeth Hannah Martin was my grandmother – my father's mother. She was born in Balmain on 4 June 1882, the eldest daughter of Edwin and Ellen Eaglestone. She married William Thomas Martin in the Methodist Church at St Peters in 1908. They lived in the inner suburbs of Sydney – St Peters, Rockdale, Arncliffe, Banksia. William was a blacksmith, although I think his was more of a generalist metalworking role.

They had seven children, five boys and two girls, who came in that order. However, five months after the birth of the last child, Elizabeth had a breakdown. She was delusional and ranting. It culminated in her swallowing sheep dip. She was admitted to Callan Park Mental Hospital in February 1921. Although there were a couple of attempts to bring her home over the next twelve months, it did not work out, and she remained in the hospital. The smaller children were farmed out to relatives.

In 1930, a new mental hospital was opened out at Orange (later called Bloomfield), and Elizabeth was transferred there. From this time on, there was little or no contact between her and her family. She remained there until she died, on 1 August 1957, aged seventy-five. She was cremated, and her ashes are at Canobolas Crematorium, Orange. Norman Martin, her eldest son, attended her funeral.

It took a long time for me to piece this story together. No one had talked about it, so information had not been shared. I obtained relevant certificates (births, deaths, marriages), and eventually I was able to obtain Elizabeth's medical records from Callan Park and Bloomfield. Having put the facts together and written it down, I decided to visit Canobolas Crematorium at Orange.

31 July 2015

I drove out from Sydney this morning, a sunny morning that wasn't too cold, not like the cold that brought on the deep falls of snow in the mountains a couple of weeks ago. I stopped off in Bathurst to see my daughter and had morning tea with her.

Then I drove to Orange and found the crematorium, after one failed attempt. First I drove along Lone Pine Avenue, right to the end, but all I found was a row of houses and a stretch of paddocks. But when I consulted Google maps, I found that Lone Pine Avenue runs across the other side of the highway too, so I found the crematorium not far along from the highway on that side.

You enter the driveway and drive up the hill to a car park and the small chapel. At the rear of the building there are two gas bottles and a chimney. At the front there are many small gardens, and plaques everywhere – in the gardens, along the pathways, on mini-walls, on and around a cube-shaped block inside a small pagoda.

As I pulled into the car park, the only other car there was about to leave, and the man asked me if I needed assistance. He said he had been about to leave for lunch. He was happy to come back and open up his office again, next to the chapel. The crematorium opened in 1956, so my grandmother, Elizabeth Hannah Martin, was one of the first people to be cremated there. She died on 1 August 1957, meaning that the anniversary of her death is tomorrow.

He brought out the book, the register with all the names in it, with tabs to mark each letter of the alphabet, and the names in date order within each letter. Elizabeth Martin was right at the top, August 1957, on the "M" page. He allowed me to take a photo of it with my phone, but the light was poor and the picture is very blurry.

I had brought one large native flower with me, a type of waratah, which I asked my daughter to give me from the bunch that I had given her. It seemed appropriate for the flower to pass through her hands that way, Elizabeth's great grand-daughter. The man from the crematorium walked me out to the wall and located the plaque for me before he left.

It is called the Florentine Wall. It is a long oblong-shaped alcove, with walls about seven feet high, roses in the middle space, and a colonnade of cream-coloured pillars down the side that is not enclosed. When you walk down the path towards the wall at the eastern end, she is there in the middle, at about waist height.

Most of the wall is full, of course, with plaques around her commemorating people who died from around 1957 to the 1960s, but there was one place left vacant right next to Elizabeth, so I had a place to put the waratah. Then I took some photos, her and the flower. Fifty-eight years ago she died. The plaque says she was seventy-three, but she was born in 1882, so she was actually sevnty-five.

She was admitted to Callan Park Mental Hospital in February 1920, four months after the birth of her seventh child (her second child had died as an infant). She never went back home. She was at Callan Park until 1930 and then she was transferred to the newly built mental hospital on 600 acres outside of Orange. She remained there until her death; she was thirty-eight when she went into an institution, and she then spent thirty-seven years in custodial care. I am tempted to believe that she died when she did so that the years of her confinement would not exceed the years of her freedom.

On the plaque it says, "Always remembered by family. God bless." When you know that she spent all those years in an institution, far away from her husband, her children and her mother, those words hold much significance: "Always remembered".

Elizabeth's husband died in 1955, two years before her. I wonder if they told her that he had died, and that she had actually outlived him. He is buried at Woronora Cemetery, at Sutherland in Sydney. On his gravestone there is also something significant: the single word, "Married". Despite the fact that they had been separated for thirty-seven years, and I wonder if he even saw her again after she went to Orange. I doubt it.

I have copies of a couple of letters from him to the hospital, which were bundled in with the hospital's records for her, and in one letter he is responding to the hospital's request for him to come and visit, because she is not well, and could even die (this is sometime in the 1940s). But he says, "I am sorry, I cannot come. I do not have the money for the journey, and I cannot get time off from my job." And we know that at this time he was a man in his sixties.

I walked about for a while, not to look at other plaques – I wasn't of a mind to do that – but to take in the place, Elizabeth's "final resting place", on the side of a broad hill looking west, among tall native eucalypts and exotic fir trees.

Another man had driven into the car park, which was empty except for my car, while I had been doing my humble homage to a long-gone soul. He drove a small car and he was in his thirties. He walked up to the same area where I was – the Florentine Wall. He was actually quite close to me, but on the other side of the wall. At first it was quiet, but then I thought I heard him talking quietly. As I was walking around the gardens, I saw him squatting down in front of a plaque. Then he was sitting cross-legged in front of the plaque, and he was weeping. And soon I heard him sobbing. He was sobbing to the plaque.

These plaques, they all look the same, little brass rectangles in the cream-brick wall, neatly spaced on a uniform grid. A wall that is filled in over time. The wall knows that they will come, it expects them. And the plaques do what they can, with their limited capacity to honour the lives of the dead. Their families may offer the name of the deceased, and the date of their death, and embellish it only with a few brief words – "In God's care", or "At peace", or "Loved by her husband and children" or some such.

The man from the crematorium told me that in the days when my grandmother died, the words on the plaque used to be stamped with hand tools – a set of steel letters and numbers, a hammer, and a steady hand.

I wonder why the message does not say "Always remembered by **her** family". That would be the natural expression. Why does it not say "her"? I don't believe it was to save the cost of those letters to be punched by the artisan's hand. I think this was a decision of some torment, and I think it reflects an ethereal status that she attained over those thirty-seven years of absence. She no longer belonged simply to her husband and her children; she assumed wider connections. Her life was an event that caused waves of mystery and fear to flow through the wider family.

In the spirit world, perhaps it was my father who came and sat on the other side of the wall and sobbed. When Elizabeth began raving and screaming that her husband had died, and had lost the sense of how to look after her new baby, and then drank the sheep dip and ended up in the mental hospital, my father was only seven. In the chaos that followed her admission to hospital, he was sent to live with his Uncle Paul (his father's brother) and his wife Auntie Maud. They were only in their twenties and had been married less than a year.

Dad's oldest brother, Norm, was the one who organised the funeral. In finding out all these little things from the hospital records, I realise that Norm was only eleven when the crisis happened and he lost his mother. It was Norm who said that he wanted his mother to be cremated, and he would pay for any additional cost it might entail.

I don't know why he wanted a cremation. I don't know why the ashes weren't brought back to Sydney to be taken to Woronora Cemetery to be with her husband. Perhaps he didn't know that that was an option. Perhaps it was all too difficult to arrange. Perhaps it would have brought back too many terror-ridden memories about something that still wasn't understood. Perhaps it was best that Elizabeth stayed in Orange, although never forgotten.

I was seven at the time of my grandmother's death. I never knew that she had been alive during my lifetime, or that her death had occurred. I thought her death had happened a long time beforehand, before my mother and father were even married. Now it seems strange that we children were not told, but how would it have been explained? It was all so fearful and inexplicable.

But it was "always remembered". My mother told me that when she and dad got married, they went to see a doctor to get his advice on whether there was a genetic problem that could be passed onto their children, that his mother's breakdown could have been a genetic fault that dad carried too. (The doctor assured them that this could not be the case.)

This told me that they did indeed "always remember" Elizabeth and that her madness made them afraid. It also made me wonder if dad held himself responsible in some way for his mother's breakdown, as young children often do when their parents break up, for example.

It was improbable that he carried a fault that would be passed onto his children. He had been married before and had two children already, who were both fine. But then, his wife had died when she was only thirty-two years old, so perhaps he thought he was responsible for her death and he was carrying a bad gene that made awful things happen around him. (I don't know if they knew about genes then, that's a history-of-science question, but they certainly had knowledge of heredity.)

I think that the question of Elizabeth was too big for anyone to handle, and that is why her ashes and her plaque are in Orange, not in Sydney. I can feel the tensions – she is left in Orange, but her children tell her, on the plaque, that she is always remembered. They don't talk about love. How could they? They were all so young when it happened, and they were left behind. The household was broken up, and some of the children were sent elsewhere to live, with whatever relatives would take them in.

The children don't remember her by talking about her when they get married and have families, so the message "Always remembered" is a secret message to her, spoken through the plaque on the hillside in Orange, whispered among the eucalypts, a message left just for her. And there is a wish as well: God bless.

I recognise that there were most likely seething oceans of guilt swirling around among all of those who were "family". There may have been all of the accompanying emotions over time – anger, rejection, helplessness, bewilderment. "I could have done something. I should have done something." All pushed aside in order to "get on with life" and its many duties.

So, I accept the wish at the last, the mere two words – God bless – imprinted with a firm and precise hammer, as the heartfelt wish of a family saddened, a wish for consolation by those who themselves had received little of it.

Days later

After I left Orange, I travelled up to Ballina to visit my mother. I did not tell her where I had been. Nothing would have been served by it. It would have disturbed her, perhaps even angered her. I stayed with my mother for a few days. I had been there at least two days when I realised that I did not have my jacket with me anymore. Where was it? Where had I left it?

I do not often lose things, in fact, so infrequently that I can remember previous occasions. My father died when I was sixteen, and a while after his death my mother asked me if I wanted his corduroy jacket. It was dark green, a few years old, and not a fashion item at all. But I liked it, I think perhaps because he used to wear it when we went together to watch soccer matches on Saturday afternoons when I was younger.

I wore that jacket a lot, and probably had it for about four years when I lost it, unaccountably. I wanted to look for it, but I could not remember where I might have left it. I just had to accept that it was time enough for the jacket to be retired. It had been a comfort to me. I thought, perhaps this is a signifier that it is time to stop grieving, my silent grieving, for my father.

When I bought this current jacket about six years ago, I saw it in the shop and I instantly liked it. And yes, I remembered the old jacket of my father's, with affection. And I wore this jacket a lot, every winter. It had been the natural thing to bring it with me on my trip.

I thought about it for hours – where had I left it? There was only one place – at the motel in Orange. It must have been hanging over the back of the chair when I was writing my account of my visit to the crematorium and the hospital. I must have left it on the back of the chair the next morning, even though it was a chilly morning, crisp and clear, with breath taking shape and hanging in the air before me. And I didn't think of that jacket until I was well gone, many miles gone.

So I had left something behind to honour the life lost and the family that remembered. I shed something, something that signified my father to me. At some point, sadness and bewilderment can be put to rest, and if we are still alive we can reach out to feel peace. Life is about breathing in sunny days and the beauty of blue skies and wind in trees.

When my mother found out I had lost my jacket, she insisted on shopping. We went to shops in Ballina and when that failed, to Lismore. We saw all manner of appalling jackets and inappropriate ones. She kept the pace with her walking stick, her ninety-one years not forestalling her, for the mission must be achieved, to buy a new jacket for her son. But a jacket is not an insignificant purchase, and I held my poise.

Finally, it was the last quality menswear store, and if this failed, she would not have the strength for more. This would be the only expedition. But I still had hope. I shouldn't have worried at all, because the right jacket was there, in the last shop. It was soft and light-coloured, it was made of the best materials, it was warm, and it was cut right. It fitted me as if it had been waiting, and my mother was pleased to use her money for the purchase.

It goes like that. Much sadness, but always a new dawn. I bring the past into my present as my companion. You do not hurt me. I honour you and I stand tall.

2 September 2015

And there's always more to the story. I had dinner with my friend Roselle at the house of one of her neighbours the other night, and Roselle invited me to talk (briefly!) about my investigations into my family history. I mentioned Orange, since it was recent, and it turned out that the guy, Anthony, is the grandson of a lady who worked at Bloomfield Hospital for fifty years – she was a seamstress. She would have had to have had contact with dad's mum at some point. Life is full of surprises.

12 September 2015

Last week I put together a set of slides using images from the crematorium and the hospital at Orange, and selected pieces (medical records and letters) from the hospital records I looked at from State Archives, and sent it to my children and a few friends. I needed to do something to honour my grandmother. That story has been locked up for a long time.

This was my first foray into using the medium of slides to tell a story, using images, artefacts and some text. I am pleased with what it allowed me to do.

I think my grandmother probably didn't have it as bad as it could have been. She could have been tied to a post in a quadrangle for hours, which was common at Parramatta Psychiatric Centre in the 1940s, or heavily drugged with lithium or Largactil, or lobotomised.

Currently, I am not happy with saying that people like my grandmother have a "disease"; I think that is a mask over ignorance.

Anyway, you open your arms wide, and then manage what comes the best you can.

Online at Slideshare: slide set of my grandmother and her time at Orange Mental Hospital:

http://www.slideshare.net/glennmartin9678/elizabeth-martins-death

Image: The remembrance wall at Canobolas Cemetery, Orange

Photo of my mother as a baby

Context
My mother was born in 1923. She did not have many photos of her early life, and there are only a few of her childhood. You can explain this partly because of the time: photos were still an expensive business, and unless your family was well off, you probably couldn't afford to have many photos. Also, my mother was the fifth of six children, and I suppose that, by the time she wanted to have some photos of her childhood, they were mostly gone.

This photo was in my mother's oldest photo album. It is captioned on the back, so the people in the photo are all identified.

Formal analysis
This black-and-white photo shows a group of five children, the youngest being a baby and the eldest about twelve. It is a smallish photo: 107 x 60 mm. It may have been taken with a box brownie camera. The setting is the backyard of a weatherboard house. The yard has mature bushes, somewhat scrappy. The lawn is rough.

The oldest child, a girl, is sitting in a cane chair with the baby on her lap and the others are standing in a group around the chair. There are no adults. It is a sunny but coolish day, as they all (except the baby) seem to be wearing long sleeves. They are all smiling –

sweetly. They are looking to the left of the photographer rather than looking directly at him/her. Who is it they are looking at?

Contextual analysis

This is a photo from my mother's oldest album. On the back it has the date 1924 written in pencil. My mother was born in November 1923 and she looks about six months old here, so it is probably May-June 1924. It is most likely at Meeks Rd, Marrickville, where the family lived for several years.

This is my favourite photo of my mother and her siblings. As the baby, she looks very comfortable on the lap of Frances, her eldest sister (aged twelve). Mum said that Frances was really her mother, meaning it was Frances who always looked after her. When my mother was twelve, her father died; when she was seventeen, her mother died, as I have learned from the certificates I have acquired. Mum told me that when she was about twelve, she went to live with Frances, who was married by then with maybe two daughters (the timing is not quite clear, from what one of the daughters (my cousin) has told me).

This is the only group photo I have of mum and her siblings. There was another child, Jackie, born later. Around the chair are Pearl (nine), Tommy (ten) and Victor (four).

I don't know who took the photo, but the children all seem to be comfortable with the photographer and the photographer's companion. They are relaxed and pleased and seem 'natural'.

Note: My mother died in 2017, so I can't ask her.

A perplexing family photo from 1928

Formal analysis

This black-and-white photograph is very small: 37 x 58 mm. It was probably taken with a box brownie camera. The setting is the living room of a house. Two adults are sitting in cane chairs and a third person is standing behind. The furniture in the room looks old (even for the time), with a sideboard, and pictures are hanging on the walls. The seated woman is looking at the camera with her hands folded in her lap.

The man is not looking at the camera; he is slouching with his chin in one hand and the other hand holding an open book. He is looking down at the book. The standing woman is looking at the camera, more behind the seated man than the woman, but her right hand is resting on the chair behind the seated woman's head. No one is smiling, but the scene does look relaxed.

Contextual analysis

This photo came from my mother's oldest photo album. The date 1928 is pencilled on the back of it. There were only three photos that my mother had from this period; the other photos are ten years or more later. The photo was loose in the album, but the corner tags in the album for a photo of that size suggest that the correct label for the photo is "MUM, DAD, FRANCES".

Accordingly, the man is mum's father, Thomas Richard Archer (aged forty-two in 1928). The woman sitting next to him is his wife, Margaret Florence (forty-one), and the woman standing is Frances, their oldest child (sixteen). My mother was five at this time.

Mum's father died in 1936, when she was twelve; her mother died in 1941, when she was seventeen.

What is the location? In 1928 I think they lived in Meeks Rd, Marrickville. When Thomas died, in 1936, they were living in Gerard St, Marrickville.

What about the children? Thomas and Margaret had six children, and Jackie (the youngest and the last) was born in March 1928, so the photo is after that. Where are the children (ages: fourteen, thirteen, nine, five, and the baby)? Is someone else looking after them? Do we assume it is after dinner?

The photo is perplexing. In the 1920s, photos were still invariably posed, and the subjects are always focused on the camera. Why is the man reading a book and not looking up? He seems indifferent rather than offended, as if he were used to having his photo taken by this photographer.

And what is he reading? It is a foldable book, not hardback. He was a painter; it could be a manual about painting, but it could also be anything else! I think he is still in his painter's gear, and I think those are paint splashes on the legs of the trousers. This would suggest that the photo was taken in the afternoon or early evening.

Why would two chairs be arranged like that, to take a photo of three people, with one person having to stand behind? Who was the photographer?

It seems highly unlikely that the photographer was a child – in 1928, you needed a good slice of money to buy the camera, then you had to have money for consumables: to buy film and get the film developed. Photography had not got to the stage where it was a child's hobby. So, was there an adult who either lived in the household or visited frequently, who could have established this kind of familiar relationship? And whose photographic propensity had got to the stage where it was accepted to the extent of occasional boredom and indifference? In this photo, it looks as if Thomas is tolerating having his photo taken, while the women are being polite and dutiful.

And also, why did the photographer think the photo was worth taking?

I thought George Henry Archer was the man; he was nine years younger than Thomas, and I thought he did not get married until 1929. But, I had the details wrong; he actually got married in 1918, so I assume that the photographer is not him.

Out of Margaret's siblings, there were two living, unmarried brothers in 1928: William Percy Mackie (born 1894, married 1935) and Robert Mackie (born 1903, married 1932). When they did get married, they lived reasonably close to Marrickville: Newtown and Rockdale. Could either of them have been living with the Archer family, or been a frequent visitor? I can't say, but it is certainly possible.

I am afraid the trail runs out here. It just seems as if the photo is part of a project. Someone is recording family for posterity. And it has indeed been preserved and handed down, to amuse us with its perplexity. And my mother thought it was worth putting in her photo album.

I was right about one thing – the possibility of extra members of the houseshold. When I corrected the details in the family tree for George Henry Archer, I discovered that he and his wife had adopted his wife's nephew after the child's mother had died. Families often had extra members of the household, even if the house was already crowded. So, my theory still stands, even if I can't prove it.

Section 3: Great grandparents, paternal (1)

Thomas Martin (1856-1945) and Philippa Dower (1857-1931)

Introductory notes

Thomas and Philippa Martin both had parents who were born in Cornwall. Thomas himself was actually born in Cornwall and came to Australia as a child. Philippa was born in South Australia. They met in Bethanga, Victoria and were married there. They were both from mining families.

The first story in this section is about artisans in my family tree – miners, carpenters, stonemasons and other tradespeople – and the ethic that seems to go with that.

Thomas and Philippa eventually moved from Bethanga to Sydney. The gold had run out, as it often does, and the future seemed to be in the big city. Philippa died in Sydney, but the event was still news in their old diggings. This story is based on the news clipping.

The third story is of a different kind. It presents a map of Cornwall showing where the ancestors of Thomas and Philippa lived. Remarkably, there was no inter-marriage between the two families (Martin and Dower) before Thomas and Philippa met in Bethanga.

The artisan ethic

Going back six generations and more in my family, a common theme seems to be skilled tradespeople, rather than leaders, the powerful or the wealthy. I think my ancestors shared "the artisan ethic". I take that to mean they believed in trade skills, practical experience, commitment to excellence, and honest living. On dad's side, the Martin ancestors were miners from Cornwall, where copper and tin had been mined for thousands of years.

Thomas Martin emigrated to Australia in 1857 with his wife and one child, Thomas (my great grandfather).[2] He travelled around various goldfields for about twenty years. I believe he was gaining knowledge.

Thomas settled at Bethanga (northeast Victoria) and became manager of the goldmine there. Young Thomas had grown up, and father and son worked together. The mine was difficult to work; the gold had to be extracted from quartz.

They eventually solved the problem and made the mine profitable. June Philipp wrote about it in a book.[3] She observed that Thomas the elder and his son worked so closely together that it was often hard to know whether the father or the son had been responsible for an innovation.

When the father died in 1904, a lengthy eulogy appeared in the regional newspaper, praising his work and his character.[4] His gravestone, paid for by the mine employees, has an inscription that ends: "WE LOVED HIM".

When the gold ran out, Thomas the younger had to make the difficult decision to leave Bethanga and move his family to the city and re-establish himself. I am inspired by both men.

---

[2] Passenger list for *Carnatic*, from Plymouth, 24/1/1857, arrived at Port Adelaide, 28/4/1857, The Ships List,
http://www.theshipslist.com/ships/australia/carnatic1857.shtml Accessed 18/10/2021.

[3] June Philipp, *A Poor Man's Diggings: Mining and Community at Bethanga, Victoria, 1875-1912*, Hyland House, Melbourne, 1987.

[4] 'The late Mr Thomas Martin', *Wodonga and Towong Sentinel*, Friday 6 May 1904, p. 3. Retrieved 23/8/2021, from http://nla.gov.au/nla.news-article69544961

Reflection

Across my family tree there are stonemasons, carpenters, painters, dressmakers, publicans and plasterers. In some cases, I can sense the commitment to the ideals of the artisan ethic. With the two Thomas Martins, it is shown clearly in Philipp's book.

I grew up knowing nothing about my father's past, and he died when I was sixteen. But I think the artisan ethic was the unspoken texture of our lives – modest expectations, willingness to work, and not getting ahead at the expense of other people. Now I can look back and recognise these qualities in my father.

Thomas Martin: a reflection on his wife's death

(Told from the perspective of Thomas Martin)

I got a newspaper clipping this week, dated 30 January 1931, from my daughter, Martha. It was from the *Wodonga and Towong Sentinel*.[5] My wife died in January (in Sydney) and the newspaper reported it. Considering it's been fifteen years since we lived at Bethanga or Chiltern, I had to smile. My wife was described as "a well-known district personage". I got a mention too, having been the manager of the Lady Rose mine at Chiltern.

It was really my father who was well-known. He was the manager of the Bethanga goldmine for over twenty-five years,[6] and it was his persistent engineering tinkering that solved the problem of how to extract gold from the local quartz efficiently. Not to be too modest, I did work alongside my father, and I played some part in it too.

The mine finally became profitable. The problem had been tackled by engineers from around the world: France, Germany, America, Great Britain. But dad was the one who figured it out.

He was proud of it too. He said it was the dream of his life. And everyone loved him, because he was also a good man. They called him the "Father of Bethanga". But I suppose I had thirty good years there. That was where I married Philippa, and all our eleven children were born there.

The Lady Rose was never a success. There just wasn't much gold there. We left and came up to Sydney in 1915, to make a new start. I've got an interest in an engineering firm, but I am feeling my age. I was born in Cornwall; I came to Australia as a one-year-old. What would the people at home think of me? I guess I can say I moved to the big city and re-established myself. I must send Martha a thank-you note for the clipping.

---

[5] 'Personal', *Wodonga and Towong Sentinel*, 30 January 1931, p. 3, http://nla.gov.au/nla.news-article69607362 Retrieved 23 August 2021.
[6] 'The Late Mr Thomas Martin', *Wodonga and Towong Sentinel*, 6 May 1904, p. 3, http://nla.gov.au/nla.news-article69544961 Retrieved 23 August 2021.

Reflection

This Thomas Martin is my great grandfather. He was seventy-five at this point, but he lived until 1945, dying when he was close to ninety. When I first started to think about him, I mostly thought about the major disjunction of having to leave a place of mining and move to the city. Mining had been in the Martin family for hundreds, and probably thousands, of years. It must have taken great courage to make the move.

However, then I saw that he had spent a good thirty years at Bethanga, mining, and much of that in collaboration with his father. So, I saw that he had had a good working life there; it wasn't a life of loss. So, I think his attitude, as shown here, is more philosophical, even laconical, and accepting of the way life moves on. And I think that he never lost sight of his roots in Cornwall.

A map: Martin and Dower ancestors in Cornwall

Introduction

When I began family history, I knew nothing about my father's background other than that the family had probably been Methodist, and I was probably fourth-generation Australian-born on his side. (These facts were correct.) My family tree for the Martin family now extends in some cases back to the 1500s; they are natives of west Cornwall, and tin miners as far back as I have records.

Thomas Martin (my great great grandfather, born 1834) emigrated to Australia in 1857 with his wife and family – one son, called Thomas, aged one. The wife died young, but the father remarried and ended up in Bethanga, northern Victoria and became the manager of the gold mine there. His son had grown up and he worked with him. Another Cornish family also moved to Bethanga: William and Elizabeth Dower, and young Thomas married one of their daughters, Philippa.

This is the curiosity: the Martin and Dower families had lived within twenty miles of each other in Cornwall, but before Thomas and Philippa met and married, there had been no inter-marriages between the two families, going back as far as the 1500s. Thus, I have analysed the places of birth and death for the Martin and Dower ancestors and mapped it. I limited this to generations 4 to 8 for convenience (taking myself as Gen-1; Gen-4 is my great grandparents, and Gen-8 is my 5 x great grandparents (early 1700s); Gen-4 and Gen-5 were the generations who came to Australia from Cornwall).

The map and its meaning

The map is of west Cornwall. It has a grid to help in naming places. The relevant places are labelled. Black dots are for Martin places; grey dots are for Dower places.

The places on the map and the instances of Martin and Dower

In the table below, *Martin data* and *Dower data* count the number of instances of births plus deaths of direct ancestors in each place. *Other* refers to scattered instances of towns not named (number is < 3).

Town	Map Ref	Martin data	Dower data
3 Towednack	E4	14	
4 Ludgvan	F4	5	
5 St Ives	D4	7	
6 Phillack	E5	3	
(Other: Martin)		4	
7 Crowan	E7		12
8 Wendron	F7		14
9 Mullion	H7		3
(Other: Dower)			3
Totals		33	32

Data: Counting only people born in Cornwall (not Australia), there are 49 known persons and 12 not known. Of the known persons, 23 are from the Martin side, 26 are from the Dower side.

The table shows the absence of overlap. Among the 'Other', there was one instance of overlap: Martha Chellew (Martin side) and Joseph Pascoe (Dower side) both died at the same town, Penzance, but at separate times, fifty years apart – no connection. The separation between the two families is despite the closeness of the places in distance, eg from Towednack to Wendron is nineteen miles. You could walk this in five to six hours; and much faster by horse. Penzance to St Ives is eight miles. Note, too, that miners sometimes had to walk several miles to work.

The family names exhibit the same absence of overlap. There are no cross-overs before Thomas and Philippa met in Bethanga and married. The ancestral family names are (first five sequentially are given):
- Martin side: Williams, Chellew, Morcom, Roach, Berryman
- Dower side: Pascoe, Walters, Willey, Roberts, Moyle.

Despite the lack of overlap, the occupations and lifestyles of the two branches were very similar. The occupation of the men was tin mining (back as far as I have occupations recorded), and women were also involved, in above-ground processing of the ore; they were called 'bal maidens'.

Neither the Martin nor the Dower men seem to have been involved in other occupations – farming, fishing, seafaring merchants, or clergy or administration.

Tin mining in Cornwall is said to go back over 3,000 years. Thomas Martin (born 1834) was progressive – he was a stationary engine operator in Cornwall; they worked machinery, including pumps that pumped water out of the shafts, and the man-engine that brought men up and down the shafts.

Visiting Cornwall

I visited Cornwall in 2018, starting at Penzance (at F3). From there I went to St Ives – the younger Thomas Martin was born in Street-An-Garrow in 1856. I visited the church at Towednack and its cemetery, which had many Martin family names. I missed Wendron and Crowan because I hadn't done this analysis yet. I went up the coast to Tintagel, the place associated with King Arthur and Merlin. I went to Levant mine (E2) and saw a working beam engine: the type that Thomas Martin (the father) had operated. At Bethanga he was the mine manager.

The guide at Levant said the man-engine kept moving, so the men had to step on and off at the right time. He said they sang songs because it kept you in rhythm.

When I went to the church at Towednack (800 years old), inside there were little cards with copies of the Lord's Prayer in Cornish. Many of the Martin ancestral family names were on the graves at Towednack – Martin(!), Curnow, Berryman, Quick. One grave had an inscription for a young family member who had gone to America in the mid-1800s, gold-mining, and been killed.

Reflection on the history of the Martin and Dower families

It wasn't until I considered the question of what the Martin ancestors would look like on a map that I got clear about the tale it tells – about how people lived so locally but might not be known to each other. The map shows the dynamics of the families' lives. Maybe they married someone from the next village, but twenty miles away was mostly another world. At the same time, there was a way of life that was common to the Martin and Dower folk, with common elements, eg language, singing, mining, religion.

What also became clearer to me was the tension between continuity and change in the 1840s-1850s. The Cornish language had largely died as the spoken language, the steam engine was transforming mining, the railway was on the way. Thomas Martin (the father in my account) had taken on the operation of the beam engine – it was only introduced in Cornwall in the early 1840s – so he was ready for change.

And, of course, both families made the momentous move to Australia; migration had been going on from Cornwall since the late 1700s. The Dower family emigrated in 1848, and the Martin family in 1857, so both families left before tin mining in Cornwall collapsed due to cheaper overseas imports. They left before the railway arrived (1859), which made Cornwall open to mass tourism (a Victorian dream).

I think they left before the old ways atrophied. I have a book of Cornish legends first published in 1856 by Robert Hunt, who collected them by wandering around Cornwall. They indicate a people with respect for the power of nature and a belief in virtue, along with a dry sense of humour.

A book by June Philipp about mining in Bethanga (1987), in which Thomas Martin and his son feature, discusses the community's way of life, their sense of honour, modesty and the way they looked out for each other. I think that the Martin and Dower families embodied this, and that it came as part of them from Cornwall.

References

Atkinson, R.L., *Tin and Tin Mining*, Shire Publications, Botley, Oxford, 1985.

Deacon, Bernard, *The Real World of Poldark: Cornwall 1783-1820*, CoSERG, Redruth, Cornwall, 2021.

Hunt, Robert, *Cornish Legends*, Tor Mark, Redruth, Cornwall, 2017.

Philipp, June, *A Poor Man's Diggings: Mining and Community at Bethanga, Victoria, 1875-1912*, Hyland House, Melbourne, 1987.

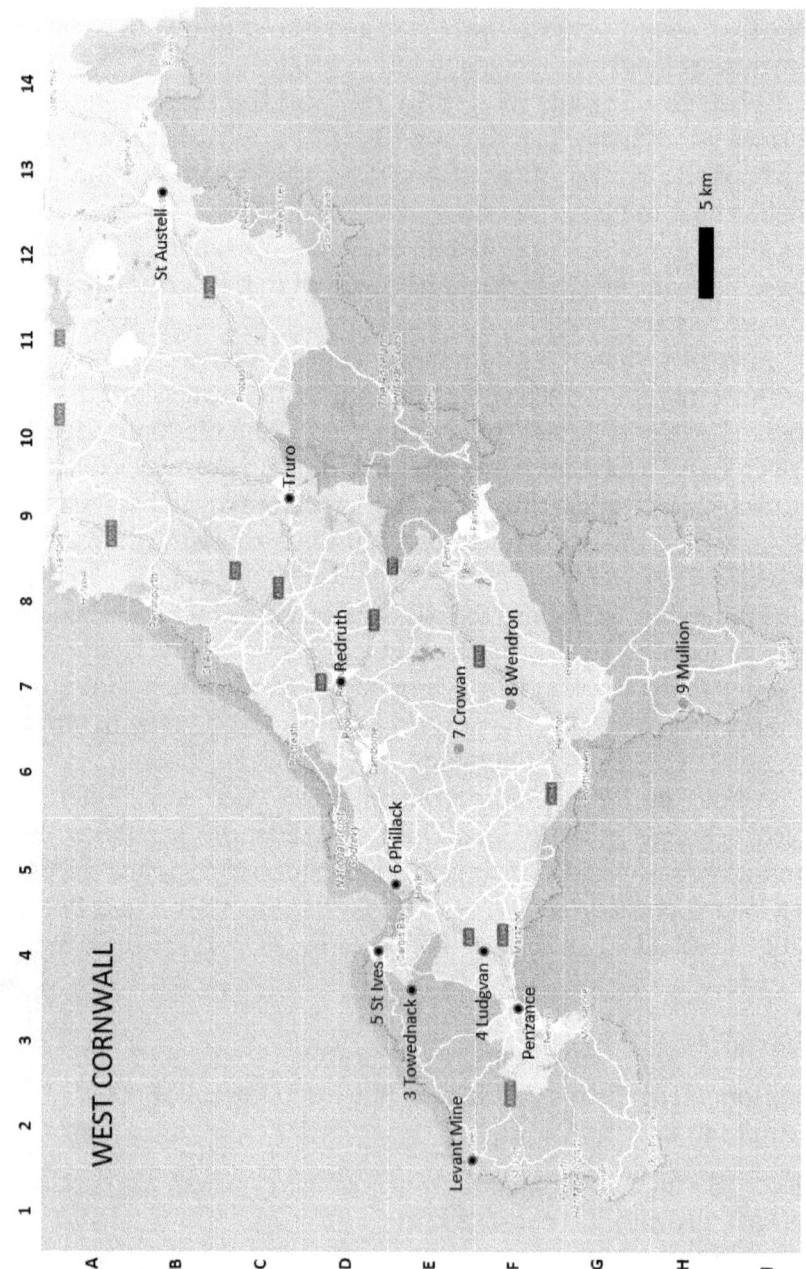

Section 4: Great grandparents, paternal (2)

Edwin Eaglestone (1858-1916) and Ellen Elizabeth Lewis (1857-1937)

Introductory notes

Edwin Eaglestone and Ellen Elizabeth Lewis were both first-generation Australians, if we take that to mean that all of their parents were born elsewhere and migrated here – in England for Edwin, and in England and Ireland for Ellen. Edwin had been born in Oxfordshire and came here aged two; Ellen had been born in Launceston. Her parents had both been convicts.

There are six stories in this section. Edwin and Ellen were establishing themselves as a family in a colonial society which had elements of both vigour and roughness. People were striving for work and money and a new way of life that exhibited a Victorian understanding of culture.

I started to wonder about the generation that follows two convicts, but it can become too easy to see every issue as the result of that past. I think the ordinary business of family life is the foreground – housing, work and income, the relationship between the parents, babies, sickness, bringing up children, deaths. But it's an open question: does having convict parents show in the children's offspring and so on? The first story simply presents all the children of Ellen and their pathways in life.

The second story looks at Edwin's life from the end-point, his death. Through the death certificate, notices in the newspaper, and a visit to the cemetery, much of his life started to become evident. Had he been alone, or was he surrounded by family? What work had he done? Had he moved during his life? Did it all seem satisfying? Bold questions, but interesting answers emerged.

The third story, about morning tea and death certificates, is an imagined conversation between Ellen Eaglestone and her youngest sister, Margaret Leonard. It's a long story because theirs had been complicated lives. This was the generation that had to decide how to memorialise their parents, both in death certificates and at the cemetery. There were choices to be made. Sometimes, we guess that children are ignorant of certain aspects of their parents' lives, so they are wrong about things like when they were born or where they got married. But for this generation, there was a widespread feeling that convict pasts should be buried. Ellen and Margaret's conversation discusses the options they faced.

The fourth story comes from the period when I went searching cemeteries for graves. I realised that gravestones could tell me things that were not on the death certificates. And it became a form of ritual and homage to the ancestors. Sarah Lappan was one of Edwin and Ellen Eaglestone's children. She died young, having given birth to four children.

In the fifth story, Margaret (the youngest of the children of Edward and Sarah Lewis) visits the grave of her mother at Rookwood. She talks to her mother about her father. They were the ones who had both been convicts in Tasmania. Edward became a policeman and detective after his sentence ended. He ran into trouble with people in powerful positions, and then became a legal clerk. I suspect there was a rift between Edward and Sarah, and I suspect that it was because, later in life, Edward went back into the police force. But it seemed as if Edward saw it as his mission. Margaret makes the case for him to the spirit of her mother.

The last story has the grand title, "Truths about searching for family history". It does discuss that proposition, but it does so through the lens of the lives of Ellen and the other of Edward and Sarah's children.

Ellen Lewis's children

Ellen Lewis was my great grandmother (on my father's side) (1857-1937). Her parents had both been convicts in Tasmania. She was the fourth child after twin girls and a boy. The family moved to Sydney. Somehow, Sarah-Ann, the elder twin, met a goldminer from Gulgong (where? in Sydney?). They were married at St Mary's Cathedral. They called their first child Ellen, and in 1875, my Ellen went out to Gulgong to visit them.

During her stay, Ellen became pregnant to an unknown man, and had a baby (at nineteen). She went back to Sydney and the baby got sick and died at six months. Then she met Edwin Eaglestone, a young stonemason working in Lithgow (where? in Sydney?). They got married in Paddington at 'Friendville', a Presbyterian house-church.

Their first child, Charles (named after Edwin's father), died at six months from "hereditary syphilis". Who had syphilis, Ellen or Edwin? Congenital syphilis affects male children more than females. They had three more children, all girls. What happened to these children – Sarah Ellen, Blanche Ellen, and Elizabeth Hannah?

Sarah Ellen grew up, married and had four children, then died at twenty-five, seven months after the birth of her last child. Cause of death: "Incomplete abortive septicaemia".

Blanche Ellen grew up, married and had nine children. She left, there was a divorce; it was messy. She died at sixty-three.

Elizabeth Hannah, the eldest, was my grandmother. She married William Thomas Martin. They had seven children. After the birth of the last child, she had a breakdown and went into Callan Park Asylum. She never came out, dying in 1957 at seventy-five.

The sources

New South Wales Births, Deaths and Marriages: certificates
Tasmanian Names Index (Ellen's parents)
Google eg Friendville; medical websites
New South Wales State Archives: Divorces
Graves at Woronora, Rookwood, and Orange crematorium
New South Wales Health (at State Archives): Medical records for Elizabeth Martin

Upon the death of Edwin Eaglestone, 1916

Edwin Eaglestone is my father's mother's father, so he is a great grandparent of mine. I did not know about him at first. I was filling gaps in a family tree chart, and his name showed up as being a parent of Elizabeth Hannah Eaglestone, my grandmother. I had no other information, and I had no idea how many persons by the name of Edwin Eaglestone there were, in what was still an elastic span of time.

I was conscious of place as well. I certainly didn't blithely assume that the Eaglestones, Edwin and his wife Ellen, had conveniently conducted all of their business (their lives, my business) in New South Wales, although I hoped so. When you are short on skills and experience, you hope. I went searching in Births, Deaths and Marriages. I went looking for deaths (it sounds macabre). What I found seemed to help, but it was both more and less than I hoped for.

There were three entries. The first was the death of Charles Eaglestone in 1881. The parents were Edwin and Ellen. Okay, so they had a child and it died. Information to be examined further. Sadness. Reason?

The next entry was for Edwin Eaglestone's death in 1916. That's the man, isn't it? He would have been fifty-eight (which is fine; that's some kind of life). I obtained the death certificate. He died at Rockdale, and his parents were Charles and Gladys A. He was born in Oxfordshire, England and he was thirty-seven years in the colonies. But he had lived in both Victoria and New South Wales. When had he lived in Victoria? Did he and Ellen go there after the birth of Blanche? Yes, I had found her birth, too; she was born in 1887; she was the youngest child.

Oh, the third record was Ellen, her death in 1937. She was living at Hurstville, and her parents were Edward Lloyd and Sarah Ann – quite correct, as it turned out.

There was a death notice in the newspaper, the *Sydney Morning Herald*, 8 January 1916. For Edwin. In fact, there were six notices. It seems that Edwin was loved or respected, or both. The funeral procession was to leave from his daughter's residence at Rockdale (Blanche) for Woronora Cemetery. (There were three daughters, one of whom had died already.) There was a notice from Mr and Mrs W. Martin of Sans Souci – William Martin had married Edwin and Ellen's daughter Elizabeth.

There was a separate notice from Blanche as Mr and Mrs Royall – Herbert Royall had married her. Mr and Mrs Chalmers inserted a notice as well – Frances was one of Edwin's three sisters; she had married Arthur Chalmers and they lived in Sydney.

Mr and Mrs John Philipson of Leichhardt also inserted a notice. Sarah Ann was Ellen's oldest sister; She was "the responsible one" in their family.

Lastly, there was a notice from the Lodge, the G.U.O.O.F., the Grand United Order of Odd Fellows, a Friendly Society that predated social security, supporting members in adversity through mutual charity. Edwin was a Brother in the Lodge.

The gravestone says: "In loving memory of my dear husband, Edwin Eaglestone, died 7 January 1916, aged 58 Years. May he rest in peace. Erected by his loving wife." One of my sons and I went to the cemetery one day and located the grave. The gravestone was faded sandstone, just over one hundred years old. We struggled to read the words. We took it in turns, and lay on the ground to look at it in the sun's different light, and I had my notebook ready to write down the words.

Another struggle I had was the certificates. Just because I had a certificate (and I had paid for it), it didn't mean it was correct. The death certificate said Edwin's mother was Gladys. That was not even close. Her name was Hannah; I found that out later. 'Gladys' was purely and simply wrong. So, who said it? The informant was Blanche. I wonder: why, how, did she get it so wrong? I have since explored the story of Charles and Hannah, and it is a beautiful story. There is no reason why their story should be mangled. There simply is no Gladys; or rather, the only Gladys is a daughter of one of Edwin's younger sisters. She was therefore a cousin of Blanche's.

One has to think about Blanche now. Was it something that she misheard, or heard in a different context? Was she inclined to mishear things? Was she an adamant kind of person? Did she not think to check with other people? Why was she the informant anyway? She was not the eldest child. Was everyone else too busy with their own lives? Oh, then I realise the question is narrower;

since Sarah was dead (at twenty-five), Elizabeth was the only other sister/sibling. Did Blanche not want to perform this role, but was saddled with the burden?

Then I realise I have to take into account that Edwin seems to have been living at Herbert and Blanche's house. They had five children at the time, so the house must have been crowded. Ellen must have been living there as well. Perhaps in this matter, Blanche and her husband were the responsible ones.

It was good that Edwin was laid to rest with apparent dignity. The gravestone is a loving monument. It shows, after a hundred years. Ellen joined him twenty-one years later. As it goes with these things, the words for her on the gravestone are simple: "Also Ellen Elizabeth, wife of the above. Died 6 June 1937. Aged 78 years".

The death certificate said that Edwin was born in Oxford in England. That was unexpected. It also gave his occupation as stonemason. I think, there is 'stone' in his name. Does that mean that the men in the family had been stonemasons ever since surnames began? Next, I think, stonemasons must generally be fixed in one place rather than itinerant, because stones are heavy to move. Also, one gets used to the types of stone in a particular area, and learns how to select them and work them.

Migration must have been a big move for Edwin, I thought. At this point I thought that he migrated when he was around twenty, based on the information on the death certificate. However, when I finally explored Edwin's parents' lives, I saw that they had emigrated when Edwin was two; Edwin was one of four children at the time. So, yes, it was a big move, but he probably didn't remember much about it.

Charles and Hannah, the parents, went to New Zealand first from England, on the *African* in 1860. They didn't stay long, and ended up in Geelong, where they settled for the rest of their lives. That reinforces my idea that stonemasons don't like to move house much. Charles lived to be very old – ninety-two, but Hannah died when she was sixty, in bizarre circumstances: she died in a February heat-wave in Geelong – an English rose in a harsh country. Apparently this was not an uncommon event at the time, either heat-waves or deaths thereof.

Edwin was not there when his mother died. He had left Geelong as a young man and made his way to Lithgow, across the Blue Mountains in New South Wales, where he got work as a stonemason. There are many stone buildings in and around Lithgow, mainly due to Alexander Binnings, who was recruited to come to Australia in the early 1830s by the Scottish minister, John Dunmore Lang (who is always described as 'fiery').

Binnings worked on buildings in Sydney before moving to Lithgow and establishing himself there. There were many other Scots in the district, due also to the recruitment work of Lang. Binnings was responsible for numerous churches, other public buildings, and private houses, but in the 1870s he was getting older. It would be no surprise if he looked for younger men to take over some of the stone work. The timing would have been right for Edwin to take up work around Lithgow.

Somewhere, either in Lithgow or in Sydney – I haven't fathomed this – Edwin met Ellen, and they got married after only a short acquaintance, it seems, on 30 December 1878. The marriage certificate reveals an oddity – they were married at a place called 'Friendville' at Paddington. Friendville was an initiative of the Presbyterian Church. I think it was what we would call a 'house church'. So many times I have discovered that what I had thought was a 'modern' initiative had been done long ago.

Edwin came from Oxford, and his religion was Church of England. What about Ellen? Her case was not so simple: her mother was Irish, and Roman Catholic, but her father was from Essex and he was Church of England. I suspect that the question of religion was not completely settled in the Lewis household. Perhaps Friendville was a convenient alternative. For the sake of clarity, Edwin and Ellen are buried in the Church of England part of Woronora Cemetery. Records give us but a thin slice of people's lives.

The location of Friendville was also interesting: Paddington. Ellen's family had been living in the inner-city streets – Sussex Street, Kent Street, Bathurst Street. Edwin had not lived in Sydney before. So, Paddington was an odd place for them to hold their wedding. However, I think the clue is in Edwin being a stonemason. I suspect stonemasons tended to network among themselves; I think they were an exalted throng. So, I suspect that Edwin's father had made inquiries in Sydney about work for his son before Edwin packed his bag to leave Geelong. I am sure that Charles's pedigree as a stonemason from England, whose father was a stonemason before him, stood him in good stead.

Aaron Loveridge had been a builder and contractor in Sydney since 1852, and he specialised in stonework. Among his buildings was the St John's Church of England church in Darlinghurst Road, Darlinghurst. The building business was taken over by his son, Thomas Loveridge, and Herbert C. Hudson, in 1882, forming the esteemed firm of Loveridge and Hudson. They were responsible for the sandstone gates of Centennial Park, built around 1883.

This puts Edwin in the right place to be working on the church, and the sandstone gates. Loveridge and Hudson were responsible for many fine stone buildings in Sydney, such as the Bank of Australasia on the corner of Martin Place and George Street, the Great Hall of Sydney University, portions of St. Andrew's Cathedral, and the Museum, the Synagogue and the former AMP building. (This information came from a *Sydney Morning Herald* article on the Jubilee (50 years) of the firm, 12 October 1932.)

The marriage certificate for Edwin and Ellen is also interesting because it asserts that Edwin was born in Victoria. I knew that Edwin had been brought up there, in Geelong, and that he had been only two when he arrived in Geelong, but I also knew that he had been born in Oxford. Ah well, that curtailment was probably just for the sake of simplicity. Naturally I was a little annoyed, because the information was more important to me than it was to Edwin and Ellen at the time.

Edwin had not emigrated when he was twenty, then; he had been only two. His death certificate should have said fifty-seven years in the colonies, not thirty-seven.

However, the marriage certificate did convey some essential facts. Edwin's occupation was stonemason, even at the early age of twenty. Edwin moved to Sydney from Lithgow, and at some point the couple moved into a large, lovely stone house in Norman Street, Balmain. Very appropriate. They stayed here until late in life. One assumes failing health was involved in their move to Blanche's home at Rockdale.

The house in Norman Street is still there (in 2022), as one would expect a well-built stone house to be. Did Edwin build it? Perhaps, or perhaps he supervised other people to build it for them. It has three chimneys and a considerable amount of living space. A solid home suggests a solid family. Alternatively, it suggests a solid façade behind which many pains transpire. Edwin died of an aortic aneurism rupture. Ellen, fourteen years later, died of chronic myocarditis. You could read that, both deaths, as unresolved afflictions of the heart. Or you could say that is mere speculation.

Image: Gravestone of Edwin and Ellen Eaglestone at Woronora Cemetery

Morning tea and death certificates

Ellen Eaglestone and Margaret Leonard, sisters, were having morning tea together. It was Wednesday 30 October 1935, the date chosen because it was one week after Ellen's birthday (her seventy-eighth) and one week before Margaret's birthday (her seventy-fifth). Neither of them was poor, at least at this point in life, but one must be economical with effort in advancing years. Morning tea consisted of good tea: Bushells, of course, served with a dainty tea service, along with a slightly decadent and most delicious cake.

They were at Margaret's house at Mortdale, the house with the name: *Malolo*. It was only three minutes' drive from Ellen's place at Penshurst. Ellen had come by taxi, the driver known to her. Both women were widows. Ellen's husband had died a long time ago, in 1916, but Margaret's husband had died more recently, in 1929.

Ellen said, "You remember when Joseph died? And your son had to complete all those details for the death certificate?"

Margaret remembered, because the past was a delicate commodity. Joseph, her second husband, had been a cartoonist for the *Bulletin* at one stage, and one's public reputation was important. It had not mattered so much with Joseph – his father had been a respectable Congregational Minister in South Australia.

It had not mattered so much with Edwin Eaglestone either. He was a stonemason whose parents had brought their children out from England when he was two. His father, and all the fathers before him, apparently, had been stonemasons in Oxfordshire. Nothing to hide there.

But Ellen and Margaret had more serious matters to consider. Margaret took another sip of her tea, then put the cup down. "Yes, we have to think about this, don't we? One day we are both going to die, and the same questions will be asked."

"Exactly," said Ellen.

"What do you think mum and dad would have wanted?" asked Margaret.

"Yes, I suppose that's the question. We don't have Sarah Ann to take charge anymore." Sarah Ann had been the oldest one, the responsible one, ever since she was a child. When their mother had had another baby in 1865, Sarah Ann, at age eleven, had been the one to go to the Registrar with the information about the birth. And ten days later, when the baby died, she had gone there again to let them know.

"Well, what happened when Sarah Ann died?" asked Margaret. "That was only in 1931."

"One of her sons was the informant," said Ellen. "I asked him later what he had said. He just threw a sheet over the whole question. He stated that Sarah Ann was born in Sydney, got married in Sydney, apparently spent her whole life in Sydney." Ellen was a trifle scornful. She knew it was a difficult question, but perhaps one had to at least leave clues, give some kind of indication.

"But you know how mum and dad felt about their past. I'm not that clear about the details. I was the youngest, well, the youngest that lived. And there are things I still don't understand. Why was I born in Adelaide? We grew up in Sydney. I know that mum and dad were convicts, and that was in Tasmania. Or Van Diemen's Land."

"It's hard, I know," said Ellen. "I don't even know whether to call it Tasmania or Van Diemen's Land. And you know why you were born in Adelaide. Mum told us. She was upset about it, and didn't understand what dad had been involved in. He went to gaol in Sydney, and he thought mum would be safer away from Sydney. Why? I think when he was a policeman he was involved with some rough criminals, and maybe some undesirable people in the upper class as well, the squatters, who might have wanted to harm him."

"Do you know what Sarah Ann said for mum's death certificate?" asked Margaret. Their mother had died in 1897. She was buried at Rookwood.

"Yes, I got the certificate from Sarah Ann's things after she died."

Ellen sipped more tea. She was thinking it over. She had memorised the information on the certificate. Margaret was more interested in hearing what Ellen would say than sipping more tea. But she had learned to be patient with her older sister, remembering that she had been married to a stonemason for a long time, and stonemasons are slow with their thoughts. It might take them six months to bring one idea to fruition. Margaret had been married to a cartoonist, and they are the fastest of all to bring an idea to fulfilment, maybe within five minutes.

"There was the part about parents," said Ellen. "I think she got this a little bit wrong, but I don't think it was intentional, and I think the right information is actually there."

This wasn't really the heart of the problem, but Margaret was interested. "What do you mean?"

"She said that mum's father's name was Martin Fitzgibbons, and mum's mother's name was Sarah, and she didn't know her maiden name."

"So, what's wrong with that?"

"Can't you see? Mum's father's name had to be Crosby. That was mum's maiden name. So, the name 'Fitzgibbons' must have been mum's mother's maiden name."

"Ah, yes, of course, I see. Now, what did it say about where mum was born and how long she had been in the colonies?"

"The first part is correct: she was born in County Waterford, Ireland. We know that. Mum was proud of it. It's carved onto her gravestone. The rest of the section says twenty-six years in New South Wales, ten years in Victoria, and nine years in South Australia."

"Wait a minute. Let me write that down. And, you said ten years in Victoria. We never lived there!" Margaret reached for a writing pad, and wrote it down, and started putting dates against the places. Ellen was happy to let her carry on with it. She sipped her tea and finished eating her piece of cake.

"Oh, and one more thing,' said Ellen. "In the marriage section, the certificate says mum and dad got married in Waterford when mum was nineteen, and then they came to Australia together."

"But dad was never in Ireland. He came from London. They got married in Australia, didn't they?"

"Yes, but where?"

"You're teasing me," said Margaret. "Come on, you're the older one – what do you know?"

"To tell you the truth, I'm not sure, but I know we were in Tasmania when I was born, because Sarah Ann let me know that later, so I guess they got married there."

Margaret went back to her writing pad. After a few minutes, she said, "Well, someone put a lot of thought into this, because all the dates add up perfectly. Mum was sixty-four years old when she died. The dates and places just don't correspond with reality."

"Indeed," said Ellen. "Well, we both know that Victoria played no part in it, and Tasmania did. But I couldn't be sure about dates. I only remember living in Sydney."

"Then there's the question of what mum and dad would want," Margaret noted. "And I want to mention South Australia. I was born there."

"I want to name them properly on my death certificate," said Ellen, "but they wouldn't want me to reveal their convict past. If it was ever mentioned, they both got emotional about the injustice of it all, and the harsh times they had had."

"Would you want the truth on your death certificate about all the dates and places?"

"No. Well, I would, because it's my life, but some things are more important. I want to respect mum and dad."

Margaret and Ellen finished their morning tea. These had been troubling matters they had discussed, with conflicting responsibilities at play. However, they could both view all of it from the position of having lived full lives, both having had family, both of them coming out of poverty, and neither of them living under cruel authorities. But they remembered their parents, so there was little difference in their minds between the authorities who could be so cruel and righteous, and the authorities who collected information for death certificates.

"Happy birthday, Margaret," said Ellen, kissing her and smiling as she left.

"Happy birthday, Ellen," said Margaret, kissing her and smiling back.

Notes on the story

This is a fictional account of a conversation that must have taken place. All the facts in the story are correct. Including Bushells tea? Well, that is a guess. I could argue for it.

Ellen Eaglestone, born Ellen Elizabeth Lewis in 1857 in Launceston, Tasmania, died on 6 June 1937. Margaret Leonard, born Margaret Lewis in 1860 in Adelaide, died on 30 April 1946.

They were both children of Edward Lloyd Lewis and Sarah Ann Crosby, who had been convicts in Hobart. Edward (1829-1897?) was transported to Hobart in 1846, sentenced to ten years for pickpocketing a purse from a woman at Kensington in London. Sarah (1833-1897) was transported to Hobart in 1850, sentenced to seven years for stabbing a policeman in London outside a Refuge for the Houseless Poor (she had made her way to London from Ireland during the potato famine).

Ellen Eaglestone's death certificate names her parents correctly as Edward Lloyd Lewis and Sarah Ann Crosby. As to where Ellen was born and how long she had been in the colonies, it says she was born in Sydney N.S.W., and that is all. The informant was James Pearson, no relation. Ellen must have instructed him prior to her death.

Margaret Leonard's death certificate in 1946 says her parents' names are Edward Lewis and Sarah Crosby. It states that she was born in Adelaide, South Australia. That is all – it makes no attempt to state how long she had been there or when she came to New South Wales. The informant was Mr Jean Brial, a son-in-law from her first marriage, to Louis Deleuil. Mr Brial was seventy-two at the time, and perhaps knew better than to delve into the distant past; he was, however, precise about the details of his mother-in-law's two marriages and the children born.

There may be a question as to why Ellen and Margaret were the only persons at their birthday morning tea. Were there no other siblings or children alive? Apart from two babies who died young, Ellen and Margaret had had three other siblings, one being the Sarah Ann mentioned in the story. In 1935, all of their siblings were deceased.

Margaret had not had any children with Joseph Leonard, but she had had four children with her first husband, Louis Deleuil, a French chef who had moved to Sydney in the 1870s. Three of the four children were still alive in 1935 and all were married. There were eleven living grandchildren. So, perhaps the tea for two was a peaceful respite for her.

Ellen's tale is somewhat different. She and Edwin had four children, a boy who died young, and three girls. One girl, Sarah Ellen, had grown up, married, had four children, then died suddenly at age twenty-five. Blanche Ellen had married and had nine children, but was divorced and living apart from her children. Elizabeth Hannah married and had seven children. After the birth of the last child, she had an emotional breakdown and went into Callan Park Mental Asylum. She never came out. In 1930 she was sent out to Orange to a new facility called Bloomfield Hospital, so she was essentially unreachable by Ellen.

Tea for two with her sister was a welcome respite, a solace.

Visiting Sarah Lappan's grave

It was a spring day, the first of October, a rare day when the wind was more obtrusive than either heat or cold, so it was the sound that was most immediate – the wind among myriad leaves, talking, talking, and I don't know the words. I had been to Rookwood Cemetery before, but it is a vast field of stones and it is often difficult to find the precise one you are looking for.

I was looking for the grave of Sarah Lappan. Sarah's sister, Elizabeth Hannah Eaglestone, was my father's mother. Elizabeth's life was a troubled one, as was that of Blanche Eaglestone, the other sister. Sarah was the middle child. But Sarah died young. She married at seventeen and died at twenty-five. She married Herbert Lappan in Sydney in 1902 and they had four children.

Neville, the last child, died as a baby, thirteen weeks old. Six months later, Sarah became violently ill with "incomplete abortive septicaemia". I assume she became pregnant again soon after Neville died. My understanding is that this condition can be due to either an intentional termination or a miscarriage, so we don't know the exact circumstances. We just know that her life ended suddenly and tragically.

I wanted to see her grave. I was already deeply involved with finding out about her parents and their parents. Sarah Lappan was part of the picture. She was named after her grandmother, Sarah Crosby, who married Edward Lewis. They had both been convicts in Van Diemen's Land, he from London, she from Waterford in Ireland. Sarah Lappan's husband, Herbert, was also from Irish stock. He was a second-generation Australian, just as his wife was. His forebears came from Tyrone .

What happened after Sarah died? Herbert was left with three young children. His job was manufacturing harnesses for horses. But I think Herbert's parents must have stepped in. They lived in the same suburb, Annandale, and Herbert was the eldest of nine children. Of them, Ruby was twenty-three and Olive was twenty, and they were probably still at home; they could have had a hand in looking after the children.

In these circumstances, many men get married again soon afterwards, to someone who is willing to look after the children.

Herbert did get married again, but not for thirteen years. One could argue that this was circumstantial – he just didn't find the right lady until then – but perhaps the death of his wife shocked him and made him numb for a long time. In 1923, he married Kathleen Goodwin. Even so, it was not a long-lived marriage. She died just three years later, at the age of thirty-two.

Today I am interested in Sarah Lappan. I know the facts of her life, but I am touched by the fact that her life was so short. Her living children were aged eight, five and three.

I knew Sarah was buried in the Presbyterian section at Rookwood, but it was in 1910, and chances were that her memory had been buried as well. In that span of time, graves can subside, headstones can fall over and break, and by now any trace of them may have disappeared altogether. On top of this, even if the headstone survived, in most cases it is unreadable. If it is sandstone, the words have worn off, the original etchings having leached out into the surrounding stone. If the words were stuck on as metal leaf, the letters have fallen off in the relentlessness of weather; even the small rivets are gone.

I wondered about Sarah being in the Presbyterian section. Her father Edwin Eaglestone was Church of England and her mother, born Ellen Lewis, may have been torn between Church of England and Roman Catholic, but Presbyterian was not part of the mix. However, then I learned that Herbert's grandparents had come from Tyrone, in the north of Ireland, and that is where Presbyterianism made its entrance. Ironically, when Herbert died, in 1939, He was buried in the Church of England section at Rookwood.

So, Sarah Lappan was buried in the Presbyterian section. Now there was the simple question of navigation, finding my way to the appropriate grave. In theory it is straightforward; there is a map – with sections, zones, designations, codes and numbers. The difficulty was that in practice, it was mostly hard to determine how the graves aligned with the system. I often felt that it was all planned irrationally. Moreover, the critical piece of information, the grave number, was seldom to be seen on any grave.

You can walk down a row of hundreds of graves and not find a single number engraved on the concrete perimeter of a grave. If you manage to find one number, that is not yet enough. You need to find another grave with a number on it, then work out how all the numbers between the two graves would fall – neatly and sequentially.

Only occasionally does this work. Sometimes, the sequence of numbers disrupts radically. You may have fooled yourself into thinking that you were following numbers in the 8000s when you suddenly come across numbers in the 600s. Then you realise you must have crossed a boundary between two sections. To add to your bewilderment, the names of two adjacent sections could be quite different. Section 6D, for example, might be next to Section 2C. I am looking for Zone A, Presbyterian Sec 06D, Grave 8072.

I ask myself why I am doing this. Sarah Lappan is not a direct ancestor of mine. She is a sister of a grandmother. I could say, she is *just* the sister of a grandmother. Does it matter at all? Even her children have all died, and they were only young when she died, so they had someone else who looked after them while they were growing up. But Sarah Lappan is part of my grandmother's family. Sarah is part of the picture of her family, so she matters.

What's more, I want to pay my respects to a mother who died so young, with a husband and children around her and life urging to be lived fully. The wind has eased, but the shadows are longer, reminding me that it is already afternoon. I have moved myself to Zone A of Rookwood, which includes the Presbyterian section. It also includes Ukrainian Orthodox Church graves, Chinese and Jewish. Eventually, I suppose, it makes some kind of sense.

After some wandering that seems to be aimless, I come across a stake in the ground labelled '06D'. This is the most promising thing yet. But yes, unfortunately, it is right next to the '02C' section. Sometimes it is not helpful to confine oneself to the logic of numbers, because that would drive you to consider two interacting sequences of categorisation and not know what to do with it. I know (intuitively) that it will not be helpful to think about this logically. I take my cue from the '06D' sign and venture forth. There is a row of graves. My best guidance is the dates. I assume that the graves in proximity to each other were occupied more or less sequentially in time.

I am looking for graves in the period around 1910. I walk down the slope, among the rows. I am alert enough to note that the area I am walking into is almost an open forest, with trees that would not have existed in 1910. They are smallish casuarinas, wispy she-oaks, river oaks, hill oaks – something in that family. They whisper in the wind, I know that. And they have grown up, unable to be tamed by the cemetery stewards, who have so much else to tend to. I have seen rabbits this afternoon, hopping among the graves. This is the outskirts of the cemetery.

I walk. The numbers do not make sense, the few that I have seen. I am looking for 8072, but I entertain that lightly. The reality is that I am walking into the casuarinas, the young ones that would not have been there in 1910. The graves have thinned out. There are long spaces where there are no graves at all, just casuarinas – I assume that, over time, the graves have been and gone. Young casuarinas are still coming up, just a foot high. Occasionally I note the light, long strands of it coming through the fronds. In colour it is light green, light greens, whitish yellows on a fair afternoon. I am prepared to be unsuccessful, but my determination is steady.

Just then there is a grave, standing tall, by itself. I look. I look closely, at the words on the stone. I pick out the words, one by one – Sarah, Lappan, died, 12th April, 1910. In loving memory (fainter). There is an aura around the words. They are faint, but they shine, they glow. I sit down now, beside the grave. I am absorbed. 1910. Many years. The grave is soft, because of the soft fronds of the casuarinas that fall and fall, perpetually.

How could it stand so tall, so clear, after this long? It is quietly wonderful. I sit, and I say, I have found you. I have found you. Your grandmother says hello. Your mother says hello. I am sorry your life ended so short. I suppose that is how it was in your day. Death was never very far away, even for those who were young.

And there is Neville, whom she has joined in death: "Neville, infant son of the above. Died 14th October 1909, aged 13 weeks". He had preceded her.

That is all. Her husband Herbert lived on, and his grave is somewhere else in the vast stone fields of Rookwood. I take photos. I suppose that is my devotion. I say, in parting, I have remembered you. You are the sister of my father's mother. And you are part of the story.

Image: Grave of Sarah Lappan at Rookwood Necropolis

Margaret Lewis at her mother's grave at Rookwood

"I hate to say it, mum, but dad turned out to be a pillar of the community." I'm sitting next to mum's grave at Rookwood: "Sarah Anne Lewis, A Native of Waterford, Ireland".

"You came to Australia as a convict; so did dad. Then dad went on to become a policeman: Detective Edward Lewis. Not that it was plain sailing; people would bring up his past and accuse him of being dodgy: 'Leopards don't change their spots.' But dad was straight, eventually. Yes, mum, I know you might disagree. He went to prison for theft and sent the family away to Adelaide for the duration. You were carrying me at the time. I was born in Adelaide.

"Then he became a legal clerk and life was finally peaceful. But just when I was getting married in 1877, he went back into the police force. He was forty-seven. I was so angry, I refused to put his name on the marriage certificate. Why was I angry? I thought those dangerous, fearful years were over. Maybe I was picking up on your fears.

"But listen, mum. I've been collecting newspaper clippings. In this one, he's investigating a theft down at Darling Harbour. It's muddy and there's a footprint. He thinks he knows who it is and goes to the man's house and borrows his boot. It's a perfect fit. In court, he says, 'I saw there, like Robinson Crusoe, a very plain left footmark.'

"Isn't that just like dad?

"And this one. He arrested a sailor for swearing. In court (the newspaper says), 'Constable Lewis, with his customary modesty, handed the words complained of up to the Police Magistrate on a piece of paper.' Priceless!

"I eventually accepted that the police was dad's mission, his redemption. Can't you?"

Reflection

The narrator is Margaret Lewis, youngest daughter of Edward Lewis and Sarah Crosby, my great great grandparents. Sarah died in 1897 and I think Edward died around the same time (evidence is lacking). Margaret did an astonishing thing in 1877: on her marriage certificate she put a dash instead of her father's name, although she had to have known it (there were five children and Edward's name was on all the others' marriage certificates). It struck me as anger rather than ignorance. I think she feared her father going back into the police force, perhaps reflecting her mother's fear. In 1898 she got married again, and this time, she was able to provide all her father's details.

Sources

Grave of Sarah Anne Lewis, Rookwood Cemetery, Old Roman Catholic Section M1, T, 386.

[Editorial], *Empire*, 21 February 1860, p. 4. Retrieved 26 November 2017, http://nla.gov.au/nla.news-article64097680

Edward Lewis, New South Wales Gaol Description and Entrance Books, Parramatta, June 1860, p. 190, State Archives and Records. Accessed 27 July 2018.

Birth certificate of Margaret Lewis, born 6 November 1860, Adelaide, Genealogy South Australia.

Marriage certificate of Margaret Lewis and Louis Deleuil, married 3 November 1877, Registry of Births, Deaths & Marriages, New South Wales, 11496/1877.

'Footprints in the mud', *Sydney Daily Telegraph*, 24 May 1883, p. 4. Retrieved 20 November 2021, http://nla.gov.au/nla.news-article238488377

'Newcastle Police Court', *Newcastle Morning Herald and Miners' Advocate*, 10 September 1896, p. 6. Retrieved 20 November 2021, http://nla.gov.au/nla.news-article135765828

Marriage certificate of Margaret Deleuil and Joseph John Henry Leonard, married 24 October 1898, Registry of Births, Deaths & Marriages, New South Wales, 6863/1898.

Truths about searching for family history

At a certain point, it looks as if you can see everything, and it ought to make sense. Ellen Lewis is my great grandmother. She was born in 1857 of two parents who were no longer convicts, although, her father did get into trouble once, later, and spent two years in gaol. During that time, Ellen and her sisters and brother lived in Adelaide (perhaps it was safer), and Margaret was born there.

Back in Sydney, Edward Lewis and Sarah Crosby brought up five children. Mary Susannah, the younger of twins, married at fifteen, an Irish lad around the corner, a carrier in the age of horses. Sarah Ann, the older twin, met a goldminer from Gulgong and they were married at St Mary's Cathedral. Ted, the only boy, married next. Margaret, the youngest child, married at seventeen, a French chef newly in town. Then Ellen got married to Edwin, a stonemason.

This looks alright; after the time of convict servitude, life has taken shape and settled down. All the children have grown up and are married. But it was not so simple. Prior to her marriage, Ellen had had an encounter with a man and given birth to a child. Sarah Ann and her new husband had gone to Gulgong, where the gold was, and young Ellen went to visit them. The complication was that Ellen got pregnant to someone.

Back in Sydney, the baby got diarrhoea and died. Life was tenuous for infants in 1877. It was after this that Edwin came along. He had been working stone at Lithgow. They got married in Sydney, at 'Friendville', a Presbyterian house-church in Paddington. And then their first child was a boy, Charles. But Charles died at six months from 'hereditary syphilis' and there were two possibilities for that. But other children followed, all girls, who lived.

Of the other children of Edward and Sarah Lewis, Mary Susannah had six children and then she died, aged thirty-four. Her twin sister Sarah Ann had three children and lived long. Ted was not good at marriage and his wife soon left him, tired of the violence. Margaret and the chef stayed together for twenty years and had four children, but then she divorced him for adultery.

Is that everything? What kind of sense does it make? Are these the usual ups and downs of life that are to be expected? Is this a good outcome for the offspring of two convicts? Or is it unfortunate and likewise attributable to the convict past?

Perhaps I should also say that Timothy Moroney, Mary Susannah's widower, married again and they had four children together. Or that the new wife died at the age of twenty-nine, and the three of them – Timothy, Mary Susannah and Johanna – are buried together at Rookwood. Perhaps I should say too that Margaret got married again after the divorce, but they had no children together. And Margaret lived the longest, dying when she was eighty-six.

Is there a pattern in this? I do not think so. People lived, people had families, people lived in proximity – they all lived in Sydney for most of their lives, with Annandale as the epicentre. But there is nothing to say these are the children of two convicts. They could be any family, with their ordinary triumphs and disasters, mishaps and mayhem.

In the mix there is a stonemason, a carrier, a French chef and a goldminer. There is also an artist (Margaret's second husband). When the mother (Sarah Lewis) died, there were fifteen grandchildren. When Margaret died, she left ten houses in her estate. The French chef (divorced) is buried in the same grave as the mother and Ted, who became a bootmaker.

The children did their best to hide the fact that their parents had been convicts, as propriety demanded. The mother's death certificate said she had been married in Ireland, not Hobart, but the record of the marriage in Hobart still exists and offers proof of the reality, the unsociable facts.

The only shadow is Ted, the son. Was he evidence of the 'bad blood' of his parents? He had a wild and unpleasant career as a drunk and a thug when he was a youth. Just before he turned sixteen he was arrested for drunkenness and the police put him in gaol for two days. When he was nineteen he assaulted two young women, on separate occasions, and was fined both times.

After his marriage, Ted was brought to court for threatening to beat his wife's brains out and was put on a bond for six months. When he was twenty-two, in company with two other men, he assaulted a young woman. After a second assault he was sent to gaol for twelve months. He came out of gaol and within months he was back in trouble. With two other men he assaulted a man and robbed him. This time he was given four years in gaol. He was twenty-four.

Out of gaol again, within a few months he was arrested for drunkenness and put in Darlinghurst Gaol for twenty-four hours. But this was the bookend to his criminal life. He may have learned boot-making when he was in gaol, because that was his occupation from then on. As a young man he had been a mariner. I suspect that meant that he had tried it by going to sea on a ship once or twice. Perhaps a group of drunken sailors had been his inspiration.

He never got married again; and his wife had gone home to her parents. His death at fifty-one and the cause – chronic renal disease – suggest that he continued to drink heavily. I suspect that he softened somewhat as he got older. Perhaps he regretted his unsavoury actions as a young man.

His mother (she who had been a convict) died when he was forty-one and he went to the trouble of inserting his own notice in the newspaper for the funeral: "The friends of Mr. Edward Lloyd Lewis are respectfully invited to attend the funeral of his beloved mother". It was hardly necessary; there were five other such notices from family. Twelve months later he inserted a poem for her in the 'In Memoriam' columns of the *Sunday Times* (Sydney).

We cannot point the finger to the father for a history of violence. He was transported for being a child pickpocket on the streets of London. He had survived by stealing by stealth, not by beating people up. In all the many facts I have accumulated about Edward (the father), there is nothing indicating brutality, only dishonesty when his life was at stake.

Maybe Ted was led astray by rough types in inner city Sydney, up around Darlinghurst when he was sixteen. Maybe he bought into the dreams about the sailors' high life when in port. Maybe he had that type of personality that is led by a crowd. Maybe he reacted adversely to having to grow up among four sisters.

This is how it goes: the more you find out about individual ancestors, the more they start to look like ordinary people dealing with ordinary situations, difficult or otherwise. It looks as if contemporary society and luck both play a part. As ordinary people they are subject to pressures. Sometimes they win and sometimes they lose. They do good things and bad things, and with luck and perseverance, often they learn to live an honourable life.

And of course, you have never seen everything. Ellen, my great grandmother, had the three girls, and all of them had difficult lives. They all married and had numerous children. One, however, died at twenty-five after having had four children. Another had nine children but seemed unable to endure her life as a mother; she left and seemed to live unhappily. The third (my grandmother) had seven children but then had a breakdown and went into an institution.

I have changed my proposition. Now I think: at certain points, it may look as if you have seen everything, and it may seem to make sense, but that is only a temporary position. Nevertheless, we live, and it is worth asserting that it serves us all best if we seek to live honourably.

Section 5: Great grandparents, maternal (1)

James Archer (1857-1917) and Alice Neil (1862-1903)

Introductory notes

James Archer was one of the children of William Archer, the first emigrant to Australia in my family tree. William was an involuntary emigrant, that is, a convict. In Australia, he married and had eight children. James, the sixth child, is my great grandfather. Alice Neil, James's wife, was born in Sydney. Her parents came from Armagh in Ireland. James and Alice married in Sydney in 1880. They had eleven children.

William and Ellen Archer took their family to England in the late 1860s and they stayed there for several years. James was a child on that adventure. After they returned to Australia, William established a hotel at Ultimo, Sydney, and James became the publican after his father died. But James was also a plasterer.

In the first story (told in the first person), James talks about his journey to the old country (England) from the new country (Australia), and the journey back.

The second story features James again, in the first person, talking about his sister Ellen (named after her mother) after her death. She had been married twice – interesting, exciting, and then difficult experiences.

The third story tries to make sense of the estate that was accumulated by William Archer, and its fate as it passed to his wife and children. James is a central figure, as the executor of his father's will and his mother's will.

James Archer: new country and old country

> The story below is told from the perspective of James Archer (1857-1917), my great grandfather. His father, William Archer, was transported to New South Wales in 1838 for stealing. He served his time in the Hunter Valley, from Fullerton Cove to Dungog, and then had his own farm in the area.

I remember complaining to dad about the farm work: so much time I spent clearing weeds and scrub from the paddocks. He just laughed.

"Son," he said, "think yourself lucky. We've got our own plot of land. In the old country, I was just a labourer, like my own father. Don't worry. We'll make something of it."

Sometimes he would talk about the old country – Hertfordshire. English meadows, streams, the village, the White Horse Inn where he had been the groom. He didn't say much about the convict years, but I sensed that his best revenge would be to do well in his life.

After a few more years of farming, he announced, "We're selling up and going back to England." I guess that's what they mean by a bombshell. So we did: mum, dad and five kids. There were three other children, but they were older, and they already had their own lives.

I was eleven. Dad bought a farm in England, a cherry orchard in Kent, so, again I had to do farm work, but what a place – so beautiful! And there were castles nearby, like a dream!

We were only twenty miles from London and we went there. That must be the biggest city on earth – amazing! On the way to London, we stayed at the Duke of Edinburgh Hotel in Brixton. I could see dad was dreaming. Back at the farm he said, "We're going back to Australia."

That was the best adventure: a new ship, steam and sails, the *St Osyth*, 3,500 tons. She did the trip to Melbourne in forty-two days. We arrived on Christmas Day, 1874. Sister Mary McKillop and a group of about twenty nuns were also on board. Mum seemed to get on with them better than dad.

We didn't go back to farming; we stayed in Sydney. Dad had this idea of building a hotel. For a while he had the job as publican of the Spread Eagle Hotel, and he started brewing in a shed in a paddock at Pyrmont. There was a dairy farm nearby.

The hotel opened in around 1880: dad called it the Duke of Edinburgh. He was sixty-nine, but still a ball of energy. I'll be publican of that hotel one day.

Notes on the story

James did indeed become the publican, after his father died.

I am studying (2021-2022) a Diploma of Family History at the University of Tasmania (online, of course). A constructive thing to do in the time of COVID? I won't argue with that. In one of the units, we had to write a series of short pieces. Can you say anything useful or interesting in 250 words? Now I think so.

I haven't persuaded myself that this is the only type of writing (just as I am not an aficionado of Twitter), but it has its moments. I am still the same Glenn.

These short pieces often highlight the connections there can be between people and between events. This story talked about William Archer packing up his family and moving back to England. I thought that was bold, and it certainly was.

But later, I discovered there was a twist: prior to William and family going to England, the oldest daughter, Hannah, had married (in the Hunter valley) a man from Sussex, Stephen Covell, and he and Hannah went back to England with them.

So, suddenly it is not quite so random that William bought a farm in Kent. It was, as we say, in the neighbourhood. I wonder how many other connecting threads there are between my family history stories that currently look separate?

James Archer on the death of his sister Ellen, 1909

(Spoken from the perspective of James Archer)

I will have to speak at her funeral. My poor sister, Ellen, just fifty-five. It's only six months since her second husband died: George Bunce. He was a bit mad; he let the drink get the better of him. I'm a publican, I should know. He drowned in a pond at Centennial Park, having delusions about the police chasing him. And Ellen took it hard; she didn't get over it.

Everyone at the funeral will know; I don't have to say. Ellen's first husband, Arthur Gibson, died young too, only forty-three, like my first wife died aged forty-one – so young. I had expected all these years of us together. It was cut short. Same for Ellen, only, for her, twice.

I want to tell how she married Arthur. Dad and mum had packed us all up and taken us to England: me, Ellen and three of our brothers, when I was eleven, and she was fourteen. Dad wanted to clear away his convict past. We had this lovely orchard in Kent. Then she met Arthur, an Englishman, and they ran away to London. Mum and dad were aghast, but for me it was exciting.

We came back to Australia because dad wanted to open a hotel. Ellen and Arthur came back six years later. That's what I want to remember.

I've been thinking about the obelisk on the grave: there's one space left on the main four panels. I think I'll give it to her. So far there's mum, dad and Alice (my first wife). I could have had it, but there's plenty more room around it. Her children want to say:

> Hush, hush, all sorrows and weeping,
> Our mother is only at rest.

Reflective statement

James Archer is my great grandfather. Through My Heritage I met another of his descendants, a second cousin. He said James was a drunkard and lost the licence for the hotel (the Duke of Edinburgh at Pyrmont). So, I had a negative impression of James, and then I thought, there had to be more to him than that. I invented this story, but there is the business about the plaques on the obelisk at the grave. I think James gave up the place he could have had, twice: once for his wife, and again for his sister. There is generosity in that.

Notes for sources

Death certificate: Death of Ellen Bunce, 18 January 1909 at Kogarah NSW.

Death certificate: Death of George Bunce, 9 October 1908 at Randwick NSW.

Newspaper account of inquest into George Bunce's death, *Evening News*, 13 October 1908.

Death certificate: Death of Arthur Edwin Gibson, 6 November 1896 at Coast Hospital, Little Bay NSW.

Death certificate: Death of James Archer's wife, Alice, 19 October 1903 at Ultimo NSW.

Marriage certificate: Marriage of Arthur Edwin Gibson and Ellen Archer in September 1874 at Islington, London.

Passenger list for William Archer and family, *St Osyth*, arrived Port Phillip, 25 December 1874.

Passenger list for Arthur and Ellen Gibson and family, *Orient*, arrived Sydney, 20 October 1880.

The estate of William Archer

In family history there is so often a search for lost wealth: money, lands, a castle, or a precious heirloom. Is there such a story in my family tree? In general, it would appear not; the ancestors were, for the most part, artisans – tradespeople who earned their living through skills and hard work. There was little opportunity for accruing wealth beyond a family home, and there is no suggestion in any branch of the family of lucky speculation or unknown benefactors.

Yet, in the case of the Archer family, there is a suggestion that some modicum of wealth had been accumulated. William Archer, having begun his adult life as a convict, ended it as the publican of a hotel in Ultimo, Sydney. Before that, he had had a farm in the Hunter Valley, and then an orchard in Kent, England. Was there a pocket of wealth in this part of the family?

William Archer died in 1894 at the age of eighty. He was at that time the publican of the Duke of Edinburgh Hotel on the corner of Harris Street and Union Street, Ultimo. He was the one who had established the hotel in 1880. One thinks of hotels generally as being places where cash flows as freely as the beer. On the other hand, there were many hotels around at that time, and you could buy some hotels for around the same price as a modest house.

William Archer's grave suggests that he was well-heeled. It is a large affair at Waverley Cemetery with a view of the ocean. At the centre of it is a white obelisk around three metres high. There was room in the grave for around twenty people, and as at 2010 there were indeed twenty people buried there. His residence, however, does not give the impression of wealth. It was a small, two-storey building in Paternoster Row, one in a line of identical residences.

The inventory presented for the probate of William's last will and testament is also confusing, at least to me. It says that he owned just ten pounds of real estate, but he also had "landed property under lease" worth 2,600 pounds. There is not a list of the property, so I do not know what it consisted of. My understanding of property under lease is that someone else owns it and you lease it from them at a given price for a given period of time, and the inference is that you use that property to earn an income.

However, the City of Sydney Archives list William Archer as the owner, in 1891, of four houses in Paternoster Row, which is the little street directly behind the Duke of Edinburgh Hotel. Only some years of the records are available.

I got curious about the prices of houses in the 1890s, so I looked up the *Sydney Morning Herald* advertisements in the Trove database (all the scanned issues of historical newspapers in Australia), for Houses for Sale. The general price of an inner-city house at that time was around 250 pounds. That is, a normal, smallish, two-storey building with perhaps four rooms. Nowadays that could be worth one or more million dollars.

My guess is that 2,600 pounds would have equated to the hotel plus the four houses. Also, the City of Sydney records indicate that William Archer was the owner of those houses, not the lessee. Further, the inventory was obliged to list all the person's assets for the purposes of assessing stamp duty to be paid ("death duties"), so it was not in the interests of people to overstate their assets. Whatever "landed property under lease" means in the context, it has to imply effective ownership.

There are other curiosities about the inventory of William Archer's belongings. His "money in hand" amounted to four shillings and eight pence. His "money at bank" was even less: one shilling, ten pence. My thought is this: a hotel operates on cash. People pay cash for alcohol. So, where is the cash? My suggestion is: the hotel operated as a company, so it was separate from William. However, I have no evidence of this until 1907, when all the houses in Paternoster Row show up in the City of Sydney records as being owned by the Scottish Australian Investment Company. I think the hotel also was in the hands of this company at that time. But, the hotel could have been operating through a company in earlier years.

Still, it is hard to believe that William Archer had only about six shillings to his name. He may have been hiding his cash underneath his mattress.

What did William's will say? All of his estate was to be left to his wife, Helen Archer, to be held in trust by her during her life, and to be used by her as she wished. Upon her death, the estate was to pass equally to all of their children. There were eight children, and all of them were alive in 1894.

Who was the executor of the will? Two people: James Archer and Helen Archer. James was one of the eight children; to be precise, he was the sixth child and the fourth son. However, he seems to have played a central role in the family.

Why? One needs to know that William and Ellen Archer left Australia and went to live in England in the late 1860s. They lived there for several years before coming back to Australia. At the time they decided to do this, some of the male children (that is, the likely executors) were already grown up and had their own lives. William, the eldest, was already married. Edward, the next male, spent his life on the mid-north coast of New South Wales. John, the third male, did go to England with the family, but he left Sydney on their return.

James was the son who stayed closest to his parents. He went overseas with them; he was seventeen when they returned to Australia. I wonder about the others. One theory is that William came to Australia (as a convict) but he ended up in Sydney and stayed there. Perhaps the others were curious and wanted to explore further afield, to see more of Australia. Seen this way, it is a legacy from their parents, the idea of seeing what their parents hadn't seen.

It appears that John Archer was the publican of a hotel in Launceston, Tasmania in 1894. This is especially curious because there is another branch of the Archer family in Tasmania. The connection goes a long way back, to William Archer's grandparents in Hertfordshire. Was John trying to connect with them?

Helen Archer, William's wife, relinquished her right as the executor of her husband's will, leaving James to manage the affairs alone. The business was carried out through a solicitor, so one assumes it was not too onerous. The other point of interest about the will was that William recognised the agency of females. Not only did he leave Helen to manage the estate, but he specifically declared all his female heirs to be agents of their own volition:

> Lastly, I declare that the shares and interests of all females taking under this my will shall be held for their sole and separate estate use and benefit and that their receipts alone shall, notwithstanding coverture, be sufficient discharges.

Note: 'Coverture' is the legal status of a married woman, considered to be under her husband's protection and authority.

In reality, there were two things in tension. Helen Archer had relinquished her right to be the executor, suggesting that she was leaving business affairs up to James. But, on the other hand, she shows up in the City of Sydney records (1896) as the legal owner of the houses in Paternoster Row, suggesting she is still exercising her rights. And there are five houses owned now, not four.

There is more to the story of the estate of William Archer. The next puzzle is Alice Archer, who was the next to die, in 1903. Alice was the wife of James. Why is this interesting? It is interesting because Alice had money of her own. Where did this come from? Note, I had a conversation with another descendant of William Archer (a second cousin?) and he asserted the same thing: Alice had money of her own.

James and Alice got married in 1880. Alice's mother had already died, and her father, John Neil, died in 1891. John had an estate of around 200 pounds, to be split three ways – Alice and two brothers. There were connections between John Neil and James Archer, because the first ten pounds of the estate were to go to James. Perhaps James paid the deposit on the house that John owned. It suggests consideration and generosity on the part of James.

However, this does not account for the amount of money Alice had: 500 pounds in real estate, and 114 pounds in money at the bank. Did the money come from Alice's grandparents? Her grandfather, Richard Wetherell, had been a grain buyer in Armagh, Ireland. All I can say is, this is a possibility. If we use the crude measure discussed above, 500 pounds equates roughly to two houses. Accordingly, the inventory submitted for probate of her will includes 26 pounds for rent.

What happened to Alice's estate? Alice bequeathed it all to James, not to their children; there were eight living children at the time.

The next death was Helen Archer, in 1912. She was eighty-nine. She was no longer living in Paternoster Row; nor was James. James was living at Westbourne Street, Petersham. I suspect James had the house built, and at the time it would have been one of the nicest houses in the street. It was a two-storey house in a street of mostly single-storey houses. It had an ornate wrought-iron railing on the upstairs balcony, and arches over the downstairs windows and doors, just as the Duke of Edinburgh Hotel had had when it was built. Like father, like son.

Helen Archer was living with James. So was Margaret Storey, whom James had married in 1905. There were still young children at home, from James and Alice's marriage, and Margaret Storey did not have any children of her own.

I thought that when Helen died, the bounteous estate of William's would be realised and passed onto their living children, of whom there were seven living in 1912. However, the estate consisted of 102 pounds and some jewellery, that is all. Helen left specified jewels to the women in the family – her daughters and daughters-in-law. There was one bequest to a male: "I bequeath to my son William Archer [the eldest] my gold scarf pin".

There was some novelty for me in this will; I had not seen such items described in a will before. For example: "to Elizabeth Archer, my daughter, one gold brooch (forget-me-not) and one pair of earrings set with stones all around them" and "to my daughter Ellen Bunce, my small keeper ring, also my watch and chain and my gold brooch with two red stones in the centre".

Where had all the real estate gone – the houses, the hotel? The will left the money to her children equally. Were Helen's real estate interests now operated by the Scottish Australian Investment Company? No, they weren't, or it would have shown up on Helen's inventory as shares. The company was established in Scotland in 1840, and it invested in properties in Australia. It bought up the family's assets, either because the family was in trouble financially, or because the family was ready to sell and the company thought that the investment was attractive.

Alternatively, was James dishonest with the money held on trust for all the children by Helen? Or was he negligent or foolish with the money? Or, had the estate already been dispensed among all of William and Helen's children? I am inclined to the latter view. Perhaps I am being unduly kind, but we have the knowledge that James helped John Neil to buy his house, and we know that he had taken his mother into his household in her last days to care for her.

James died in 1917, aged sixty, plagued with several diseases. His youngest child was seventeen. The estate was left to his children equally. There were six living. His occupation was plasterer. For a period of eight years (1897 to 1905) he had been the publican of the Duke of Edinburgh Hotel. He had also been the publican of the Green Park Hotel at Darlinghurst for a period of two years (1908-1909).

What did his estate consist of? Ten pounds' worth of real estate, and some money. I don't know what ten pounds of real estate looks like, even in those days. The odd thing is, his father likewise had had ten pounds' worth of real estate in the inventory of his possessions. Was it the same item, or was it the same token or gesture? Like father, like son.

James made a donation in his will of forty pounds to the Lodge Mission. I knew he was a member of the Masons. It is a generous donation considering that it amounted to about one-third of the estate. He had eighty-three pounds in the bank, aside from the donation. There is no mention of the nice house he lived in at Petersham, just the mysterious ten pounds real estate.

Either James had very little property at the time of his death, or it had been distributed to other people already. The fact that he gave a substantial donation to the Mission Lodge suggests that his family were not desperate. As to his new wife, Margaret Storey, they must have had an agreement about what was going to happen upon his death. She married someone else two years later.

Money comes, money goes, like water. The question is, did James's conduct in relation to his parents' estate or his own lead to acrimony within the family? The associated question is, how would I know? This was all over a hundred years ago. But it is amazing what persists over time, and comes down to us through stray stories or bits of stories.

There is the descendant I know about, who said that James was a drunk and he frittered away a lot of the inheritance. But I think about what came down to me via my mother. There was the story about there being no convicts in the family. There was the story about the hotel that the first ancestor to Australia had built. So, some of the stories were true, and when they were not true, there was a reason for that.

However, there is no overriding story about an ancestor who lost all the wealth. What seemed to be the case, instead, is that there were many children in each generation, and people were expected to grow up, learn a skill and make their own way in the world. And this seems to be what they did, without rancour.

The hotel was seen as an interesting phase of the family's life, not to be appropriated by the whole family except as a story. People would still have to work hard. And I think, well, even James was a tradesman, a plasterer. What do I think of James? Did he seek to take over his father's exploits and extend his success, and did he fail in this?

I think William was extremely successful with what he achieved in his life, in terms of property. Then James took over as the central person in the family, while his siblings went in other directions. Perhaps there was some play of ego in this, and perhaps he often had to remind himself to think of the best interests of the family rather than attempting to replicate his father's extraverted personality. But I think the interest in the Masons was an expression of wanting to live up to high ideals, rather than merely being the expression of a desire for higher social standing.

I think James struggled with himself, and that at his best he had the capacity to bring people together. I think he probably took on more than he could master; you have to be sure that you are equal to a task. At the end he might have said that he had achieved part of his goals. I find it interesting that his parents lived to be eighty and eighty-nine, considering their hard beginnings, and James died at sixty. I don't think he left peacefully.

Nevertheless, although little materially was left to be passed down – little money, and no lands, castle, or precious heirlooms – there are gifts of the spirit. What the various people of the family were trying to do with their lives, in their families, and what they were doing it for, still stand as admirable ideals. The family continues.

One small thing passed down: a printed "memorial card" given out to attendees at James Archer's funeral. I received a copy of this from the descendant with whom I had been in contact. With a cynical eye, one can take this with a grain of salt. With modern scorn, we could say it was a trite expression of current cultural norms. Whilst I do not eye the world with the same perspective as the people of James's time, I am sympathetic to the sentiment:

The Lord gave, the Lord hath taken away, blessed be the name of the Lord.

In loving remembrance of James Archer, who departed this life, 26 August 1917, aged 60 years.

    One of the best that God could send,
    Beloved by all, a faithful friend,
    Called Home from those who deeply love,
    To gain a glorious Life above.
    With aching hearts, with tearful eyes,
    We linger where our dear one lies,
    And breathe those sacred words once more,
    "Not lost, but only gone before."

There is love in that, worth something.

Section 6: Great grandparents, maternal (2)

George Briggs Mackie (1863-1926) and Frances Emily Bulling (1865-1934)

Introductory notes

George Briggs Mackie is one of my great grandfathers. He was only six months old when his father (Robert Mackie) died in a mining accident in Melbourne. He was one of four brothers, with one older sister. The death of their father affected the family profoundly, indicated by the fact that all the boys left Melbourne when they grew up.

The first story looks at the situation from George's point of view. He speaks here as a young man, asserting that he is an individual among his three brothers; he is not just a pea in a pod.

In the second story, George is helping his mother (Catherine) to carry a parcel to Margaret's place – his older sister. Clothes for a new baby. Margaret and her husband have been away from Melbourne, and they have just come back. Margaret is living a surprising and interesting life. George's mother is catching him up on family history, including his nieces' and nephews' names.

The third story is called "Alice and Alice – two cousins". Alice Maud Mackie and Florence Alice Mackie were the children of two sons of Robert and Catherine Mackie. They were fourteen years apart, and each of them lived a very unconventional life, involving several partners. Were they influenced or inspired by each other? Perhaps. It is good to wonder.

George Briggs Mackie and his brothers

My brothers and I are like peas in a pod? I don't think so. To start with, there were four peas: four brothers, not two, so it would be improbable. We were alike in some ways. We were the sad ones whose father got killed in a mineshaft, a ridiculous, fruitless goldmine in Collingwood, Melbourne.[7] I knew the least about it; I was only six months old. Alexander, the eldest, was seven. He remembered.

We grew up, and we were just holding back the urge to escape. I suppose we were like peas in a pod in that respect. James bolted. He went to Sydney, found a girl, and got married in December 1882.[8] Alexander did the same in 1884.[9] But me, the youngest, I beat them all, at least to marriage. I married Frances Bulling at Fitzroy in May 1882.[10] I was nineteen and she was seventeen. I was more than just a pea in a pod.

I'd become a house painter. I was definitely not going to be a carpenter like my father. My brothers felt the same. There were some ways in which we were alike.

James was the grand one. He went to Newcastle and opened a furniture store. It was a big success.[11] Alexander became a painter in Sydney. Uncle Bill had taught us both. But we were not two peas in

---

[7] Death register entry of Robert Mackie, died 2 Nov 1863, Registry of Births, Deaths and Marriages, Victoria, South Melbourne 8/35.
[8] Marriage certificate of James Hood Mackie and Mary Kendrick Murray, 29 Dec 1882, Elizabeth St, Sydney, Registry of Births, Deaths and Marriages, New South Wales, 1950/1882.
[9] Marriage certificate of Alexander Mackie and Annie Maria Elizabeth Stooss, 9 Oct 1884, St Paul's Church of England, Sydney, Registry of Births, Deaths and Marriages, New South Wales, 1504/1884.
[10] Marriage register entry of George Briggs Mackie and Frances Emily Bulling, 2 May 1882 at Registry Office, Fitzroy, Victoria, Registry of Births, Deaths and Marriages, Victoria, Collingwood 3094.
[11] A Pioneer of the Furniture Trade, *Newcastle Sun*, 19 October 1954, p. 3 (Furniture Spring Fair Supplement). Retrieved 25 October 2021, from http://nla.gov.au/nla.news-article167653441

a pod. Nor was Robert. He went up to Sydney to live, but he didn't get married. Then he took himself off to Johannesburg, South Africa.

I never understood Robert. He wanted to go to a goldfield. How could he, after what happened to dad? And he got himself killed there. Was it like staring into the eyes of a snake, hypnotised? I could have told him – don't do what dad did! But I was the youngest.

I wasn't so quick to leave Melbourne. I went to Sydney in the 1890s. I lived just seven kilometres from Alexander. He married a German girl. I married an English girl. He had a big wedding in Elizabeth Street; Frances and I got married in a registry office in Fitzroy. You see; not two peas in a pod!

Maybe Alexander was disappointed he wasn't a big success like James. Good luck to James, but I'm happy with my life, and I'm happy with my work. I put on my suit for church on Sunday, and I remember I'm Scottish. My middle name, Briggs, goes back to Gran,[12] and I know the Mackie tartan. I am an individual pea.

Reflection

George is my great grandfather (on my mother's side). George's father got killed when George was still a baby. The boys' childhood must have been difficult. I wondered how that childhood affected all of them – they all left Melbourne. I wondered if George felt there was a shadow over his life that he had to overcome.

I have one photo of him and his wife. The feeling I have of it is: "Life has had its trials, but I have done okay, and I have tried to be a decent man."

---

[12] Gran is Rachel Bridges who married Alexander Mackie, grandfather of George and the brothers in this story. 'Briggs' and 'Bridges' were names that were used alternatively.

The last one to stay

George Mackie was the last one to stay at home, although that was mostly a matter of age. In 1878, he was fifteen. It's an uncomfortable age, because it is old enough to be thinking about an occupation, but still young enough to be a comfort to your mother. This morning Catherine, his mother, had asked him to accompany her on a visit to Margaret, because Margaret and her husband were back living in Collingwood and she had just had a baby.

Margaret was George's older sister, ten years older than him. He knew her father was not his father, not that it was a big deal, and it was seldom talked about, because who needed to talk about it? Margaret had always been his sister. She was three years old when Catherine and Robert, his father, got married. She was there at her mother's side at the ceremony, all dressed up and happy. Catherine and Robert were happy too, in the sombre precincts of the Presbyterian Church in Melbourne. They both came from Fife in Scotland, even the same part of Fife.

George was the youngest of four boys. He was only six months old when his father got killed, in late 1863. Margaret was ten. It had been a sudden accident and a lingering death. It put some distance between him and his brothers, because they had been old enough to have some idea of what was going on, while he was the oblivious infant. And when you grow up with a shadow around you, you never know it is a shadow until much later on. For you it is just how the world is constructed, and you accept it, the weight of it, without knowing what it's about.

Catherine had a parcel of new baby clothes for Margaret, because Catherine was a dressmaker. George knew that being a dressmaker was important, because his mother had to have some way of earning money after her husband died. Robert had been only thirty-one, as was she. She had Margaret plus the four boys to look after. It also meant they always had visitors to the house, people coming for fittings of clothes in the process of being made. Was that a good thing or a bad thing? George just accepted it; it was how things were. And so they all grew up.

George was happy that Margaret was back. She and her husband, John Skelly, had been away for years. Was he really her husband? George didn't know. Catherine had her doubts. Margaret had said they'd got married in Ballarat in 1873, but why was there no celebration? Why were there no invitations to the wedding? Ballarat was not so far away. Or even, why did they not get married in Melbourne?

It was shocking anyway. John Skelly had worked with Robert's father, Alexander, in his stonemason's workshop in Melbourne. John was thirty years older than Margaret; he would have been around fifty years old when they got together, and she was around eighteen. And he had known her since she was three.

Alexander had announced he was closing up the shop because he was too old to be a stonemason. He was going to be a grocer. So, John had to figure out what to do, because he wasn't quite old enough to retire, or even semi-retire. He decided he was going to check out the goldfields, and before you know it he had left town, and Margaret had gone with him.

Is that why there had been no announcement of a wedding? It would have been too shocking? But Catherine's own past had been, shall we say, unorthodox? Still, you never know how people will react, notwithstanding their own past.

John and Margaret came back a couple of years later, and they had a baby, a boy. This was not something George paid much attention to; he was more intent on working out his occupation. He would not become a carpenter, because that was what his father had been.

Catherine was telling George, "The new baby is called Catherine Isabella." They had named it after her. You could tell she was pleased. And she reminded him, "The others are called John Luke, he's four, and Alexander is aged two."

"Oh," said George. "Yes, they named Alexander after our grandfather." This was funny, because Alexander Mackie was not the boy's biological grandfather. That would have been.... it was unknown. But Catherine was pleased about the name. Margaret was unquestionably part of the Mackie family.

George didn't think he was the appropriate one to be asking his mother questions about who Margaret's father was. That was Margaret's place. George was a fifteen-year-old boy walking down the road with his mother. He was just carrying the parcel, the gift she had made with her own hands.

George asked, "Who was Isabella?" That was the new baby's middle name. They probably got that name from someone too, although George didn't really expect an answer. Surely, sometimes, people just liked a name, or it sounded good. And it would be new.

"It was your grandfather Alexander's little sister," said Catherine. George smiled.

"Where was the baby Alexander born?" he asked. He had an idea it was somewhere up in New South Wales.

"He was born in Gulgong."

"The goldmining town?"

"Yes, John must have had gold fever," she replied. She was being ironic. John, after all, was a stonemason, more inclined to shape stone than dig it up and throw it away in the search for something small that glittered.

"Are they back here for good?" asked George.

"I hope so," said Catherine, quickly.

George was thinking about his older brothers. They were all out working. None of them was a carpenter. Alexander, his oldest brother, was a painter. He learned off Uncle William. Alexander had told him once, how their father had come home from the hospital with his left hand and half his left arm gone, how it was all wrapped up in bandages. And their father was like an empty shell from the shock. And how it had sent the whole household into a daze. And his father got worse and worse, until he had to go back to the hospital, and he died there.

"But what happened?" George had asked. "What happened?"

Alexander had told him how there had been a goldmine in Collingwood, a deep shaft in the ground behind the Royal George Hotel in Hoddle Street. It got very wet at the bottom. After you go down fifty feet or so, the water just seeps in, so they had a pump to pump the water out. But the pump used to get clogged up all the time, and you had to take it apart to clean it out. The pipes were heavy and one of them fell hard onto their father's hand.

It was their father's job, with his carpentry background, to shore up the walls of the shaft. The memory of seeing his father's amputated arm made Alexander feel sick. He would never be a carpenter, and he couldn't wait to get out of Collingwood, to get out of Melbourne.

George realised that that was part of the reason he was glad Margaret was back. He recognised, with a sense of shame, the selfishness of it. Now, if he left Melbourne, he would not be leaving his mother by herself. As they came to the gate of John and Margaret's house, young John Luke ran out to meet them, a cheeky grin on his face. "Grandma!" he shouted.

Closing notes

George is George Briggs Mackie (1863-1926), a great grandfather of mine on my mother's side.

George did leave Melbourne eventually, although he stayed in Melbourne long enough to marry and have four children. He became a painter. After the family arrived in Sydney, four more children were born. All of the children had names from predecessors in the family except the last one: Vera Lillian just sounded nice.

George's three brothers also left Melbourne and went to Sydney. Margaret stayed in Collingwood.

John Skelly and Margaret were, in fact, not formally married, but they stayed together and had eight children. After Margaret's mother, Catherine, died (in 1900), they did finally get married, in 1906, at the same Presbyterian Church in Melbourne where Catherine and Robert had got married in 1856. Margaret was fifty-three and John was eighty-three. For what it's worth, making peace with the Lord?

Margaret was born in Melbourne in 1853, sometime after her mother came ashore from the ship the *Wanderer* from Scotland. The father? My guess is that he was a Scottish lad from Airlie. Why? Margaret was the informant on her mother's death certificate, and on it she said her mother was born in Airlie. She wasn't born in Airlie, and everyone knew that. The whole family came from Largo in Fife. So, why say Airlie, unless it was a clue to where Margaret's father came from? Margaret and her mother had obviously had many conversations about the past.

Alice and Alice – two cousins

Alice and Alice were cousins, the daughters of two brothers: James Hood Mackie and George Briggs Mackie (George is my great grandfather). They were the sons of Robert Mackie and Catherine Hood, who were immigrants to Melbourne from Scotland in 1852 and 1853 respectively. Both sons left Melbourne and came up to Sydney to live. James then went to Newcastle and established a very successful furniture store. George stayed in Sydney and became a house painter.

James Hood Mackie married Mary Kendrick Murray in 1882 and they had thirteen children. Alice Maud was the second child. She was born in 1885. She was born in Sydney, but she grew up in Newcastle.

George Briggs Mackie married Frances Emily Bulling, also in 1882, and they had nine children. Florence Alice was the seventh child. She was born in 1899 in Arncliffe and she grew up there.

Alice Maud was fourteen years older than Florence Alice. Both of their lives were complicated in terms of relationships, extraordinarily so. I wonder how much they knew of each other, and how much the younger cousin looked up to her older cousin as a person to whom she could relate. Certainly, there were times in their lives when they lived not far from each other, in the Rockdale/Arncliffe area of Sydney.

Putting each of their stories together was not easy, because much of their lives took place outside of the bounds of the records of the Registry of Births, Deaths and Marriages (BDM). In the case of Florence Alice Mackie, it wasn't until I received contact through my family tree from a person who said he was a descendant of hers that I knew she had any children at all. Thus, I discovered she had had a de facto relationship for around twenty years.

When I started acquiring certificates for Alice Maud, among them was a birth certificate for a child born in 1918, but the certificate was not created until 1934. I am still not sure if the designated father on that certificate was in biological fact her father, or whether he was affirming that role through his current relationship with Alice Maud. However, it might have been a belated recognition of what had always been a fact that was unable to be admitted at the time.

I have learned that the norms are not always the norm. Also, I have learned that the norms of society lurk behind much family history work. The model of a child growing up, marrying someone and having children of their own, and staying together with the one person for life, is strong, and understandably so. But there are assumed attitudes about all of this, and these days, many people who contest those attitudes. I try to approach my discoveries, instead, with a sense of wonder. I think that, whatever the norms, people very often manage to live intriguing lives.

People also manage to leave questions in their wake. For all that I have found out about Alice and Alice, I could not say if they were nice people, or loving, or happy or unhappy. Would I like them, would I admire them, would I feel compassionate towards them? Yet the facts that we do know tease us and suggest.

There are also questions about exposure. These two women lived what we might call complicated lives. Moral judgements invariably hover around. Should I have just let it all lie? Do I "have the right" to expose these facts? Even if Alice and Alice are dead, they have children and grandchildren. Yet, their lives are there to be seen. In fact, all of my searching has been in records that are now public.

Even my own life will one day be public in the same way, through the records. There is no defence against that. So, there is no point in arguing about it. We have to accept that it is okay to view the records, whatever the records may say. We also have to accept that such exposure is not the same as understanding. When they say "History is written by the victors", it is just a way of recognising that the records have their limitations. Finally, it is us as the observers who carry the final word, with whatever sensibility we care to bring to the material. One hopes to learn, and appreciate.

Story 1: Alice Maud Mackie, 1885 to 1947

Child of James Hood Mackie and Mary Kendrick Murray.

Alice was born on 1 August 1885 at Surry Hills, the second of thirteen children. Her parents later moved to Newcastle. James established the Federal Furniture Warehouse in Hunter Street,

Newcastle in 1897, a business that prospered through to at least the 1950s.

In 1902, at seventeen, she married George Isaacs and she gave birth to a daughter the same year – Minnie Elizabeth. But Alice divorced George in 1907, on the grounds of his desertion. At the time, she was living at 5 St Marys Terrace, Lower Domain – near St Mary's Cathedral in Sydney.

In 1909 Alice married Gordon Fink (in Sydney), the son of a Jewish solicitor in Melbourne. I think that she had the child from George with her, although I have no proof for this. Alice and Gordon lived in Sydney for six months, then they travelled to Victoria, staying at Wangaratta on the way. It would seem that Gordon was wanting to present Alice to his family. They took their time getting to Melbourne, because they did not get there until 1912.

Gordon had studied law and finished his degree, but he had not yet been admitted to the Bar. One suspects that he was in Sydney because he was running away from his destiny, at least, the destiny prescribed for him by his father.

When they got to Melbourne, there was obviously a furore about Gordon's wife. It should be mentioned that Gordon's father was not just a solicitor; he was a principal of one of Melbourne's leading law firms. The story that emerges is this: Gordon has supposedly been told by Alice that her previous husband, George Isaacs, had died, but then it is alleged that he found out that this was not the case. He is allegedly outraged, and sues for an annulment of the marriage in Melbourne. A decree of nullity of marriage (as opposed to a divorce) was granted in May 1912.

Are we to believe that Alice never told Gordon that she had got a divorce from George? There was no doubt that there had been a previous partner: she had a child. Or, was the real story that his family didn't want the scandal of their son marrying a divorcee, especially one who already had a child? And she was not Jewish: was that a factor? The legal case was pursued on the grounds of Alice's bigamy.

However, when I looked at the records of Alice's divorce from George Isaacs (1907; available at New South Wales State Archives), I discovered that Gordon's father's legal firm, Fink Best & Hall, of Melbourne, had issued a subpoena for those records in February

1912, which means that they not only knew Alice had got a divorce from George, they actively suppressed the knowledge. They committed perjury. Alice's marriage to Gordon was not bigamous; she was not still married to George. And although one might argue that it is possible she told Gordon that George was dead, this would not explain why Fink Best & Hall went searching for the divorce in the New South Wales legal records.

In the wake of this legal decision, Gordon and Alice split up. It seems clear that Gordon's family forced him to end his marriage, and most likely he couldn't stand the shame of the situation; maybe he still loved Alice, but it was now immaterial.

Gordon went to Perth (as far away from Melbourne as he could go, it seems). Alice and Minnie went back to Newcastle (to the suburb of Waratah), back to her family. Gordon was finally admitted as a solicitor in Western Australia, but he also got involved in farming, and somehow served in the Malay States Rifles as well. Perhaps going to Malaya was the first thing he did after the annulment happened.

When the First World War started, and Australia joined the war, Gordon enlisted immediately in the Australian Army (September 1914), and he was sent to Gallipoli. He died on 2 May 1915. The reports said he performed an act of heroism during an assault at Gallipoli. His battalion was engaged in fighting during the night, and he volunteered to carry ammunition to his comrades up on a ridge when he was shot and killed. Out of a battalion of one thousand, eight hundred soldiers were wounded or killed (letter from Major Mansbridge published in *The Eastern Recorder*, Western Australia, 13 August 1915).

Alice kept the name Fink. She met another man, David Thomas McLoughlin, who had been born in Tasmania. Both David's parents had been born in Tasmania; there may have been a convict past there. Alice and David got married at Kensington (Sydney) in 1916, a Church of England marriage, although David was born Roman Catholic. Minnie, her daughter, was now fourteen. Alice and David did not have any children (later, in their divorce papers, it is said there was "no issue" of the marriage).

However, there is a parallel, conflicting story here, in which Alice meets another man, Joseph Beirman, whose family had emigrated from London sometime in the previous few years. They were Jewish, and tailors. Joseph was born in 1892; he was seven years younger than Alice. And a birth record says that Alice had a child to Joseph in 1918, called June. But, this is not a typical birth record. This one was not created until 1934, even though the date of birth is stated to be 20 June 1918. The informants are the two parents, Joseph and Alice. The certificate is dated 15 May 1934, and signed by R.W. Willis, Registrar General.

However, Alice was still married to David McLoughlin in 1918. These two stories do not reconcile easily. We know that David petitioned for divorce in 1921, on the grounds of her adultery with another man, Jack Buckworth, who is named as co-respondent. Alice was living at North Sydney, and David was living at Merewether, near Newcastle. He was a commercial traveller, or sales manager, for Barnet Glass Rubber Company, a seller of car tyres.

Alice sued David for maintenance, but he did not pay her anything. He claimed he gave her 200 pounds when they separated; she denied this. David applied for bankruptcy as the divorce was finalised, despite the fact that he had a well-paying job.

Alice reverted to the name Fink. It was 1921; June was three, and Minnie was nineteen.

In 1926, David McLoughlin married Minnie! After I obtained records for this marriage, I discovered that David and Minnie had had a child in 1921, so the evidence in the divorce case starts to look questionable, and perhaps fictitious. Did Jack Buckworth really exist or was he a name of convenience just to satisfy the conventions of divorce cases under the laws of the time?

(Another such person was "Annie Message", named in a divorce case elsewhere in my family tree. There is no such surname in the BDM records over a 100-year period, that is, she was a fictitious person. I think it was a lawyers' in-joke: "Any message?") The reality was that David was already with Minnie. Did Alice know this? She may not have, because David and Minnie were in Newcastle, and Alice was in Sydney.

Or, was Jack Buckworth the real father of June? This would fit if the divorce was on the grounds of desertion, because a spouse had to be deserted for three years, which brings us back to 1918 when June was born. But the divorce was based on adultery, and

Buckworth must exist because he has a solicitor. In contrast to the name 'Message', Buckworth shows up in the BDM records. In fact, to make it even more interesting, one John B.M. Buckworth married Eileen B. Milligan at Mosman in 1921 (of all the years it could have been). The truth may have been very complicated indeed.

Even with the little we do know through the records, the truth is at least complex. The marriage certificate of David McLoughlin and Minnie Isaacs in 1926 gives 'Maud Isaacs' as one of the witnesses. The ages of David and Minnie check out – he is thirty-two and she is twenty-four, so there is no mistake about who they are. And Maud Isaacs can only be Alice Mackie, David's former wife and Minnie's mother. How extraordinary! Was Joseph Beirman present as well?

Then, in 1932, Joseph Beirman reappeared on the scene (according to the records), and Alice and Joseph got married – in the Congregational Church in Sydney, despite him being Jewish. I suspect that this was a secret marriage, and that Joseph's family thought they had been married years earlier.

The wedding was in July 1932. The next month, an odd thing happened: David and Minnie McLoughlin registered the birth of the daughter they had had in 1921 – Peggie. Perhaps this was the prompt for Joseph and Alice to register (in 1934) the birth of their daughter, June, who had been born in 1918.

The *Hebrew Standard of Australasia*, in June 1936, reported Mr and Mrs Joseph Beirman attending the Montefiore Home Ball at David Jones store in Sydney, among 800 others, and June, aged eighteen, was also present. The report described many of the gowns worn by the ladies present.

Alice and Joseph remained together until death. Alice died in April 1947, aged sixty-two, and Joseph lived until 1964. Alice was not buried in Sydney, and her husband was not buried with her. Joseph was buried at Rookwood in the Jewish section, while Alice's body went to Sandgate, the cemetery at Newcastle, where she was buried in the James Hood Mackie family grave (Church of England) along with her parents and several of her siblings, returning to the fold of the family in the end.

The informant for Alice's death certificate was Joseph Beirman. Her life story had been simplified, with Joseph being named as the only spouse. Her two children are named: Minnie and June. June's age is twenty-eight, which is consistent with the birth certificate I have – born in 1918. Minnie, however, is unexplained. Her age is said to be thirty-five, but she was actually forty-five – born in 1902. In any case, her stated age still predates Alice's relationship with Joseph; her imputed birth is 1912, six years before Joseph and Alice made their connection.

A descendant of June's told me (via my family tree) that Alice had worked in the theatre and she had worked with quite a lot of the stars of the day, such as Gladys Moncrieff. I wonder if this was where Alice and Gordon Fink had met – Gordon on the run from his family in another city, and looking for a place to meet people. This is a fact that puts an entirely different perspective on Alice's life. It suggests a cohesive centre, an ongoing theme, and a passion that enlivens all the events and twists of her life.

Now, when I am looking at a person in the family tree, and the life that I have built up for them through the records, I wonder whether there is one other significant fact that would throw a different light on it all – they were interested in theatre, or they got killed at Gallipoli because they despaired of their life. I think there is always something like that.

Story 2: Florence Alice Mackie, 1899 to 1978

Child of George Briggs Mackie and Frances Emily Bulling.

She was born on 18 December 1899 (just two weeks before the end of the nineteenth century) at Rockdale. She was the seventh of nine children. Her parents later moved to Arncliffe and stayed there until George died in 1926. Frances lived until 1934.

At the age of eighteen, Florence Alice had a child, father unknown. It was 1918 (the same year that Alice Maud's child June was born) and she was living at Rockdale. She called the child Marie Mackie. Marie grew up; she married Leslie James Hayward in 1939.

Somewhere between 1918 and 1924, Florence Alice started a relationship with Thomas Charles Denning. He was seventeen years older than her. He had been born at Dubbo and he had worked in a cotton mill. He had also been married, to Edith Beatrice Moore; they had got married in 1902 in Sydney (the same year that Alice Maud Mackie had married George Isaacs). Edith was just three years younger than Thomas, and they had six children together. There is no record of their divorce, or Edith's remarriage, and Edith did not die until 1960, at Erskineville.

Thomas Denning and Florence Alice did not get (legally) married. One assumes that this was because he was still legally married to Edith. Nonetheless, she became known as Florence Alice Denning, and they had a child in 1926: Noreen Mary. The relationship continued for perhaps twenty years.

Noreen grew up and married: Albert James Small at Chatswood in 1947. That's according to the BDM records. However, according to a person who contacted me through my family tree, Noreen (also) married Edward James Robert Hallam. This person is a direct descendant of the latter couple, and he says this is supported by DNA testing. My digging indicates that Albert Small died in 1952, and that Noreen married Edward Hallam in 1951. How is this possible, legally? But one assumes that Albert and Noreen had separated, and that legal niceties do not determine everyone's life.

There was a child of this marriage, satisfying the DNA link required by the existence of the descendant, but there was also a subsequent divorce of Edward and Noreen Hallam, in 1956. I do not know what happened to Noreen after this.

Thomas Denning and Florence Alice had another child: Allan, who was born in 1936 at Enmore. He also grew up and married. His occupation was 'brushmaker'. He died in 2013 at Kingswood, west of Sydney. However, later I obtained Florence Alice's death certificate, for which Allan was the informant, and he named five other children that I did not know about: Charley, Shirley, Jim, Gladys and Eileen. So, there were several more children than I thought. Nevertheless, the time frame for the relationship remains about the same.

The other thing that Allan Denning's completion of the death certificate informed me about was Florence Alice's partners. No, not that exactly, but the accepted notion of who her partners had been. Marie was mentioned as being the first child, meaning that she was accepted as part of the family with no questions asked about who her biological father was. Two partners are mentioned: Thomas

Denning and Francis Brennan. But there was one more partner: Thomas Sidney Robinson. I assume that Allan knew about this relationship, but I suppose that he considered it unnecessary to include it.

What happened to the relationship between Thomas Denning and Florence Alice? Well, we know it ended, because Florence Alice married in 1948. The husband was Thomas Sidney Robinson, aged thirty, of Marrickville. Florence Alice was now forty-eight, significantly older than him. Interestingly, the BDM record doesn't give her family name as either Mackie or Denning, it gives it as "Mackie known as Denning". This is very unusual.

Thomas Robinson had not been married before. Despite his youth, he died within three years of the marriage, in 1951. The inexplicable factor is that he died in Goulburn. It is not as if Thomas Robinson was born in Goulburn. He had been born in Sydney. Had he split up with Florence Alice? Was he working on a job at Goulburn? Did he die en route, while he was travelling to somewhere else? These questions are unanswered.

What had happened to Thomas Denning? He had not died before Florence Alice married Thomas Robinson. However, he died on 11 August 1952 at Marrickville. He was seventy.

Florence Alice married one more time. She married Francis Norman Brennan, a hospital attendant, in 1953, at Bankstown – at the registry office. He was aged fifty, three years younger than her. Francis did not live all that long either. He died in 1960, aged fifty-seven.

Florence Alice did not die until 1978, when she was seventy-eight. Her first child, Marie, had died in 1975 at Bankstown District Hospital, indicating that she and her mother lived close to one another, if not with one another.

Florence Alice was survived by the children she had had with Thomas Denning. She was living at Alexandria (in Sydney) when she died, but she died at Bankstown District Hospital. One gets the feeling that she had been staying with one of her children when she got sick. She had had "congestive cardiac failure" for two years.

Did Florence Alice's body "go home" when she died? Not intentionally. Allan Denning, the informant on her death certificate, did not know her mother's name. He only knew that her father's name was George Mackie. But in fact, George and Frances Mackie are buried at Woronora Cemetery, and so is Florence Alice. Francis Norman Brennan is buried there; I think that was the reason why she was buried there. Ironically, David McLoughlin (one of Alice Maud Mackie's husbands), is also buried at Woronora.

What I do not have for Florence Alice is an informant who can tell me something that brings more life to her. The descendant who contacted me told me he knew almost nothing about his forebears until he did a DNA test and got lucky. For Alice Maud, I eventually had an image of her life, in the world of live theatre. It served as a compass to guide me through the tumult of her relationships. Florence Alice still feels largely unknown – what was her defining centre?

It is easy to see a succession of relationships as repetition – a person who repeats the same mistakes. But one does not get this image of Florence Alice's relationships. The first one was youthful – the (presumably) young man by whom she got pregnant. Either he disappeared or she chose not to enter into a permanent relationship with him. That would signify some sense of strength and independence. And also, the fact that she kept the child, at a time when so many illegitimate babies were put up for adoption and the mothers felt compelled to do so. Was her cousin the inspiration for her to do this?

Her next relationship was with a much older man, so we might conclude that she had a need to be looked after by a father figure. It was not the easiest of choices – he was coming out of a marriage where he was the father of six children. Were there occasions when Florence Alice had to play the part of the children's father's new wife? Was she labelled as the usurper?

Florence Alice and Thomas Denning stayed together for perhaps twenty years. Did they split up because she realised that he was becoming an old man long before she was ready to become an old woman? One way of reading the scant facts is that this is exactly what happened, and then he lost his enthusiasm for life, or he couldn't live without her, so he died. Pure speculation.

You could say that she erred in the opposite direction on her next choice. She decided it would be better to have a man who was younger than her (eighteen years younger, as opposed to Thomas

Denning, who was seventeen years older). Does this fit with the idea that a succession of relationships is repetitive, or does it support the idea that there is some kind of development or evolution evident? The person is not making the same mistakes, but is at least making new ones? You could say she was still experimenting.

It could be that the relationships were not mistakes at all, but episodes from which one learns, and there are certain satisfactions and challenges along the way. As to break-ups, one view of modern times is that a break-up is preferable to a lifetime of steadily being ground to dust by one's partner. Then there is the view that when the fire goes out, one should move on.

Florence Alice's – and Alice Maud's – relationships could be seen as unorthodox. In narrow conventional terms, their relationships might be seen as unusual, or even inappropriate. Some people would say scandalous. Some societies and religious groups are sterner than others when it comes to ostracising couples considered to deviate from the norm. Sometimes, cities make it more possible to survive as an atypical couple, and sometimes, a couple can win people over through their personality and presence.

In some ancient societies the emperor could, during a celebration, sanction even unorthodox unions. It was deemed an act of wisdom to occasionally loosen up the tightness of the reins, and allow room for generosity. It was better both for those feeling constrained, and for those too inclined to judge others.

Sometimes, a person who has lost a partner (for whatever reason) will get married again quite soon, and we think that they just find it too difficult to be alone. There is some sympathy for that perspective. That was not the case with either Alice Maud or Florence Alice. Alice Maud stayed married to Joseph Beirman (officially) for the last fifteen years of her life. In practice, they may have been together for nearly thirty years.

After Francis Brennan died, Florence Alice did not have another partner, and she lived for a further eighteen years. Accordingly, any theory about her dependence on having a partner fails.

At the end, one hopes mainly for the affection of one's children. This could be one conclusion, but by itself it would be trite and sentimental. Moreover, it would dismiss the wide sweep of their lives. What I really found compelling about their lives was what I saw as the felt necessity to live their own life, even though it was outside of the trodden paths.

There is a saying in an old Chinese book: "She steps on the tail of the tiger and it does not bite her". I think Alice and Alice both stepped on the tail of the tiger. They both felt the necessity to step forward, despite the dangers of the path itself, and the disapproval of other people. And in doing so, I suspect they lived well.

Section 7: Great great grandparents, paternal (1)

Thomas Martins (1834-1904) and Mary Ann Williams (1832-1860)

William Dower (1825-1907) and Elizabeth Pascoe (1826-1920)

Introductory notes

These two sets of great great grandparents are my father's father's grandparents. Both couples were born in Cornwall and migrated to Australia. The 'Martins' name was occasionally 'Martin' in Cornwall and permanently 'Martin' in Australia. Most of the stories here are about the Dower and Pascoe families, because this was an area of relative ignorance for me before this book.

The first story is about the Pascoe family coming to Australia to continue their tradition of mining. They went to South Australia, where copper had been found in the 1840s. Elizabeth Pascoe, their eldest child, was already married to William Dower when her parents decided to emigrate with their whole family, so Elizabeth and William joined the throng. The place they went to, Burra, came to be known as Australia's little Cornwall.

The second story focuses particularly on William and Elizabeth Dower, who eventually left Burra and went to Victoria to mine for gold. They ended up in Bethanga, where Thomas Martin (along with his son Thomas, born 1856) had established himself as the mining manager of a goldmine that sought to extract gold from quartz.

The third story traces a monumental change – the time when mining ceased for the Cornish families (Martin, Dower and Pascoe) in Australia, after hundreds, if not thousands, of years.

The fourth story concerns Thomas Pascoe, who was a son of one of the Pascoes who stayed in South Australia, and his is a great pioneer story – his journeys to the goldfields in Victoria and his return to buy a farm, and his eventual election to the South Australian Parliament.

The last story is about Thomas Martin (born 1834). I think he followed a conscious, long-term pathway to develop his knowledge of Australia from the perspective of a miner, and then to apply that knowledge when he became the mining manager at Bethanga. So, I have called it "The long journey to fulfilment".

The Pascoe family: Cornish miners in South Australia

All of my direct ancestors came to Australia between 1838 and 1860, on eleven separate voyages. All of them came from the British Isles. Most of them were my great great grandparents, but among them were two sets of great great great grandparents, and two voyages brought families from Cornwall.

Francis and Elizabeth Pascoe were great great great grandparents of mine from Cornwall. They came on the *Abberton* in 1848. They were taking a big step: both aged forty-eight, they brought their nine children with them. Of the children, Elizabeth was the eldest, twenty-two, and she was married to William Dower who, of course, came with them. They had one child of their own, and Elizabeth was pregnant with another, who was born at sea, four weeks before arrival in Adelaide.

Thomas and Mary Ann Martin were the other family from Cornwall, and they also sailed to Adelaide, on the *Carnatic* in 1857. They were young, and had one child, also called Thomas. He was one year old (he was my great grandfather). I don't think the Pascoe and Martin families knew each other back in Cornwall. The Pascoe family came from Crowan and Wendron, east of Penzance; the Martin family came from Towednack and St Ives on the northwest coast – only about thirty kilometres apart, but far enough to be strangers.

Nevertheless, they were Cornish, and moreover, both were mining families, so there were strong commonalities. There are sayings about this. One is, "Wherever there's a hole in the ground, you'll find a Cousin Jack at the bottom of it, searching for metal." Cousin Jack is a generic term for a man from Cornwall. Women were called Cousin Jennies. Certainly, it is true in my family tree that the same names came down through the generations, although not expressly Jack or Jennie.

Another characteristic is that Cornish miners had a highly developed sense of their prowess as miners, like the dwarves in Tolkein's *Lord of the Rings*. When the world opened up in the 1800s to accelerated migration around the world, Cornish people were there in droves. They went to America, Canada, South Africa, Peru,

Mexico, Chile. And South Australia and Victoria. They believed they "were innately and uniquely equipped as skilled hard-rock miners".[13]

Oswald Pryor says the greatest wave of emigration from Cornwall started in about 1830 and was at its height during the period from 1845 to 1880.[14] In the 1840s, Cornish prospectors in South Australia had found silver, lead, galena and copper. The greatest discovery was made at Burra Burra (now called Burra), 160 kilometres north of Adelaide, where copper ore was found.

Some Cornish immigrants had arrived as agricultural labourers, but Cousin Jacks could switch as occasion warranted to mining. However, experienced miners were required to work the copper mine, and Francis Pascoe was attracted by the opportunity. Mining in Cornwall was already under threat from cheaper imports of copper and tin from overseas, and in 1866 the industry collapsed. The Pascoe family picked a good time to go.

The Burra workforce grew to around 1,170 miners (as Pryor notes). Francis and Elizabeth Pascoe stayed at Burra until the end of their lives. As many mining families did, they lived in a hollow dug out of the banks of Burra Creek.

Pryor describes the dug-outs as follows: they "consisted of two, three or four rooms, the largest being only nine feet square. The miners roofed them with layers of stout sticks, and over these they placed thin, flat slabs of stone, made more or less watertight by means of a thick layer of puddled clay.

"These homes were snug in winter, and cool in summer. There were, of course, some disabilities: straying cows and horses broke through the roofs, practical jokers dropped stones down the chimneys, or poured water down them, and a severe thunderstorm flooded them out. There were also many cases of typhoid fever..."[15]

---

[13] Martin Greenwood, Appendix 3: Cornish emigration, in *The Promised Land: The story of emigration from Oxfordshire and neighbouring Buckinghamshire, Northamptonshire and Warwickshire 1815-1914*, Robert Boyd Publications, Witney, Oxfordshire, 2020, p. 127.
[14] Pryor, Oswald, *Australia's Little Cornwall*, Rigby, Adelaide, 1962, p. 16.
[15] Pryor, pp. 21-22.

One must remember that Francis and Elizabeth would have had several children living with them. The youngest was five when they arrived in South Australia.

The Burra mining population was strongly Cornish, but there were also other nationalities. A great deal of equipment and stores were required for the mine, and these were hauled by bullock teams from Adelaide. Augmenting them were teams of mules, whose drivers came from Spain. One of the camps had the name *Mintaro*, which is Spanish for *resting place*.

There were Indians in the area too, who invariably worked as shepherds. The name *Burra Burra* comes from them. It is Hindustani, and means *very large*. So, despite the occurrence of 'burra' in Aboriginal languages (eg kookaburra), the name is not Aboriginal.

When gold was discovered in Victoria in 1851, many of the miners abandoned Burra and it almost came to a standstill. Some of the miners "made it rich" from gold, but most of them made only ordinary returns, and by 1855 many of them were drifting back to Burra.

By the 1870s, the Burra mine was petering out, but in 1861 copper had been discovered at Moonta and Wallaroo on the upper Yorke Peninsula, about 150 kilometres southwest of Burra, and this was an even bigger find than Burra. Cornish miners flocked there, and the engineers and managers (called captains) were wholly Cornish, so much so that Moonta became known as "Australia's Little Cornwall".

For the Pascoe parents, it was too late to move. They were old and they stayed put at Burra. There was an incentive for younger people to move away, because of the way land was managed at Burra. The land on which the mine was situated was tightly controlled by the company, called the South Australian Mining Association (SAMA). It refused to grant freehold title to anyone – for businesses or residences, and the leases it did grant were short-term. This was one reason many miners chose to live in dug-outs along the creek.

SAMA's attitude persisted until the 1870s, despite the fact that the peak population was around 4,000. Its hold also meant there was no local council to plan, construct and manage infrastructure.

This led to a number of small townships springing up around Burra, including Kooringa to the south, and it meant that these small townships were scattered and divided. It wasn't until 1872 that a District Council was formed, which had some effect in bringing the settlements together. The Town of Burra was proclaimed in 1876 and the first Mayor and town councillors were appointed.

Francis did not live to see the change. Perhaps he would have seen the irony, that the change did not come until the economic life of the mine was virtually exhausted. Francis died of dysentery in 1871, a testimony to the difficulty of maintaining good sanitation in their dug-out shelter. He was seventy-one. Elizabeth died in 1878 of apoplexy, when she was seventy-eight.

References

Greenwood, Martin, Appendix 3: Cornish emigration, in *The Promised Land: The story of emigration from Oxfordshire and neighbouring Buckinghamshire, Northamptonshire and Warwickshire 1815-1914*, Robert Boyd Publications, Witney, Oxfordshire, 2020, p. 127.

Pryor, Oswald, *Australia's Little Cornwall*, Rigby, Adelaide, 1962.

William and Elizabeth Dower: a mining family

William and Elizabeth Dower, great great grandparents of mine, came to Australia from Crowan in Cornwall. William was a miner, although his father, William, had alternated between mining and farming (in the 1841 Census he was a yeoman, meaning that he owned some land). William (the son) was one of ten children. Elizabeth was one of nine. When they got married, he was twenty, and she was nineteen. But movement was afoot. Elizabeth's parents, despite being in their late forties, were considering emigration to South Australia, with all of their children.

William and Elizabeth were only too happy to join them. They all came out on the *Abberton*, arriving at Adelaide in August 1848. They already had one child of their own, and Elizabeth was pregnant with another, who was born at sea, four weeks before arrival in Adelaide.

The Pascoe and Dower families made their way to Burra Burra (now called Burra), 160 kilometres north of Adelaide, where copper ore had been found in 1845. Francis Pascoe and William Dower went to work as miners – a new country and an old occupation. The mine was regarded as a successful endeavour: although it did not last, over a period of thirty years, nearly five million pounds' worth of copper ore (money, not weight) was produced.

The families lived at various places in and around Burra. Some lived in dug-outs in the banks of the Burra Creek. Some lived at Kooringa, to the south of Burra. Francis Pascoe and family lived in one of the dug-outs.

William and Elizabeth Dower lived at Kooringa, and they stayed there for around twenty years. Several of their children were born there. The children included Philippa, who was born in 1857. She is important, because she is my great grandmother. There is a problem with her: the birth records in South Australia say that she is a boy called Phillip. This is not true.

The records say that William and Elizabeth had a baby girl called Phillipa in 1852. However, she died in 1855. I have no dispute with that. And note, it was customary to reuse a name if a child died, so it would be nothing unusual for a later child to be called Phillipa. My point of difference from the records is that the baby born in 1857 was definitely a girl, not a boy. Why? Because, in later records (marriage, births of her children, death), my great grandmother's age consistently corresponds to her having been born in 1857. Another unusual feature was that her name, according to these later documents, is spelt Philippa with one 'l' and two pp's.

Is this discrepancy about the sex a transcription error in the records? The indexed records have been transcribed from handwritten documents by mere humans. Maybe. I know that it upsets other family historians, because they have gone to the trouble of looking up the records, and why shouldn't they accept them as being true? I have been told that I am wrong, that the baby born in 1857 was a boy: "It's in the records!" – but when the person involved is your great grandmother, you become a little bit more adamant.

So, I assert: the Phillip Dower who was born on 30 October 1857 at Kooringa was a girl, and her name is Philippa! For example, on her marriage certificate, January 1879, she is twenty-one, indicating she was born in or close to 1857. And for those who still wonder, she is not a twin (Phillip and Philippa!) – according to the records.

Philippa got married in Bethanga, Victoria, so how did she get there? Her parents had fourteen children over a period of thirty years. Philippa was the seventh. The first child was born before they left Cornwall and the second was born at sea, before the parents arrived in South Australia. The next ten children were born in the mining district of Burra/Kooringa. The last child born at Kooringa was a girl, in 1867. There were two more children to come: boys, who were born in Victoria, and who both died young.

William and Elizabeth Dower had finally moved from Kooringa. I have a theory that people often make radical moves in their late forties. It is as if to say, "If I don't do it now, I never will." As illustration: Francis and Elizabeth Pascoe, both aged forty-eight, packing up all their belongings in 1848 and boarding a ship to Australia with nine children.

William and Elizabeth had come all the way from Cornwall for a new start, and they had settled quickly at Burra and stayed there. However, I suspect their living arrangements were not much better than Elizabeth's parents, given that the mining company prevented people from acquiring their own land to build their own houses. One could make a dug-out comfortable, but one could not prevent some disasters from happening, such as flooding.

Around 1868, William made an excursion to Broken Hill, to a place called Thakarinka. Broken Hill then was not the massive mining site that we think of now. Silver and lead were only discovered in the 1880s. Burke and Wills had passed through the area on their expedition in 1860–1861. There were a few pastoralists around, and the Darling River was the avenue for bringing in goods and sending out harvests. Silver ore was discovered at Thakarinka in 1875. Perhaps William was prescient.

A baby was born to Elizabeth in 1871; she was forty-four. The birthplace was Kyneton, Victoria. It is in the Macedon Ranges, northeast of Ballarat and south-south-east of Bendigo. Kyneton was established in 1850, before the gold rushes started. It became a supply point for people trekking from Melbourne to goldmines at Castlemaine or Bendigo. One of its few claims to fame was that Ned Kelly was tried there in 1870 for robbery under arms. Mount Alexander is also to the north of Kyneton, and gold was mined there too.

A little to the west of Kyneton is a smaller place called Lauriston. Gold was mined there, although it was never a big magnet for prospectors. It was what was referred to as "a poor man's diggings" – if you were a good worker you could make a modest living and enjoy a peaceful lifestyle if your tastes were not presumptuous. William and Elizabeth Dower were not the only ones to make the move from Kooringa; their eldest son John also came.

John had married Mary Jane Brokenshire at Kooringa in 1870. Her parents had emigrated in 1846, from Liskeard in the southeast of Cornwall. The Kyneton area was known to miners in South Australia because when gold was first discovered in Victoria, there was a route from Mount Alexander, just to the north of Kyneton, to Adelaide to take shipments of gold to port. And it was a Cornishman, Joseph Blight, who quarried stone for the railway line at Kyneton, and also had some success in quartz reef mining.

Elizabeth's daughter-in-law also had a baby in 1871. She called the baby William John, after both her father-in-law and her husband. But there were other children of William and Elizabeth Dower around as well, most of them grown up. Three of the girls: Mary Ann Willey, Thurza, and Frances Ann, got married in Victoria.

Elizabeth's newest child, James, unfortunately died in 1876, aged five – in Lauriston. But, the same year she had another child (her last), and she named him James. It must have been about now that William and Elizabeth, and the accompanying horde of children, young and old, moved to Bethanga. The daughter-in-law Mary Jane gives us a clue. She had five children at Kyneton and the last was born there in 1876. The next child she had was in 1879 and it was at Bethanga.

One must imagine that all the time the Dower families were at Lauriston, and the menfolk were digging away at their hopeful ground, other things were happening elsewhere. Cornish families were gravitating to Bethanga, in the north of Victoria. It was another small town in the hills where gold was being acquired through hard labour. A Cornish miner called Thomas Martin, who had arrived in Adelaide in 1848 on the *Carnatic*, had teamed up with a flamboyant entrepreneur, John A. Wallace, who was a Member of the Legislative Council of Victoria as well.

In 1876, news of the discovery of a valuable new reef at Bethanga brought hundreds of new settlers there. It was enough to uproot William and Elizabeth Dower from Lauriston. Perhaps they were thinking of the younger people in the family, and new opportunities for them. The gold was to be found in quartz ore, and the quartz had to be processed in order to extract the gold – and the whole process had to be achieved in such a way that it was economic to do so.

Thomas Martin was determined to find the way. He was the captain of the mine, appointed by Wallace. Thomas was married and had a family. Actually, it was two families. When he had arrived in South Australia he was married to Mary Ann and they had one child. Thomas worked in Adelaide for a couple of years as a miller, rather than going to Burra to join all the Cornish people mining. But then, Thomas was one of the earliest ones to go to Victoria to become part of the gold rushes.

They went to Castlemaine – not far from Kyneton. Another baby was born there, a girl. Unfortunately, Mary Ann got diphtheria and died – sanitation was not good on the goldfields – leaving Thomas and two children alone. Thomas and the two children survived, and three years later, in 1863, he married Jane McCartin, an Irishwoman. They were married at Beechworth, a place where John Wallace owned a hotel, one of many he owned around Victoria, generally near goldfields. I surmise that Thomas Martin and John Wallace met at this time.

Although Wallace made his money from hotels, he had an interest in geology, in particular, how to identify places where gold would be found. So did Thomas Martin. Over the next few years, Thomas Martin made many expeditions around northern Victoria and up into New South Wales, looking at rock formations and reefs. Sometimes Wallace accompanied him.

By the time Thomas got to Bethanga, he was ready to settle, and Bethanga had all the right signs of being a productive site. It had its difficulties, but that was good too. It would be a challenge. And he and Jane now had five children together as well as his first two. In 1876, the son Thomas was twenty.

More people began to arrive in Bethanga. Its population grew to around 1,000. Among them were the William and Elizabeth Dower clan. Philippa was nineteen. The families settled in, and the men concerned themselves with reefs and claims and furnaces. Public meetings were held to arrange the building of a Wesleyan Church. There were few illusions about "striking it rich". This was another poor man's diggings – people were looking for steady returns.

June Philipp says they were "men for whom prospecting and gold mining were a subsistence way of life that had become habitual".[16] Thomas Harris, who was one of the partners in the town's first furnace to process ore, said he "was but a miner, and was fond of the miner's life", and this sentiment was widely shared.[17]

It was a long way from Burra in South Australia, and an even longer way from Cornwall, but the Dower and Martin families had found themselves in another Cornish enclave. Their two families had never been connected before, going back hundreds of years. The

---

[16] Philipp, June, *A Poor Man's Diggings: Mining and Community at Bethanga, Victoria, 1875-1912*, Hyland House, Melbourne, 1987, p. 53.
[17] Philipp, p. 103.

Martin family was from around Towednack and the Dower family was from around Wendron. They might as well have been in different worlds, except for the bond of being Cornish.

Thomas Martin, the son, and Philippa Dower, the girl, met. On 18 January 1879, they were married at the residence of William and Elizabeth Dower in Bethanga. It was the continuation of the tradition at Burra for weddings to be held at the residence of one or the other of the parents.

As had happened at Burra, in time the ore ran out at Bethanga, and Thomas and Philippa lived the last part of their lives in Sydney. Somewhere along the line, the past got disconnected. I grew up not even knowing that I had a Cornish past, and I even think my father did not know. But you never know what you will find when you go digging. Sometimes you strike ore. The rewards can be rich.

References

Philipp, June, *A Poor Man's Diggings: Mining and Community at Bethanga, Victoria, 1875-1912*, Hyland House, Melbourne, 1987.

The death of mining in the Cornish families

Any consideration of the family of Francis and Elizabeth Pascoe has to start with statistics rather than names.[18] They had nine children. Their children all survived to adulthood and every one of them married and had children. The total number of the grandchildren was eighty.

This is probably not unprecedented for the period – Francis and Elizabeth got married in 1825 in Cornwall – but it is still extraordinary when viewed from the current perspective, when the average size of families is less than two children. Francis and Elizabeth came to Australia on the ship the *Abberton* in 1848. They were from Crowan in Cornwall, and Francis was a miner. As was common for Cornish immigrants, they went to South Australia, and then to Burra Burra, because that's where the copper was. There was no gold in Australia yet.

Three of the nine children stayed in Kooringa, a little to the south of Burra Burra and part of the same mining settlement. The men were all miners at the copper mine. One of the children, Thomas, stayed in South Australia but became a farmer, a notable pioneer in the White Hut district to the west of Burra Burra. He had a son who became a prominent South Australian politician, the Honourable Thomas Pascoe.

The gold rushes in Victoria started in 1851, and being miners, Cornish people were drawn to Victoria to test their skills against the elusiveness of the metal that glittered. The mine at Burra Burra almost had to shut down, there were so few people left. Five of the nine children of Francis and Elizabeth Pascoe went to Victoria. Only one came back.

Curiously, the Pascoe goldminers were not attracted to the larger centres like Ballarat and Bendigo. They favoured the smaller centres like Kyneton, Lauriston and Maryborough. One of them died in 1864 whilst mining, at the age of thirty-six. The jury at the

---

[18] Francis Pascoe (1800-1871) and Elizabeth Willey (1799-1878) married at Mullion in Cornwall in 1825. They had nine children. They emigrated to South Australia in 1848 and both died at Kooringa/Burra. Francis was a miner of tin in Cornwall, and of copper in South Australia.

Coronial Inquest at Maryborough held that it was an accidental death. He left a widow and four children.

Of course, it is not curious; rather, it is an indicator of the character of the Pascoe family. Mining had been the central part of their lives for many generations. We know that mining in Cornwall had been carried out for something like 4,000 years, longer than any city in Britain had existed, longer than Christianity. Had they heard that merchants had visited Cornwall from the Aegean Sea since 1450 BC to purchase tin?

When the Pascoe family left Cornwall, tin mining was hanging in the balance. It had industrialised since the advent of steam engines, but it was also under threat from overseas tin mines. One suspects that the goal of emigrating was to be able to continue mining. In Cornwall it was facing collapse. And if your goal is to continue mining, you are not beguiled by dreams of striking it rich. You are not searching for a treasure that will transform your life so that you can put on airs and never have to work again.

The smaller centres must have seemed to offer this prospect – a modest but sustainable living where you were unlikely to be overrun by companies wanting to invest, gut the landscape, make a killing and move on. Burra Burra, unfortunately, was a company from the beginning, with investment, shareholders, equipment and the necessity of profit. A miner couldn't even buy a block of land on which to build their own home. It was all company-controlled.

Predictably, the returns faded out and the mine folded. Up to 1874, dividends totalling £840,000 had been paid out – a great success (Pryor). But by 1877, the lode had been worked out and the profits had evaporated.

Copper was discovered to the southwest of Burra Burra, at Moonta, in 1861. Many Cornish miners moved from Burra Burra to Moonta, but the children of Francis and Elizabeth Pascoe, the ones who didn't go to Victoria, tended to stay in Kooringa. However, in doing so, the understanding seemed to be that they would have work for life. If it was more modest towards the end of their life, that would be okay too.

The other feature of the Pascoe offspring and their spouses was their mobility. Considering that in Cornwall their families had spent generations not moving more than a village or two, their travel in

Australia was uninhibited. John Willey Pascoe, the eighth of the nine children of Francis and Elizabeth, lived at Kyneton and Clunes in Victoria, then in later life moved to Perth, Western Australia.

Joseph Willey Pascoe, the sixth child, went from Kooringa to the Victorian gold diggings in 1849, came back to Kooringa, got married and had children in Kooringa, then went to live in Broken Hill for twenty years. Silver and lead had been discovered there, the largest deposits in the world; it became known as the Silver City. Joseph came back to Kooringa around 1910 near the end of his life.

The motivation for the movement of all the men was mining. You could say that, whatever commitment they had to the place of Cornwall, it was more important to move, if need be, to where they could continue mining. Mining was an integral part of their identity as Cornish people.

Unfortunately, the massively expanded powers of modern technology meant that all the places they moved to were exhausted within a generation. Their children had to consider alternative occupations. Elizabeth, the eldest child of Francis and Elizabeth Pascoe, had married William Dower before they all left Cornwall. Their daughter Philippa married Thomas Martin, who ended up as the manager of the goldmine at Bethanga, extracting gold from quartz, The mine worked most industriously between 1876 and 1900, but after that it faded out.

The children of the immigrants faced an existential crisis: there was nowhere to move to if they wanted to continue mining. They had to consider, for the first time in countless generations, other occupations. I think they experienced a void. Their parents had come to Australia with a rush of energy, confident of staying a step ahead of a failing industry at home, and hoping to set down new roots. Initially, they thought they would be able to continue on, but that hope was only sustained for a few of their number. After a brief show of success, it was gone, and they could not go home.

What did the children of the immigrants do?

One, just one of the children of Francis and Elizabeth, became a farmer – Thomas. He and his wife had nine children. Of them, one became a politician and achieved renown. Some of the others became farmers or married men who were farmers, mostly in South

Australia. Two became journalists, one in Sydney and one in Melbourne.

Another one of their children's children became a painter in Victoria (a trade painter, not an artist). He died of lead poisoning aged forty-two. The children of Thomas Martin, the immigrant, apart from the Thomas who married Philippa Dower, seem to have gravitated to towns around Bethanga, such as Chiltern and Wodonga, while one went to Melbourne and one went to Sydney.

Of Thomas and Philippa's eleven children, six ended up in Sydney. One of the men stayed in Bethanga, but not as a miner: he became a hairdresser. One of the women moved to Wangaratta and one moved to Walwa, a tiny town northeast of Bethanga along the Victorian-New South Wales border.

Thomas and Philippa Martin moved to Sydney around 1910 and brought some of their children with them. Thomas set up an engineering works and it seems that three of his sons worked there. On his death certificate, his occupation was shown as "stationary engine driver". This meant he was in charge of the engine at a mine that drove pumps and other machinery. That had been his father's occupation back in Cornwall. His occupation would have been historically true, but he was also described as being an engineer, which is probably closer to the truth after he moved to Sydney.

Two of his sons were described as blacksmiths, which is probably also related to the engineering works in Sydney.

In one generation, mining disappeared from the family, and a variety of related occupations took its place, along with a host of unrelated occupations. Toby, the youngest son of Thomas and Philippa, born 1900, was described as a fruit juice mixer in a letter regarding probate of his father's will. He lived in Sydney.

Thomas Pascoe: pioneer farmer in South Australia

Thomas Pascoe is an unusual story for my family tree, because most of my forebears who came to Australia were not outback pioneers. Generally, they lived in cities and worked as trades people. But Thomas started a farm in rural South Australia; he was the first one to farm that land. He also went to the gold rushes in Victoria and brought back gold. So, in the Martin family tree, he is exceptional.

His story starts with his parents, Francis and Elizabeth Pascoe. They were immigrants to South Australia in 1848, bringing their nine children with them from Cornwall on the *Abberton*. The connection to me is their eldest daughter Elizabeth, who married William Dower. Their daughter Philippa married Thomas Martin, and they were my great grandparents.

Thomas Pascoe was a brother of Elizabeth; he was the third child of Francis and Elizabeth Pascoe. He was born in Cornwall in 1830, so he was eighteen when his parents brought the family to Australia. The family initially stayed at Glen Ormond in Adelaide, then moved to Reedy Creek before settling at Burra, 160 kilometres north of Adelaide. Burra was a copper mine. The Pascoe family were continuing the Cornish tradition of mining. All the other boys grew up to be miners, and all the girls married miners.

This story quotes extensively from an obituary for Thomas in the *Northern Argus* (Clare, South Australia) on 8 March 1918. Thomas had died on 1 March. The article states that Thomas's adulthood began in mining, alongside his father and brothers. Thomas "was one of a party of three who blasted out from the Burra mine the large mass of ore – red oxide of copper — which was sent home to the Great Exhibition of 1851 in London.

"In that year Mr [Thomas] Pascoe went to the Victorian goldfields [he was twenty-one], making one in a party of five. Their first essay was highly successful; they followed good advice given them, and from one hole they cleaned up 36 lb (pounds; 16.3 kg) of gold; in several others they had vicissitudes, but in the last hole bottomed they struck it rich, and left the digging with 14 lbs (6.4 kg) of gold per man of the party. This was not a bad return for a fifteen weeks' sojourn at Forest Creek, now Castlemaine. Mr Pascoe then returned to South Australia and married."

Thomas married Frances (Fanny) Roach on 21 February 1852 at Penwortham, fifty kilometres southwest of Burra. Frances's family came from Cornwall as well, from around St Ives. There was an earlier connection between the Martin and Roach families: John Martin had married Elizabeth Roach in 1788. All the rivers come together.

Thomas was now twenty-two, and Frances was nineteen. Her father, also called Thomas, had become a farmer, switching from mining. He owned Penbetha Farm at Penwortham. But he died later in 1852, aged fifty-nine.

Thomas and Frances left again for the goldfields in Victoria.

"These were strenuous times; if there were big prizes there were also big expenses. Going to the fields from Melbourne they paid £6 10s (six pounds, ten shillings, or $13.00) per cwt (hundredweight; 50.8 kg) cartage for their belongings. There were three others in the party, all four were married, and the ladies rode on the luggage cart, while their husbands walked with the teamster. The passage money per lady was £5 (five pounds; $10.00). This time they remained eleven months on the fields; their good luck stuck to them, and though they had to pay as high as £14 ($28.00) per bag for flour, and 1s 1d a lb (one shilling and one penny, or $0.11 per 454 gm) for salt, and proportionately high for other things, they cleared £100 ($200) per month each."

When Thomas and Frances returned to South Australia, they bought 150 acres (61 hectares) of land at White Hut, a little to the northeast of Clare (Note, this is not White Hut down on the Yorke Peninsula; they were still roughly in the vicinity of Burra; there is currently a White Hut Road at Clare). Having done this, they returned to the diggings in Victoria.

The obituary continues:

"On this venture their luck was not as good; they merely cleared expenses. Mrs Pascoe lived in Melbourne while her husband was at the goldfields, and can today relate interesting stories of life in that city. The conveniences of civilisation were not what they are now, nor were the buildings; instead of being a city of edifices it was one of 'shedifices'. However, late in 1854 the young couple returned to South Australia, and in the following year they began work on their 150 acres of land at White Hut.

"At first they lived in a tent on one bank of the White Hut creek, while Mr Pascoe cleared a piece of ground for a home. They made the journey from Adelaide to Clare per medium of a bullock dray. After the home site was cleared, more forest was cut down for cultivation purposes and the first crop of wheat— only a few acres— having matured, it was reaped with a sickle and threshed, partly with a flail, partly by being trodden out with bullocks, and partly with a threshing roller.

"The grain was carted to Port Adelaide on the bullock dray, the trip occupying a fortnight. An orchard and vineyard were laid out and planted in the next year, more land was placed under wheat, and the following harvest saw Mr Pascoe the possessor of a £160 ($320) stripper, the first in the district.

"It was at first drawn by six bullocks and two horses, later by eight bullocks and one horse. Mr Pascoe reaped his first harvest, then went out and reaped those of his neighbours. As a fact, he was reaping during that harvest from January to April, and his earnings almost paid for the stripper. Time went on, good crops, some of them giving as high as forty bushels per acre (2,511 kg per ha), others as low as six, when red rust intervened to trouble the wheat grower. As his family was growing, Mr Pascoe took up another farm at Farrell's Flat, and to this day, though he sold out more than forty years ago, a turn of the road is known as Pascoe's corner.

"Later Mr Pascoe took up land for himself and his sons at Terowie, still later he leased a block at Cavenagh. The Terowie land is occupied by his son, the Hon. T. Pascoe [see below], and by his grandson; another son, Mr Paul R. Pascoe, has the home farm at White Hut. About twelve years ago Mr. Pascoe retired from active work to live in Clare, and died here, as already stated, the cause of death being heart failure. His remains were buried on Sunday,

March 3, in the White Hut Cemetery, where he rests after eighty-seven years of life.

"His widow and nine out of ten children followed their father to the grave. He left five daughters and five sons. The former are — Miss Pascoe, Clare; Mrs H. S. Stephens, Queensland, the only absentee; Mrs. A. J. Pearce, Adelaide; Mrs. S. J. Pascoe, Adelaide; Mrs. J. Flower, Canowie Belt. Of the sons, the Hon. T. Pascoe retains the Terowie property; two others, Francis and John, are in journalism, the former in Sydney and the latter in Melbourne; and two others, Mr. P. R. Pascoe and Mr. S. S. Pascoe, are on the land at Clare. The Rev. S. K. Rooney conducted the burial service, and the funeral arrangements were in the hands of M. P. McDougall."

A question that arises out of the obituary is, who was "Hon. T. Pascoe"?

He was Thomas Pascoe, the second son of the Thomas Pascoe whose obituary is above. He was born in 1859 at White Hut. Articles about him on Wikipedia and Wikitree say he may have been educated at Stanley Grammar School, Watervale (in the Clare district). He took over management of the Terowie farm of his father. He became a considerable authority on wheat growing. He spent a couple of years farming and mining in Western Australia, but otherwise his whole life was spent in South Australia.

In 1900 he was elected to the South Australian Legislative Council, and he retained the seat unopposed for thirty-two years. In 1909, Mr Pascoe was made Minister of Agriculture, and in 1912 he became Minister of Agriculture and Irrigation. Later, he was Minister of Irrigation and Minister of Mines, and in 1923 he was appointed Commissioner of Public Works and he became the leader of the Legislative Council as Chief Secretary.

Mr Pascoe travelled to every State in the Commonwealth exchanging knowledge regarding the cultivation of wheat, and attended many conferences called by Ministers of Agriculture in the various State Governments. Upon his death, Sir David Gordon, the President of the South Australian Legislative Council, said, "He was always regarded as an authority on agriculture, and he was a man who had a good knowledge of rural industries generally."

The leader of the Government in the Legislative Council, Sir Walter Duncan, said that "Mr Pascoe always had a big influence over the other members of the House because of his knowledge of the requirements and needs of the man on the land".

Mr Thomas Pascoe married Florence Eliza Rayner in 1886 at Canowie. They had five children. He died on 23 February 1939, aged eighty. He is buried at Payneham Cemetery, Adelaide.

Sources for Hon. Thomas Pascoe
Wikipedia article.
Wikitree profile.
'Death of Mr Thomas Pascoe', *Border Watch* (Mount Gambier, SA), 25 Feb 1939.
'Obituary: Mr. Thomas Pascoe', *The Advertiser* (Adelaide, SA), 24 Feb 1939, p. 14.

The long journey to fulfilment: Thomas Martin

Thomas Martins was brought up to be a miner. He lived in a mining community that had existed since time that was unwritten. It was not as if one chose, or had to choose. The path was in front of you. He was born in Towednack, in the west of Cornwall, just to the south of St Ives on the north coast. Other people became fishermen or farmers. The Martins became miners. Many people's lives consisted of a mix of all three, depending on the weather, the price of tin or copper, and other such variables. There was an easy fluidity about it, which is not to say that life was easy.

Thomas was born in 1834. His home was Chyangweal; his parents were Paul and Martha. In the end he had six siblings; he was the third child. But the times were changing. It was the nineteenth century and steam engines had come. Machinery had come, and pumps. It changed things, for now you could pump much more water out of the mine shafts, so you could dig deeper, much deeper. And there was machinery to crush the tin ore and copper ore, so you could process much more material.

Of course, in parallel, the need for tin and copper was increasing. A manufacturing society is a hungry one. And there was competition: cheaper ore began to flow in from overseas. In time, the ore would run out, but not for a while. Now the focus was on improvement. Even the ships were improved – with steam as well as sails – so that ships were bigger, and voyages were faster.

Thomas did not lag behind. When an engine came to the mine, he volunteered to man it. He learned, and he was called an engine worker.

Some things he did according to tradition. He married, as young people did; he was twenty, and Mary Ann Williams was twenty-two. She had been born in the township of St Ives. And some things were not quite according to tradition: they were married in the registry office in St Ives. Why not at the Methodist Church? It is clear from later on that the Martins family were Wesleyan Methodists. Or, alternatively, why not at the Church of England?

Thomas and Mary Ann lived in town, in St Ives, not at Towednack. Perhaps this reflected the changing times of the nineteenth century, when British people were starting to gravitate towards cities. In a modest expression of the trend, Thomas moved to town. Their first son was born in Street-An-Garrow, two years to the day after they had got married. It was 13 May 1856. They named him Thomas, according to tradition: first son, father's name, just as it had been for at least four generations.

Around them, life was accelerating. From the 1830s, Cornish people had been emigrating to Canada and America. From the 1840s, Cornish miners were emigrating to Australia. In 1842, copper was discovered at Kapunda in South Australia – an attractive place for the Cornish because no convicts had been sent there. In 1845, a bigger discovery of copper was made at Burra, one hundred miles north of Adelaide.

The discovery of copper in Australia was of interest in England, not just for commercial reasons, but because science was beginning to take an interest in geology. This was in the years just prior to the publication of Charles Darwin's book, *On the Origin of Species* (1859). Sir Roderick Murchison had been appointed president of the Royal Geological Society, and for the first time there was a developing global perspective on the location of minerals.

Murchison inspected ore specimens brought back from Australia by Count de Strzelecki. He compared them to samples he had seen from the Ural Mountains in Russia that were of an auriferous nature, that is, they contained gold. In 1845, whilst visiting Falmouth in Cornwall, he met several Cornish miners who were going to Australia. Believing that there might be gold there, he asked them to send back likely samples. They did this and thus Murchison knew of the existence of gold in Australia before Edward Hargraves' discovery.[19]

In 1846 (when Thomas was twelve), Murchison gave a lecture in Penzance, urging local tin miners to migrate to New South Wales "and there obtain gold from ancient alluvia".[20] As a youth, Thomas Martins must have been familiar with this talk going on around him, and seen neighbours join the exodus to foreign countries.

There were also some difficult years in Cornwall because of the failure of potato crops in 1845 and 1846. (This didn't only happen in

---

[19] Sir Roderick Murchison, Wikipedia.
[20] Hill, David, *The Gold Rush*, William Heinemann, Sydney, 2010, p. 25.

Ireland.) This had led to food riots, and Thomas was old enough to be an intelligent observer considering his own future.[21]

Thomas and Mary Ann made a decision: they would go to South Australia. Better to do it now before they had a handful of children and it became harder, they tell themselves. The ships have been getting better, the voyages a little faster and easier. Lots of people are doing it, and surviving. Lots of families in Cornwall are being helped by "homepay" – remittances being sent home by their relatives in the colonies. This suggested that the colonists were doing okay.

They packed up and left on the *Carnatic*, a sailing ship of 632 tons, departing from Plymouth on 24 January 1857 under Captain C.R. Suckling. Even the place of departure was easier. Earlier, emigrants had had to go all the way to London or Liverpool. Plymouth was just down the coast in Devon.

They arrived at Port Adelaide, South Australia on 28 April 1857. In those days, the lists of passengers were published in the newspapers. It was an event when a ship arrived; it was newsworthy. Accordingly, the names of Thomas, Mary Ann and Thomas Martin were published in the *South Australian Register* (Adelaide, SA) on Wednesday 29 April 1857.

Note that the name Martins has become Martin, and also, even the baby Thomas's name is published. Whether the change to Martin was intended, or the result of a journalist's predilection for the more familiar, the change was permanent. The family name in Australia was Martin, another dividing line from the past.

So, of course they went straight to Burra so that Thomas could take up mining. But they didn't. They did not do what everything suggested they would do – join the hordes of Cornish going overseas to take up mining in new country, heed the exhortations of leaders like Sir Roderick Murchison to seize the opportunity, and accept the attraction of still being part of a Cornish community overseas, symbolised by the Wesleyan Methodist Church.

Instead, in Adelaide, Thomas "built a large flour mill and established and carried on a brisk and flourishing business" (from an article in the *Wodonga and Towong Sentinel*, 29 April 1904, upon

---

[21] Greenwood, p. 127.

his death). Had Thomas made a break forever from the ways of his Cornish family? We know that he was forward-looking, for he embraced the new machinery at the mine in Cornwall. And there were other Cornish people around in Adelaide, among English and Germans and Scots. In choosing a different occupation, he would not have been isolated.

However, already much of the chatter in the community would have been about gold. Some gold had been discovered in South Australia, at Echunga, east of Adelaide, but it paled into insignificance against the finds in Victoria beginning in 1851. So, Thomas would have heard stories from Cornish men on their way back from Victoria, often with gold in hand, coming back to visit family and restock for another expedition to the goldfields. Sometimes they took family with them, sometimes they formed parties of men and spent a few months away at a time.

I think the flour mill was a project in Thomas's life, something that he could mark as an achievement, rather than something he wanted to spend his lifetime doing. I think that once he heard about the goldrushes, the old Cornish miner sentiments would have kicked in. If there was mining going on, then as a Cornish man he should be part of it, because all of those lifetimes of experience lay there, awakened back to life by a new challenge. He should be able to do well at it.

Perhaps if Thomas had been at Burra, he would have joined a party of men to go to Victoria. As it was, he went with Mary Ann and young Thomas. And, to add to the situation, Mary Ann was pregnant, and she gave birth to a daughter, Martha Ann, at Forest Creek, Castlemaine on 6 September 1858. On the birth certificate, Thomas's occupation is "Engineer". I take this to mean a generalisation of his mining experience in Cornwall to the running of the mill in Adelaide. He chose not to describe himself as a miller. Rather, he focused on the mechanical aspects of it.

I think it also showed where Thomas's mind was heading. He was thinking of the running of a mine, not simply the act of digging and hoping for sufficient returns from the dirt. But he was still young. He needed more experience. He needed to know about different kinds of ore and different methods of extracting gold and other minerals from it.

Two years later he was at Fryers Creek, Chapel Hill, one of the many smaller goldfields in Victoria. He had his family with him. Suddenly, Mary Ann got sick. The medical historians say that diphtheria first spread across the world in 1856-58, identified as a new disease, although it had probably first appeared at least a century earlier. It could devastate a family in a week. Usually it was the children who died, but in this case it was Mary Ann who succumbed. She died on 8 May 1860.

Her death certificate said she had only had the disease two days. Young Thomas was four years old; Martha Ann was poignantly described as "1 year 11 months" old. Thomas was described as a miner. He had come full circle. But he was devastated. He had not expected sudden death, not of the wife with whom he had come to Australia, not of the mother of their two young children. At such times, one questions everything and wants to go home. He had done nothing wrong, but he had brought her here. The long, future life together was extinguished, as easily as the candle a miner holds up to lighten the dark mineshaft.

At Fryers Creek today there is an "engine house" called the Duke of Cornwall, built by Cornish miners in 1869. It was a gathering place for people from Cornwall. Here, Thomas had found himself among familiar people, carrying out a familiar activity in a familiar way. The Rowe family who owned the mine came from Camborne in Cornwall, less than fifteen miles from St Ives.

Thomas wasn't quite ready to settle down in one place yet. Somehow he managed to look after his two children – one assumes that his Cornish kinship was a major factor in this, with women in the community willing to help. I suspect they caught the whiff of his dreaming and wanted to do what they could to enable him. It would be a gift to Cornwall and the old ways, of mining, the fairies having now turned golden in the colonies.

I think he travelled to other goldfields in Victoria, but I know for sure that he travelled to Beechworth, because on 4 April 1863 he married Jane Elvira McCartin there, the daughter of a carrier. At twenty-four, she was five years younger than him, and Irish – from Armagh. (She was also Roman Catholic, and in his last days, stricken with incurable cancer, Thomas found some comfort through the local priest. Love and death shook the roots of his life as much as his great adventure, his emigration.)

Thomas was exploring the various quartz reefs in northern Victoria and southern New South Wales. It was his mission, no one else's. Over the years 1863 to 1878, Thomas travelled to and spent time at Barrambogie, near Chiltern, and Golden Bay in Victoria, and Hawkesview and Yarrara (near Germanton, now Holbrook) in New South Wales. In fact, two children were born to Jane in 1873 and 1874 at Hawkesview.

By 1878, the two children of Thomas with Mary Ann had grown up. Martha Ann was twenty, and she got married in May 1878, in Albury. Thomas, the son, got married in January 1879, aged twenty-three. What was significant about this marriage was that Thomas married a girl from Cornwall, Philippa Dower, and that the marriage was in Bethanga, where both Thomas the son and Thomas the father were to spend the next twenty-five years. The father was made manager of the gold-mining company there. It was the culmination of his dream, to run a goldmine.

Image: Map of Bethanga in north-eastern Victoria

Source: Philipp, June, *A Poor Man's Diggings*, Hyland House, Melbourne, 1987.

Section 8: Great great grandparents, paternal (2)

Charles Eaglestone (1819-1911) and Hannah Palmer (1830-1890)

Edward Lewis (1829-1897) and Sarah Crosby (1833-1897)

Introductory notes

These two sets of great great grandparents are my father's mother's grandparents. They all had extraordinary lives. They were all born overseas and came to Australia. Charles and Hannah were married before emigrating. Edward, from London, and Sarah, from Ireland, were both convicts, and they discovered one another in Hobart.

The first story, "The two loves of Charles Eaglestone", explores the Eaglestone family in Oxfordshire. Most of the Eaglestone men were stonemasons. Charles got married, then lost his wife to rheumatic fever. And Hannah turned up. It looks like two loves in his lifetime.

The second story gives an account of the Eaglestone family from the local vicar's perspective, the Reverend Thomas Dand at Bletchington in Oxfordshire. He was uniquely qualified to observe his flock dispassionately and compassionately. (Yes, I made this story up, but Rev. Dand was real.)

The next two stories are about Edward Lewis and his convict days in Van Diemen's Land. I have written a book about Edward and Sarah, about their whole lives, but I only learned recently about how Edward had served his time as a convict. (The book is *The Search for Edward Lewis*.) In the first story, we learn about Point Puer, which was a place established near Port Arthur for juvenile convicts. In the second story, we learn about a small slice of time after Point Puer was shut down and Edward was seeking (successfully) to avoid being consigned to a work party doing heavy manual work.

The next two stories are about Sarah Crosby. In the first story, she is being tried at the Old Bailey in London for stabbing a policeman. It sounds as if she was dreadful, but she was not. In the second story, I discover her grave at Rookwood; it was one of those magical moments in the family history search.

The two loves of Charles Eaglestone

A short history of the Eaglestone family, centred on Charles Eaglestone (born 1819 at Kirtlington, Oxfordshire, died 1911, Geelong, Victoria)

Once there was a stonemason in Oxfordshire, in the little village of Bletchington, not far north of Oxford. His name was Thomas Eaglestone. He was born in 1742 and he married Martha Payne. They had five children: two who must have died young, and Thomas, Edward and Mary. Thomas and Edward, not surprisingly, grew up to be stonemasons.

Thomas and Edward both married. Although Thomas was the elder, Edward was the first to get married. He married Ann Stevens in 1795, at St Giles' parish church in Bletchington. Thomas married Mary Rogers in 1799, also at St Giles. But Thomas and Mary moved. Not far – to nearby Kirtlington, where Thomas set up as a stonemason. Edward stayed with his father.

Both families had children. Edward and Ann had eight children over a period of about twenty years. Unfortunately, five of them died young. Thomas and Mary had four children and all of them lived to grow up. All the parents were in their forties when the last child was born, and that was Charles, in 1819.

Thomas the father died in 1830 at the age of eighty-eight: a fine innings, as a cricketer would say. It is not known when Martha died, but she did die. The Census tells us that by omission.

The first British Census was held in 1841, recording who lived in every house, so we know which children were still living at home. At Kirtlington, Thomas at this stage was sixty-nine years old, and Mary was sixty-seven. Nevertheless, all of their four children were still living at home.

The eldest was Martha, thirty-five, Joshua was thirty-four, Caroline was twenty-four, and the youngest was Charles, at twenty-two. Charles had trained with his father to be a stonemason. Joshua was likewise a stonemason, and one suspects that he had taken over much of his father's work.

At the household of Edward and Ann in Bletchington, only one child was still at home: Elizabeth, who was thirty-one. She was a dressmaker. The other living children were Caroline and Sarah; they had husbands. Edward was sixty-five years old and, one assumes, no longer spry and strong. One wonders how often the two families met. It was only a short horse ride between the two villages, and the roads in the area go back to Roman times. Both Bletchington and Kirtlington are mentioned in the Domesday Book of 1086. Locals could argue about the spelling of the two village names. Should it be 'ton' or 'don' at the end?

What was it that stonemasons did in this period of time? Of course, they made gravestones, but they also built walls and gate pillars, stone buildings, both public and private, and played a part in other building works. They were sometimes involved in roadworks as well. With churches they did repairs, restorations and additions, which never seemed to be completely done with.

St Giles, the church at Bletchington, was built in the eleventh century and it featured both Norman and Gothic styles. The church at Kirtlington was St Mary the Virgin; it predated St Giles, with Saxon features, and Norman arches that were added in the twelfth century. Changes were still being made to the churches in the nineteenth century, designed during this time by Charles Buckeridge.

If you are the son of a stonemason, while the vicar is giving his sermon, with more or less passion and fire, you can silently build up the walls of the church in your mind, stone by stone. You can mentally trace through all the steps required. If you are an older stonemason, you can still do this.

Stonemasons were once associated with the Freemasons, with their secret ways and lore, occult mystique, and prestige. The Freemasons formed at about the same time that the churches at Bletchington and Kirtlington were built. In the Middle Ages there were craft guilds that oversaw the practice of stonemasonry, recognising three stages of expertise: apprentices, journeymen and master-craftsmen. Stonemasons' skills were held in more respect than the skills in many other trades.

By the nineteenth century, a shift was occurring towards unions which would protect the wages and working conditions of members, govern training requirements, and provide for injured workers. The Friendly Society of Operative Stonemasons of England, Ireland and

Wales was founded in 1833. By 1838 it had almost 5,000 members – around sixty percent of those eligible to join. There was a branch in Oxford.

Perhaps the matter of Edward's age and declining strength was discussed. Stonemasonry is a heavy business. Thomas had both Joshua and Charles to help him. In Bletchington, Edward had the help of William Palmer, a fellow stonemason. William had probably been Edward's apprentice.

Then William Palmer died, in 1843, and Edward had the work by himself. Charles moved to Bletchington and began working with his Uncle Edward. This was the original stone yard and workshop of Thomas Eaglestone, the father of Thomas and Edward. Apart from Aunt Ann, the wife of Uncle Edward, his cousin Elizabeth was there. She was nine years older than Charles.

Where do husbands come from? None had come for Elizabeth. Her older sister Caroline had married James Fenemore, a man from Berkshire. He was a 'pound keeper', which drew them back to Berkshire. Her other older sister Sarah had married John Lay, who came from Hanborough in the west of Oxfordshire; he was a quarrier of stone. No doubt he had turned up at Bletchington in the course of a day's work.

Thomas and Mary also had a child they called Caroline, who was eighteen years younger than her cousin. Perhaps the two Carolines were named after the princess who married the man who became King George IV in 1820. She was born in 1768 and married George in 1795. It was a tempestuous marriage, and she died in 1821, but she was very popular with the people.

The Caroline who was the daughter of Thomas and Mary married George Killey, who had come from Lambeth in Surrey; he was a carpenter and maker of cricket bats. Why was he in Bletchington? It is difficult to say. Did young men cruise around the shire in those days in search of a bride? Who was that young man in church this Sunday?

There was an aunt, a rather younger sister of Thomas and Edward Eaglestone. Aunt Mary got married when she was thirty-one, to Benjamin Bullock, who seems to have been some kind of local maestro. He was the victualler of the Black's Head pub in Bletchington, and the village schoolmaster, and a stalwart of the local church. It was he, as well, who was responsible for the collection of Census data (1841, 1851, etc).

This is the way husbands turn up. But a husband had not turned up for Elizabeth. Or had he? Charles had come to stay, and they saw each other every day. In the mornings there were just Edward and Ann, and Charles and Elizabeth, having toast and tea or whatever was for breakfast. Perhaps fresh fruit in season from the orchards. Edward, sixty-five, Ann, about sixty-eight, Charles, twenty, and Elizabeth, thirty – their ages in 1841. And dinner, after a day of working with stone for Edward and Charles, and a day about the house and neighbourhood for Ann and Elizabeth.

The weeks pass, the months pass, the seasons turn. Charles and Elizabeth sit together in church each Sunday. They are comfortable. Charles is at ease with the steady plod of masonry and the demands of skill and aesthetics. Elizabeth is at ease with the routines of the household. There is an aesthetic about that, too. At some point the thought must have occurred to them, to one or the other of them, or to both of them: why not marriage?

They must have sought advice. Marrying your cousin is not forbidden, but it evokes an air of caution all around. Who could they have asked? Perhaps the Reverend Thomas Dand, who was the rector of St Giles' church in Bletchington – and the person who eventually married them? Or, the versatile Benjamin Bullock, who ran the pub and taught the children, and who occasionally performed marriages himself? Whoever it was, the adviser would have been assured that they were not flighty young things. There would have been a steadiness about both of them that was calming, even alluring.

This was a love that would warm the hearts of many. Perhaps it took months for the pathway to clear. Perhaps there were many discussions and even negotiations between family members in Bletchington and Kirtlington. But it happened, on 30 October 1847 in St Giles' church, an autumn wedding, appropriate for a bride who was almost thirty-seven. Charles had just turned twenty-eight.

Charles's father ~~Edward~~ Thomas came over from Kirtlington and he was a witness at the wedding, a man in his seventies sitting alone because his wife, Mary, was already gone – she had died three years before. Being a witness to the marriage was a vote of approval from both himself and his wife.

There were three other witnesses: Ann Hill, Joanna Smith and Emmanuel Eaglestone. Who were Ann and Joanna? Not known. Nor are Emmanuel's connections clear, but he was an Eaglestone, and he had come over from Weston-on-the-Green for the wedding; the village is only a few miles from Bletchington, up towards Bicester. An uncle, a cousin? Perhaps; he was about five years older than Charles. Another stamp of approval on the marriage? Probably so.

The story could have ended here. Contentment seems to settle in. Bletchington seems like the kind of place where life goes on timelessly, breathing in tune with the seasons. The colours are bright, the air is soft, and the water in the stream gurgles around the rocks like a child playing happily. But there are shadows in this pleasant idyll.

Sickness was one of them. Elizabeth became ill, with rheumatic fever. In modern language, "rheumatic fever is an inflammatory disease that can develop when strep throat or scarlet fever isn't properly treated. Strep throat and scarlet fever are caused by an infection with streptococcus bacteria" (from the website of the Mayo Clinic).

Rheumatic fever can cause permanent damage to the heart, and sometimes, death. Scarlet fever leading to rheumatic fever was common in England and Wales in the mid-nineteenth century. It is associated with crowded living quarters and less-than-ideal sanitation. Scarlet fever features a bright red rash that covers most of the body.

Help was needed, and young Hannah Palmer came to the house to look after Elizabeth in her feverish state. Hannah was a daughter of William and Elizabeth Palmer – William, who had been the stonemason. His widow Elizabeth was by herself, but Hannah was one of ten children, most of whom were still alive, so Elizabeth could probably spare her for a while.

Elizabeth the patient did not get better, and after sixteen days of illness, she died. Hannah was present with her until the last; it was Hannah who was the informant of the death for the registrar, so that is her statement. It was a weighty matter, especially for a woman of just twenty, to have the care of a person whom she could not heal, and to sit with her unto death. It was a weighty matter to be the responsible one to go to tell the registrar the sad details, a different kind of seriousness.

Death is a large presence. It seeps through a household so that one often forgets what one is supposed to be doing. It doesn't matter anymore. Death sits like a deep, encompassing cloud that won't shift and won't rain. It gets stuck.

Messages would have been sent out to inform relatives, certainly over to Kirtlington, to Charles's father, Edward's brother Thomas. Messages of shock and consternation would have returned. Messages would have said that other relatives needed to be informed. The Reverend Thomas Dand was the one who would officiate at the funeral. But the funeral was not held until eighteenth March, a week after the death, unusual in the days when funerals were usually held within a day or two of the death. It sounds like it needed to wait until relatives from further afield could make their way to Bletchington to share and assuage the sorrow.

Amid the pall, the second British Census was held, on 30 March 1851. It tells us, for the first time, that the name of their abode was Deamond Farm. The building is still there (2021), with the grounds serving as the home of the Diamond Caravan Park. It is an impressive, large, two-storey stone building. Living in it at the time of the Census were Edward, aged seventy-four, his wife Ann, aged seventy-eight, Charles, aged thirty-one and identified as the son-in-law, and Hannah Palmer, now aged twenty-one, 'visitor'.

The days moved into summer. Maybe Hannah stayed, because Edward and Ann were old and a little help was welcome. They may also have had ailments. Charles and Edward continued their partnership as stonemasons, probably with Charles shouldering the heavier load. Edward remained only until the following summer. He died on 20 June 1852, the main cause being a cancerous tumour in the thigh. The Reverend Thomas Dand conducted the burial service.

Brother Thomas Eaglestone also passed, of 'debility and old age' at Kirtlington on 3 February 1853. He was eighty. The person who was present at his death was Elizabeth Rogers, who had to be related to Mary Rogers, his wife, who had died in 1844. Elizabeth Rogers normally lived in Oxford town. Perhaps she was Mary's sister and had not married.

Again the feelings settle; flowers are taken to the graves at St Giles. Perhaps it is on such an occasion that Charles says to Hannah: "We could be married. I would like that. What say you?" And Hannah says yes. They decide not to hold the marriage in Bletchington; perhaps it is out of respect for the memory of Elizabeth. The marriage is held at the Church of St Mary Magdalene in the middle of Oxford on ~~4 July~~ 23 June 1853; mid-summer.

There are two witnesses: Benjamin Brickwell and Eliza Palmer. Mister Brickwell's associations are not known, but Eliza is one of Hannah's older sisters. Hannah's mother, Elizabeth, may have been present, but she may have been ailing, happy to let Eliza take over family duties. Elizabeth Palmer died on 19 March 1855 from influenza and bronchitis.

Until now there had been no children in Charles's life, but now there were babies. Indeed, one was already on the way when they were married. Fittingly, for it honoured both Charles's first wife and Hannah's mother, the baby was called Elizabeth. She was born in December 1853. The next child was Thomas, in March 1856, honouring Charles's father. Then there was Edwin, born 19 January 1858 – a twist on Edward, who had been Charles's stonemason mentor.

All of these children were born in Bletchington, so you think, life goes on as it invariably does in a rural shire. The hills roll and the rivers bubble, the pasture grows abundantly. Charles has taken over as the village stonemason. And there are great houses in the vicinity. Sir George Dashwood has Kirtlington Park; Blenheim Palace is nearby at Woodstock. Charles has a son who will likely grow up and become a stonemason.

However, 1859 comes, and Hannah gives birth to another child, Mary Ann, and Mary Ann dies. Oddly, the birth is not in Bletchington; it is in Oxford town. Did she have a feeling that there might be trouble with the birth? In the longer view, the death of a child does not seem cataclysmic: Charles's uncle and aunt had lost five out of their eight children. But something must have been brewing, because by January 1860 they are gone, the whole family. They have left England and are on their way to New Zealand on the *African*.

This was so abrupt. When I started investigating Charles Eaglestone's background, I was coming from the other end, from the colonial perspective, and Charles and Hannah's function was principally as Edwin's parents. So, the abruptness of their departure from England was not evident. In the larger family tree, they came out to Australia (for this is where they ended up) just as all the other great great grandparents in my family tree did, within a period of about thirty years, to take up a new life in the colonies.

The abruptness of Charles and Hannah's migration is also suggested by the fact that they landed in Auckland and must have almost immediately decided it was the wrong country for them, for they got on another ship and went to Melbourne, and they stayed in Melbourne for the rest of their lives. There might have been discussions taking place in Oxfordshire generally about the question of emigrating to the colonies, because Hannah's youngest brother and his family ended up at Invercargill, New Zealand, about as far south on the globe you can go without standing on an iceberg. But that was much later, in 1873.

Charles set up a workshop in Geelong (near Melbourne) as a stonemason, and he and Hannah had four more children – Emmanuel, Albert, Frances Emma, and Charles – the colonial contingent. So, Emmanuel Eaglestone had to have been somebody in the family, for him to be memorialised in an infant. And finally, Charles had a son who would carry on his name. Sadly, the young Charles died at age two.

Edwin, however, did grow up to be a stonemason, and he and his family lived in a stone house in Sydney. Charles and Hannah Eaglestone are my great great grandparents; Edwin is my great grandfather.

There is just one last niggle: had Charles and Hannah already decided to emigrate before Mary Ann was born, or was her death the trigger for making the radical decision? Family research involves working with very thin slices of people's lives. Can the question be answered? I think not. There was a generalised conversation in the Oxfordshire community about emigration. It had been going on since the early 1800s, and many local people had left for America and Canada, and Australia – once it became less of a convict colony.

It could have been a long-mulled-over decision befitting a stonemason, or an act of impetuosity. Perhaps the loss of a baby led Hannah to reconsider her life in the house of her husband's former wife, and perhaps Charles was ready to listen. He was forty-one: if he was going to take a big step, now was the time. Perhaps England was starting to feel tired or over-wrought, and the Australian colony would offer a fresh outlook, for them and their children.

The advent of the Friendly Society of Operative Stonemasons signalled a new age, not just for stonemasons, but for all work relationships in society. Perhaps Charles thought this was a good time to go. Ironically, there was more chance of him being a traditional stonemason in the new land than in the crumbling old world.

Once there was a stonemason in Oxfordshire. Now there would be a stonemason from Oxfordshire in Australia.

Family tree with key people
(Dates of birth are shown)

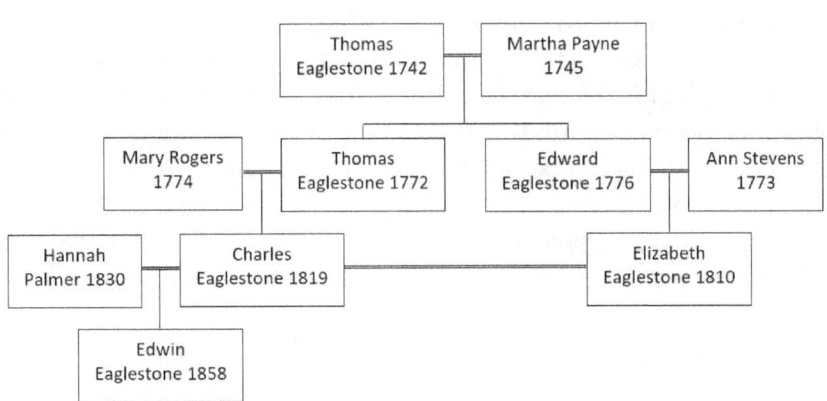

Notes on the Eaglestone family by Rev. Thomas Dand

Introductory note

My initial interest in the Eaglestone family was Edwin, who is my great grandfather on my father's side. His family emigrated from Oxfordshire while he was a small child; he turned two just before the ship *African* reached Auckland. The family soon moved to Australia (Geelong), and young Edwin grew up and became a stonemason in Sydney.

Searching his father Charles Eaglestone's life in Oxfordshire, I found a first marriage, to Elizabeth Eaglestone. This is the only case I know (in my family tree) of cousins marrying.[22]

Then I found records (in 1851) indicating that a woman called Hannah Palmer had been present at Elizabeth's death, and this was the person he subsequently married and with whom he had children. It started to look like a story of serendipitous love. I know you can read facts like this in many ways, and some of them would not be so nice. Nevertheless, I think the facts bear the weight of the story I have told.

The subsequent lives of Charles and Hannah seem to bear this out. They stayed together for life, never moving from Geelong. Likewise, Edwin and his wife stayed together for life and are buried together at Woronora Cemetery in Sydney.

I noticed Reverend Thomas Dand on several family certificates (funerals, baptisms, marriages). It wasn't hard to find the pieces of his life. He was around at the critical times. I thought he might provide an insightful perspective on the Eaglestone family.

The notes below are my imagined account of the Reverend Thomas Dand's perspective. He was the Minister of St Giles' Church at Bletchington, Oxfordshire from 1846 to 1868, when he died.

Glenn Martin

---

[22] 'Cousin marriage', Wikipedia, https://en.wikipedia.org/wiki/Cousin_marriage accessed 1 November 2021.

Extracts from the notes of the Reverend Thomas Dand

November 1846: I came to Bletchington this year, ten miles north of Oxford. My first real posting: the Reverend Thomas Dand. Before that, I'd been at Oxford University for twenty years.[23]

St Giles was built in the eleventh century by the Normans. I have stonemasons in the congregation. I'm sure that when I'm giving my sermon, they are thinking about the people who built it, and how. I see them looking at the stones. They can probably tell you which parts of the church were constructed at different times.

They even have 'stone' in their name: Eaglestone. Their ancestors could have been the builders. There are two of them in the village: Edward, seventy, is married to Ann and they have one daughter living at home, Elizabeth, thirty-six. Charles Eaglestone lives there too, and works with Edward. Charles's father, Thomas Eaglestone, lives at Kirtlington down the road; also a stonemason, and Edward's brother.

Apparently, Charles came here because William Palmer died. William had worked with Edward. There's plenty of work for stonemasons around here: gravestones, walls, buildings, the church, and work on the great houses: Sir George Dashwood has Kirtlington Park; Blenheim Palace is nearby at Woodstock.

February 1847: Charles Eaglestone came to see me. He asked me whether it's alright for cousins to marry. He is thinking of Elizabeth, who is nine years older than him. I see them sitting in church; they are quite comfortable with each other, respectful but warm.

I told him that the Roman Catholic Church frowns on it, but not the Church of England. Indeed, our Queen Victoria has married her first cousin, Prince Albert.

I assured him of my support. There are instances in the Bible of cousins marrying: good material for a sermon to highlight the virtues of marriage.

---

[23] Thomas Dand, in Joseph Foster, *Alumni Oxonienses: The Members of the University of Oxford, 1715-1886* and *Alumni Oxonienses: The Members of the University of Oxford, 1500-1714*. Oxford: Parker and Co., 1888-1892. Ancestry.com, accessed 1 November 2021.

1 November 1847: I conducted the wedding of Charles Eaglestone and Elizabeth Eaglestone.[24] People came from miles around. Both their fathers were there, the brothers Edward and Thomas; Thomas alone because his wife died three years ago, Edward with Ann. Interestingly, the betrothed have mostly sisters; some with husbands, some not. The only male was Charles's older brother Joshua, unmarried, stonemason.

11 March 1851: Hannah came to see me. She is a daughter of William Palmer. She has been tending to Elizabeth Eaglestone, who had rheumatic fever which, I'm sorry to say, is not uncommon. Elizabeth has died. May her lovely soul rest in peace. Dear Hannah is only twenty and this has been a great burden.[25]

What a shock for Charles! He tells me the funeral cannot be held for a week, as there are relatives from many places who need to be informed.

30 March 1851: The second British Census was conducted. It recorded Edward, Ann, Charles and Hannah cohabiting at Deamond Farm. Charles is 'Son-in-law', Hannah is 'Visitor'.[26] Benjamin Bullock, publican of the Black's Head pub, is the Census-taker. He married Mary Eaglestone, the sister of Thomas and Edward, years ago, but she died young.

June 1852: Edward Eaglestone died and I conducted the funeral. Sad, but he was seventy-six: a good innings.

February 1853: Thomas Eaglestone died. He was eighty. My colleague in Kirtlington held the funeral.

---

[24] Marriage certificate of Charles Eaglestone and Elizabeth Eaglestone, married 30 October 1847, Parish of Bletchington, Bicester, Oxfordshire, General Registry Office, England, vol. 16, p. 67.

[25] Death certificate of Elizabeth Eaglestone, died 11 March 1851, Parish of Bletchington, Bicester, Oxfordshire, General Registry Office, England, vol. 3a, p. 334.

[26] Census record for Edward Eaglestone and others, Parish of Bletchington, Bicester, Oxfordshire, 1851 England Census, The National Archives, HO107/1729, p. 23, UK Census Collection, Ancestry.com, accessed 27 September 2021.

June 1853: It's taken time, but Charles has married Hannah.[27] Their relationship took shape slowly, like a stone-made church. The wedding was in Oxford. I might have expected him to ask me to conduct the ceremony at St Giles, but he said he thought it might upset the memory of Elizabeth.

Hannah is eleven years younger than Charles. And Elizabeth had been nine years older than him. There is a balance in life. I think, as an observer of the Eaglestone family, that they embody that balance. If you are building something that might last for 800 years, it imbues you with a sense of calmness and reverence. It was sad for Charles to lose Elizabeth, but it is blessed for a person to have two great loves in their life.

January 1860: For the Eaglestone file: Charles and Hannah have left. They packed up their family with three children last October and left for New Zealand on the *African*.[28] I am shocked; one gets used to one's parishioners, especially stonemasons. They are solid, even stolid. I know many people from Oxfordshire are emigrating, mostly to America and Canada, and some to Australia, but them? Why?[29]

Was it connected to Hannah losing a child last year?[30] I know this can be a time when one reflects on the direction of one's life.

---

[27] Marriage certificate of Charles Eaglestone and Hannah Palmer, married 23 June 1853, Parish of St Mary Magdalen, Oxford, Oxfordshire, General Registry Office, England, vol. 3a, p. 671.

[28] 'Passengers per African', *Southern Cross*, Auckland, 28 January 1860, n.p., online at https://www.familytreecircles.com/passengers-per-african-auckland-28-jan-1860-55747.html accessed, 1 November 2021. Note: They quickly decided that Australia was preferable, and shipped to Melbourne, set up in Geelong and stayed there until death.

[29] Greenwood, Martin, *The Promised Land: The story of emigration from Oxfordshire and neighbouring Buckinghamshire, Northamptonshire and Warwickshire 1815-1914*, Robert Boyd Publications, Witney, Oxfordshire, 2020.

[30] From My Heritage family tree of Ann Francis. Note: Mary Ann was not listed in GRO UK records of births or deaths. However, Mary Ann is listed (deceased) in children of Hannah Eaglestone on her death certificate: Hannah died 5 February 1890, Births, Deaths and Marriages Victoria, 2149/1890.

But their departure seemed to happen abruptly. Then again, Charles is forty-one. If he was going to make a big move, now was the time to do it. Blessings on his family.

Image: Sketch, St Giles church, Bletchington, Oxfordshire, 1790

Source: British Library

Edward Lewis at Point Puer

[This paper was written for an assignment for the Diploma of Family History, University of Tasmania, 2021]

Research question: What happened to Edward Lewis during the term of his convict sentence?

The context for the question

Edward Lewis is a great great grandfather on my father's side. He was born in Colchester, Essex in 1829.[31] He spent much of his childhood living by his wits on the streets of London, pickpocketing and fencing stolen goods with his older brothers.[32] In August 1845 he was tried for stealing a purse and ten shillings from a lady at Kensington. He was sentenced to ten years' transportation. He arrived in Hobart on the *Lady Palmyra* in August 1846.[33]

Edward was given a conditional pardon on 29 April 1852. He married Sarah Crosby, an Irish convict, in March 1853 and he became a special constable (in Tasmania)[34] and then a detective (in New South Wales).

Edward and his family moved to Sydney. He was involved in some politically charged police cases involving squatters at Wee

---

[31] Baptism of Edmund Lewis, baptised 18 October 1829, St Botolph's Church of England, Colchester, England, Essex and Suffolk Surnames, Colchester All Saints baptisms 1813-1845, p. 32 (index only). Note: I have confirmed that Edmund is my Edward Lewis. Edward did the same thing with his own son: he was born in 1855 and named Edmund but was thereafter known as Edward.

[32] Old Bailey Proceedings Online (www.oldbaileyonline.org, version 8.0, 06 August 2021), 7 April 1845, trial of John Ball, Edward Lewis, Samuel Lewis (t18450407-1021).

[33] Edward Lewis, No. 18862, *Palmyra*, 1846, Assignment Lists and Associated Papers, CON13/1/13, images 80, 81, Tasmanian Names Index. Edward Lewis, No. 18862, *Palmyra*, 1846, Indents of Male Convicts, CON14/1/36, image 16, Tasmanian Names Index.

[34] Registry entry for marriage of Edward Lewis and Sarah Crosby, married 7 March 1853, Hobart, RGD37/1/12 no 683, Tasmanian Names Index.

Waa,[35] he was charged with perjury[36] and attacked in the New South Wales Parliament and in newspapers.[37] He resigned from the police, and soon afterwards he was arrested for stealing money, presumably to live on.[38] He was gaoled for two years.

He became a legal clerk, but in his forties he re-entered the police force and served, admirably, for another twenty years.[39] Edward's life is an exciting story, but there is a missing period, namely, the period of his time as a convict, 1846 to 1850, which was when he received his Ticket of Leave.

Until recently I knew nothing of Point Puer. I visited Port Arthur and the Hobart Penitentiary Chapel in April 2021, and went to the State Library, where I learned that Edward was sent to Point Puer upon arrival in Hobart. He was fifteen and four feet nine inches (4'9"; 144 cm) tall. This paper explores what I have learned.

Research undertaken

My research was to examine the history of Point Puer, and then to explore Edward's convict records in that context. My channels of information for the prison system were the Tasmanian State Library

---

[35] NSW State Archives, Clerk of the Peace, NRS 880 Papers and Depositions, Supreme Court Sydney and on Circuit, 1824-1946, [9/6418] Regina v Charles Wentworth Bucknell and Francis Newnham Bucknell, September 1858, Wee Waa.

[36] NSW State Archives, Clerk of the Peace, NRS 880 Papers and Depositions, Supreme Court Sydney and on Circuit, 1824-1946, [9/6413] Regina v Edward Lloyd Lewis: Perjury, 7 October 1858, Sydney. 'Central Police Court', *Sydney Morning Herald*, 8 October 1858, p. 2, http://nla.gov.au/nla.news-article13016727

[37] 'The Bucknell case', *Maitland Mercury and Hunter River General Advertiser*, 26 October 1858, p. 2, http://nla.gov.au/nla.news-article18652634 ; (Editorial), *Sydney Morning Herald*, 2 June 1859, p. 4, http://nla.gov.au/nla.news-article13025655 ; 'New Notices of Motion', *Empire*, 10 September 1859, p. 6, http://nla.gov.au/nla.news-article60406172

[38] 'Central Police Court', *Sydney Morning Herald*, 26 May 1860, p. 7, http://nla.gov.au/nla.news-article13041019

[39] References to about ninety newspaper articles in Trove, between 1877 and 1897, references held by the author.

and the University of Tasmania library. My channels for Edward were the Tasmanian Names Index, Ancestry.com, New South Wales (NSW) State Archives, Registry of Births, Deaths and Marriages records in NSW and the United Kingdom, and Trove (database of Australian newspapers).

History of Point Puer

Point Puer was established in 1834, three years before Parkhurst (a prison for children) in England. The Lieutenant-Governor George Arthur and Captain Booth, commandant of Port Arthur, decided it would be best to separate juveniles from adult male convicts. The aim of Point Puer was "to reform young inmates by offering trade training."[40]

More than 3,000 boys passed through Point Puer during its operation. When it closed in March 1849, its population was down to 162, but it had also been heavily criticised.[41]

Despite the noble ideals behind Point Puer, it was under-resourced, and was unfortunately located right next to Port Arthur, the colony's penitentiary for its most recalcitrant adult convicts. It ended by reflecting the harshness of Port Arthur. Isolation cells and beatings were integral to the management of the institution, and many of the guards were convicts.[42]

At best, boys might choose a trade to learn (carpentry, shoemaking, tailoring, book-binding, boat-building, stone-masonry). Many boys did leave with useful skills, but many graduated to be convicts as adults.[43] The institution developed a culture of bullying and violence among the boys, with compliance and silence enforced through standover tactics. In 1843 a guard was

---

[40] D'Gluyas 2020; Nunn 2017; Shore 2002; Jackson 1998, pp. 82-89; Hooper 1954. Listed in References.

[41] Steve Harris 2019b, 'Silenced by an evil system: The boys the empire sent to Point Puer', *Sydney Morning Herald*, 19 October. Online at https://www.smh.com.au/national/silenced-by-an-evil-system-the-boys-the-empire-sent-to-point-puer-20190925-p52upv.html, accessed 24/7/21. See also, references for Footnote 40.

[42] Gorton 2002; MacFie 1999. Listed in References.

[43] Hooper 1954.

killed and two boys were charged with his murder, but then the case failed when the judge declared that the boys were not guilty.[44]

After Point Puer closed, boys were sent to nearby Cascades Probation Station.[45]

Edward Lewis and Point Puer

I have had Edward's indent and other convict records for several years,[46] but I have realised that to understand their full significance, I needed to compare them with other convicts' records. Edward's indent is spare, with only events like the granting of a conditional pardon recorded. On other convicts' indents I have seen, the whole page is full of incidents and punishments.

Conclusion: Edward did not serve his time with defiance. He "kept below the radar". Maybe he knew how to stay out of trouble and was aware that that was what would serve him best in the long run. Maybe he was thoroughly intimidated by the environment. Or, maybe he really experienced his time as the opportunity to learn skills and build networks – but then the question arises: why did he not learn a trade?

The indent shows that Edward stayed at Point Puer from 1846 until it was closed. Afterwards, he became a Special Constable (from his marriage certificate).[47]

Discussion

I know Edward could read and write (from records of his trial at Clerkenwell),[48] and two depositions he wrote as a detective for

---

[44] Harris 2019a; Tuffin & Gibbs 2020, pp. 87-114; Rosen 2017. Listed in References.

[45] I found some ambivalence among the sources about the location of 'Cascades' but I assume it refers to the Cascades Probation Station adjacent to Port Arthur, not the Cascades Female Factory at South Hobart.

[46] Edward Lewis, No. 18862, *Palmyra*, 1846, Conduct record, CON33/1/81, image 174. Tasmanian Names Index.

[47] from Tasmanian Names Index – marriage register. See Footnote 34.

[48] Edward Lewis, *Lady Palmyra*, 1846. England & Wales, Criminal Registers, 1791-1892, Register of all persons charged with indictable offences of the Assizes and Sessions held within the County during the

trials in 1858 showed his ease with writing, a clear understanding of process, and a beautiful signature.[49]

Kerin Gorton's PhD thesis on Point Puer states: "Those who had proven themselves to be responsible and well behaved may have been employed as messengers, clerks, supervisors or even constables or school teachers."[50] I think Edward became a clerk at Point Puer, as a path to becoming a policeman. Later in life (1860s/1870s) he was a legal clerk (from his children's marriage certificates).[51]

The indent says (once I had learned to read the abbreviations) that Edward was sent to Cascades Probation Station when Point Puer closed, but almost immediately was sent to the Prisoners' Barracks at Hobart (Hobart Depot, that is, the Campbell Street Penitentiary)[52] – I suspect, as a clerk. The end-of-year muster places him at Hobart Depot. Edward was granted a Ticket of Leave on 20/8/1850 (after having served half his sentence).

Then there is love: Edward met Sarah Crosby, who spent time at Cascades Female Factory (she had a child there, father unknown, in 1851).[53] If Edward was a clerk or special constable, he could have spent time there too. Edward married Sarah in March 1853. So, I

---

year 1845, County of Middlesex, The National Archives, Kew, Surrey, England, HO 26 and HO 27. Ancestry.com, accessed 10 August 2021.

[49] See Footnotes 35, 36.

[50] Gorton 2002, p. 322.

[51] Example: Marriage certificate of Edward's daughter Sarah Ann Lewis and John Alexander Philipson, married 17 December 1873, Registry of Births, Deaths and Marriages, New South Wales, 1873/00210. Edward is "Lawyer's Clerk".

[52] Edward Lewis, No. 18862 *Lady Palmyra*, 1846. New South Wales and Tasmania, Australia Convict Musters, 1806-1849, The National Archives, Kew, Surrey, England, HO/40, 1849 Register of Convicts for Tasmania (Van Diemens Land). Ancestry.com, accessed 29 July 2021. Edward's indent says '14/4/49 Cascades. 19th P.B.' I think this stands for 'Prisoners' Barracks' and refers to Hobart Penitentiary, and that Edward was moved to there in April. (I have found references to 'Prisoners' Barracks' in newspapers in 1850s.)

[53] Sarah Crosby, No. 1031, *St Vincent*, 1850, Conduct Registers of Female Convicts Arriving in the Period of the Probation System, CON41/1/25, image 31, Tasmanian Names Index.

don't know how Edward and Sarah met, but they clearly had opportunity to do so.

I think Edward employed the skills he had learned on the streets of London to survive Point Puer. The core competency of a pickpocket is to be invisible. He had also learned how to judge character, and how to build and use networks among people.

In investigating sources for this report, I rediscovered Marcus Clarke's book, *For the Term of His Natural Life*.[54] It was serialised in 1871-1872 in the *Australian Journal*. I wonder if Edward read it. It would have been deeply personal for him, and transformative to see the place of his own early experiences in print. Is that what inspired him to re-enter the police service – a redemptive spirit? For that matter, did he read any of Charles Dickens' books?

References

Assignment Lists and Associated Papers, Tasmanian Names Index.

Clarke, Marcus, *For the Term of His Natural Life*, Currey O'Neil, Melbourne, 1984.

Conduct records, Tasmanian Names Index.

Conduct Registers of Female Convicts Arriving in the Period of the Probation System, Tasmanian Names Index.

D'Gluyas, Caitlin, 'Juvenile Convict Labour and Industry: The Point Puer Landscape', *Journal of Australian Colonial History*, vol. 22, 2020, pp. 85-118.

Empire (newspaper).

England & Wales, Criminal Registers, 1791-1892, The National Archives, Kew, Surrey, England.

Essex and Suffolk Surnames.

---

[54] Clarke, Marcus, *For the Term of His Natural Life*, Currey O'Neil, Melbourne, 1984. (It was brought out in book form in 1874.)

Gorton, Kerin Joy, 'Carters' Barracks and Point Puer: the confinement experience of convict boys in colonial Australia, 1820-1850', PhD thesis, University of Newcastle, 2002.

Harris, Steve, *The Lost Boys of Mr Dickens*, Melbourne Books, Melbourne, 2019a.

Harris, Steve, 'Silenced by an Evil System: The Boys the Empire Sent to Point Puer', *Sydney Morning Herald*, 19 October, 2019b, online at https://www.smh.com.au/national/silenced-by-an-evil-system-the-boys-the-empire-sent-to-point-puer-20190925-p52upv.html accessed 24/7/21.

Hooper, F.C., 'The Point Puer Experiment: A Study of the Penal and Educational Treatment of the Juvenile Transportees in Van Diemen's Land 1830-50', thesis for MEd, University of Melbourne, 1954. https://data-informit-org.ezproxy.utas.edu.au/doi/10.3316/aeipt.48695

Indents of Male Convicts, Tasmanian Names Index.

Jackson, Skye, 'From Orphan School to Point Puer: A Study of the Care of Vulnerable Children in Van Diemen's Land (1828-1833)', thesis for BA(Hons), UTAS, 1998, pp. 82-89.

MacFie, Peter and Hargraves, Nigel, 'The Empire's First Stolen Generation: The First Intake at Point Puer 1834-39', *Tasmanian Historical Studies*, vol. 6, no. 2, 1999, pp. 129-154.

Maitland Mercury and Hunter River General Advertiser.

New South Wales and Tasmania, Australia Convict Musters, 1806-1849, The National Archives, Kew, Surrey, England.

New South Wales State Archives, NRS 880 Papers and Depositions.

Nunn, Cameron, '"Making Them Good and Useful": The Ideology of Juvenile Penal Reformation at Carters' Barracks and Point Puer', *History Australia*, vol. 14, no. 3, 2017, pp. 329–343. https://doi.org/10.1080/14490854.2017.1359081

Old Bailey Proceedings Online.

Registry of Births, Deaths and Marriages, New South Wales.

Registry of Marriages, Tasmanian Names Index.

Rosen, Bruce, '"Murder Most Foul": The Death of an Overseer at Point Puer', Papers and Proceedings, Tasmanian Historical

Research Association, vol. 64, issue 3, Dec 2017, pp. 51-67. https://data-informit-org.ezproxy.utas.edu.au/doi/10.3316/ielapa.356609194946152

Shore, Heather, 'Transportation, Penal Ideology and the Experience of Juvenile Offenders in England and Australia in the Early Nineteenth Century', *Crime, History & Societies*, vol. 6, no. 2, 2002, pp. 81-102. https://doi.org/10.4000/chs.416

Sydney Morning Herald.

Tuffin, Richard and Gibbs, Martin, '"Uninformed and impractical"? The Convict Probation System and Its Impact upon the Landscape of 1840s Van Diemen's Land', *History Australia*, vol. 17, no. 1, 2020, pp. 87-114.

Edward Lewis: grounds for intercession

One of my great great grandfathers, Edward Lewis, was a convict in Van Diemen's Land. He arrived in Hobart Town in 1846 aged fifteen, on a ten-year sentence, and he was sent to Point Puer. It was a prison for boys, located next to Port Arthur. Edward had been a pickpocket in London, but he had spent time at the London Orphan Asylum and learned to read and write there.

This is a story that fills in the gaps in the records, as I imagine how things might have happened. It is consistent with the records. It is Edward Lewis speaking. It is April 1849 and Point Puer has just been shut down....

Edward Lewis: a plea for intercession

This is the letter I have written to the Commandant.

April 1849: I am Edward Lewis, convict, aged nineteen. I was transported in 1846 because I was caught stealing a purse from a lady at Kensington. They sent me here to Van Diemen's Land. I was on the ship *Lady Palmyra*. I have been at Point Puer for three years and I have kept out of trouble. You should see my Conduct Record. It's clean.

When Point Puer was closed down last month, I was sent here to Cascades Probation Station. But it is not for the likes of me. All the work is heavy, like hauling huge logs with just men, no horses or bullocks. I would not be much use at that. I am too small.

However, I can read and write, and I have been very useful that way at Point Puer. I spent part of my childhood at the London Orphan Asylum, and it was a blessing, because they were very strict with learning, and I learned well.

I did clerical work at Point Puer. I wasn't assigned to learning a trade like a bootmaker or a carpenter. I would be of good use at the Hobart Depot. There's always a need for good clerks.

Dear Commandant, I humbly request that you take me out of Cascades Probation Station and send me to the Prisoners'

Barracks in Hobart. Every prison establishment needs people who are smart, and who are good at keeping records. I would serve Queen Victoria's colony best in that position.

Edward's explanation

One of the blessings of my childhood was spending time in the orphanage and learning to read and write. They used to say to us: "Remember, boys and girls, it's important to learn to read and write."

It's a shame they closed down Point Puer. I'd been there three years – in the one place! A bit different from London, where my first crime was vagrancy! I'd sorted out my routines and my consolations at Point Puer, and I had built up my useful networks.

This Cascades Probation Station is not for me. It's just an outpost where they make convicts do heavy work. Imagine, hauling huge logs with just men, not even using horses or bullocks. The only thing it will fit you for is more of the same, a lifetime of it until you are crushed. I didn't survive London, and I didn't survive Point Puer, to waste my life now.

Supporting notes (Glenn Martin)

The identifying convict record for Edward Lewis is: Edward Lewis, No. 18862, *Palmyra*, 1846, Indents of Male Convicts, CON14/1/36, image 16, Tasmanian Names Index.

The record shows he was sent to Cascades Probation Station on 11th April 1849, but transferred to 'P.B.' on 19th April. P.B. = Prisoners' Barracks, that is, Hobart Depot. So, within eight days he was transferred. And his record was indeed 'clean'. Some boys were regularly in trouble, and it was all recorded on their indent. The details are given in the Assignment Lists:

Edward Lewis, No. 18862, *Palmyra*, 1846, Assignment Lists and Associated Papers, CON13/1/13, images 80, 81, Tasmanian Names Index.

Two accounts of the history of Point Puer are:

D'Gluyas, Caitlin, 'Juvenile Convict Labour and Industry: The Point Puer Landscape', *Journal of Australian Colonial History*, vol. 22, 2020, pp. 85-118.

Gorton, Kerin Joy, 'Carters' Barracks and Point Puer: the confinement experience of convict boys in colonial Australia, 1820- 1850', PhD thesis, University of Newcastle, 2002.

Remarkably, I found Edward Lewis in the 1841 UK Census: Census record for Edward Lewis, aged 10, London Orphan Asylum, 1841 England and Wales Census, The National Archives, HO107/698/13, UK Census Collection, Ancestry.com, accessed 10 April 2021.

An article about London Orphan School (as the Asylum was known) is on Wikipedia, under 'Reed's School': https://en.wikipedia.org/wiki/Reed%27s_School The founder was emphatic about the importance of education.

It was a convention in the British legal system that prisoners might have letters of intercession written for them (scribes would do this for payment) to submit to the authorities to beg for mercy and a pardon, or a reduction in their sentence. Edward would have been familiar with this protocol, and was in the position of having the skills to fashion his own letter.

Lest it seem precocious for Edward to have written such a letter in 1849 in Van Diemen's Land, we should bear in mind that later he became a legal clerk, and also that (I am convinced) he had been working as a clerk at Point Puer. Not only could he read and write, he knew the conventions of the prison system. I also have a sample of his writing and signature from the 1850s, and they are accomplished, even beautiful.

Image 1

Sketch of Point Puer peninsula and buildings, by N Remand, "Etablissement penitentiare de Port Arthur", 1840s (University of Tasmania). Point Puer is at centre, across the water, with the Isle of the Dead (the cemetery) on its left. The buildings at right are of Port Arthur.

Image 2

Signature of Edward Lloyd Lewis, 1858

Source: NSW State Archives, Clerk of the Peace, NRS 880 Papers and Depositions, Supreme Court Sydney and on Circuit, 1824-1946, [9/6418] Regina v Charles Wentworth Bucknell and Francis Newnham Bucknell, September 1858, Wee Waa.

Sarah Crosby, a desperate spinster

My mother said there were no convicts in the family. She meant her side of the family. She didn't know much about dad's side. Dad never said much, but I don't think he knew much about his family's past anyway. You just got that feeling.

Dad died when I was sixteen. I didn't get interested in family history until mum turned ninety, and I was over sixty. I plunged in, ignorant but enthusiastic. I gradually pieced together the family members in mum and dad's generation, and then their parents' generation.

It was a long time before I came near to the possibility of any convicts. You have to remember that transportation from Britain to Australia had ceased by 1868, so we would have to be talking about my great great grandparents or even further. It was going to take me a while to get to them.

However, eventually I got there, and it was a scandal, because there was in fact a convict on my mother's side. The great patriarch of the family, the publican, William Archer, who has a large grave with twenty people in it at Waverley Cemetery overlooking the Pacific Ocean from the clifftops of Sydney, was a convict. So, the story about "no convicts in the family" was a myth fabricated by him or his descendants, and my mum must have been only a small child when she was told the story. She believed it right up to her death in 2017; it was too late for anyone to try to debunk it.

When I subsequently found two convicts on dad's side, it wasn't so much of a shock. There were no myths to contend with. I have encountered just one person who has been exploring some lines of dad's side of the family, and no one has appeared who is following the line of my father's mother's mother, Ellen Elizabeth Eaglestone (maiden name Lewis). It was her parents, both of them, who were the convicts, making it the same generation as the convict on my mother's side – great great grandparents.

Who were these two convicts? One of them was Edward Lewis, a London-dwelling child pickpocket who was transported to Van Diemen's Land when he was just fifteen years of age. Brown hair, blue eyes, and only four feet nine inches tall at the time. The judge noted that he had been convicted of offences before, namely, vagrancy. I found him in the 1841 British Census residing at the London Orphan Asylum when he was eleven. He travelled to Hobart Town on the *Lady Palmyra*, landing in May 1846.

Meanwhile, the potato blight had begun to strike in Ireland, precipitating widespread famine. In mid-1846, three quarters of the Irish potato crop failed. Both mortality and emigration exploded. It was a crisis unlike any other that had gripped the country. Into this dire landscape comes a girl, Sarah Crosby. She is about thirteen years of age in 1846, the daughter of a farmer in the County of Waterford.

By 1847 she has fled the country, told, perhaps, by her parents, to save herself (I do not know what became of them). In mid-1847, three million people across Ireland were in receipt of soup from facilities set up by the British Relief Association (run by the Quakers, not the British Government). Sarah's convict record tells us that she became a servant at a house in Bath, England in 1847/1848. But she did not last there (we don't know why), and she ended up in London in January 1849.

Did she have any siblings? The convict record from her trial tells us she had a brother, James Crosby, and I found a James Crosby in a London shipping list, bound for Boston in the United States of America in 1848. And there was a James Crosby, Irish and of a similar age to Sarah, in New York in 1860. But the convict record says that James was at Islington (London) in 1850, so this question is unresolved. Had Sarah come to London to try to reconnect with her brother and perhaps get to America in the hope of a change in her fortunes, as many Irish did?

London did not bring any such salvation. She managed to attract one conviction of three days for being drunk.

A number of newspaper reports tell us that on Wednesday 31 January 1849 at around eight o'clock in the evening she was waiting in a queue outside the Refuge for the Houseless Poor in Whitecross Street, about one kilometre north of St Paul's Cathedral. It was a week after the new moon, mid-winter, bitterly cold and already dark. She was waiting to see if she would be admitted and get a meal and a bed for the night, or be turned away. I imagine her hungry, cold, afraid, and despairing.

And what happens? Why is she in the newspaper?

There is an incident. At her trial, police constable John Smith said that he "had occasion to move her on", whereupon she abused and threatened him. Then she took a penknife out of her bag and stabbed him several times in the arm. Constable Smith was speaking to the charge against Sarah of cutting and wounding with intent to cause bodily harm.

We hear how many days Constable John Smith had to take off work (ten). And we hear at length the judge's views about the Irish – "the law provided for her relief, and very properly; but the least that could be expected was something like reciprocity and good feeling in return; but no, quite the contrary – a police constable, doing duty at the very door where relief was to be granted, and who required the prisoner to behave herself, was to be stabbed and injured in a manner that had kept him from his duty, and might have endangered his life." The judge was determined to make an example of such a case.

Image: Central Criminal Court, Old Bailey, London, 1842 (from *The Illustrated London News*)

The newspaper reporters seemed clear enough about what was at stake. In the various accounts she is described as "a desperate spinster" and "a desperate woman", although the articles never make it clear what the actual cause of the desperation was. Perhaps their readers knew only too well. She responded to the policeman's actions by abusing him, shouting threats, then taking out her penknife and stabbing him in the arm.

What did Sarah have to say about the charges? The records of the Old Bailey contain transcripts of the trials. She said she went to the refuge at five o'clock, where she was given some bread (that is all the refuge offered). She took her knife out to cut the bread, which, accordingly to contemporary accounts, tended to be dry and hard, and difficult to eat for people who were starving. The policeman, who was on duty there, told her to move out, and threw her out.

In his court statement, the policeman said he told her: "You have got your answer; to go to St Luke's workhouse or somewhere else; they will not admit you [here] again". So, yes, she was facing a night on the street in the cold, because we know from other sources, and the policeman would have known, and Sarah would have known, that St Luke's was not taking admissions that night.

One of the workers at the refuge, Ann Pike, said, "The prisoner was very noisy and ill-conducted there". In Sarah's statement in defence, she said she was not doing anything wrong. (I guess from this that she was refusing to leave.) She said that other people told the policeman that she had a knife in her hand, and he "came up to me in a passion to take it from me. The sergeant also came up, kicked me in the chest and knocked me down, and took the knife from me". That is all we hear from her. Constable John Smith said he "kept her off with my truncheon" and "in attempting to take the knife from her [that is, he and the sergeant] she cut my finger and bit my thumb".

It is convenient that we have more information about convicts than we do about ordinary individuals of that period. When a person was convicted and was to be transported, a medical examination was conducted. This was more for purposes of their identification (in the era before photographs) than with a view to the treatment of ailments. Thus, we learn that Sarah had a scar on her left cheek. Sarah had been in gaol for four weeks before the trial (31 January to

26 February); this was enough time for a wound to heal and become a scar. It is not difficult to imagine, although it is not mentioned at the trial, that this wound was sustained when the two policemen were grappling with her.

We all know what desperation is. We have all had an occasion (or more) when we have felt it. It takes you over. It is a matter of life and death, and you have to act, no matter what. You are fighting for your own life and your whole self knows it and lunges forth with everything you have inside you. But Sarah's weapon is only a penknife, a token weapon, and the policeman is much larger (she is just five feet one and three-quarter inches (157 cm) tall, young, and weak from lack of food) and he is heavily dressed in two winter coats (unlike her scanty rags), so the attack is feeble but for her passion. And a second policeman is involved as well.

I note also that Sarah stabs him in the arm. If she had intended the policeman serious harm, surely she would have stabbed him straight in the chest. Stabbing him in the arm is more like a desperate girl's way of saying, "Get your hands off me!"

What we never hear in the newspaper accounts or the transcript of the trial is why the policeman "had occasion to move on the prisoner". She wasn't a boisterous adolescent lining up to get into a dance so she could have a good time. She was lining up miserably for the chance to get a meagre meal and a bed on a freezing winter's night, at a time when it was not uncommon for homeless people in London to freeze to death overnight. Sarah had little chance of justification in the Old Bailey. She was Irish, she was but an adolescent, and she had no standing against the story of a policeman, a man who held authority.

The jury found her guilty of the charge of cutting and wounding with intent to do bodily harm. The judge (called the Common Sergeant in the Central Criminal Court), in passing sentence on Sarah, said it was "a very bad case" and it called for the severest example to be set. He continued, "Here she was, an Irishwoman come over to this country, and in distress" and he proceeded with his pompous rant about the generosity of the English to the Irish.

He concluded by saying that the prisoner was "a very fit and useful subject for the colonies" and he sentenced her to seven years' servitude. So, after all the rhetoric, Sarah Crosby is found to be 'useful' to the Empire. How convenient. Sarah would provide a benefit to the burgeoning Australian colony through her services.

Tim Pat Coogan's book, *The Famine Plot* (Palgrave, 2012) makes it clear that the English showed little generosity to the Irish during the potato famine. And certainly, the English at that time demonised the Irish. They considered them to be less than human and deserving of their troubles. And it is also true that much of the other food grown in Ireland at the time (for example, wheat) was exported to England while the native population was starving.

Sarah's sentence of seven years can be contrasted with another case heard on the same day. Twenty-five-year-old T. Roberts, a gardener, was indicted of cutting and wounding the publican who evicted him from a beer shop (a homely version of what today would be a hotel or tavern). Roberts was drunk, and fell down in the street and his clothes became soiled. He took out his knife to scrape the mud off, and whilst doing so, attempted to re-enter the beer house. The publican sought to prevent him, and Roberts turned the knife to him and cut him 'fearfully' across the nose. The publican was 'dreadfully mutilated'.

While the jury found him guilty, it recommended mercy, and Roberts' sentence was nine months' hard labour.

There was never really an answer to the question of what precipitated the incident that occasioned Constable John Smith to move Sarah on. The refuge worker, Ann Pike, said that "The prisoner was very noisy and ill-conducted there". The policeman said, "She made use of a very bad expression". Henry Mayhew, a journalist who wrote about the London poor in this period (*London Labour and the London Poor*, 1851), described the sight of the crowd of people lining up to gain admittance to the "asylum for the houseless poor". They were ragged and shivering, sad and weary. There were the cries of distressed children, mingled with "the wrangling of the hungry crowds for their places".

Image: Asylum for the Houseless Poor, Cripplegate, London, in 1851. Wood engraving from Henry Mayhew's book, *London Labour and the London Poor*

ASYLUM FOR THE HOUSELESS POOR, CRIPPLEGATE.

Another writer of this period who was describing these refuges (Thomas Archer, *The Terrible Sights of London*, 1870) reported on the case of an officer kneeing a heavily pregnant woman in the stomach. The officer in this case was brought to trial and fined, but Archer comments: "He should remember that when starving people came for relief they might be irritable and annoying; but an officer should be above such feelings, and should not give way to his temper". He speaks more generally that it was common for people dealing with "the poor who seek the scanty aid" that is available to treat them with brutality. These stories suggest the desperation in the atmosphere of Sarah's circumstances.

After the trial, Sarah was sent to Millbank Prison, which was used as a holding place for prisoners who had been sentenced to transportation. It was a dismal place, a massive brick structure built on top of a swamp next to the Thames, damp, cold and gloomy, and the fact that it drew its water from the Thames made the prisoners susceptible to disease. In 1849 there was an outbreak of cholera in the prison, which was so bad that many prisoners had to be sent away to different prisons around London. Millbank had been built as an improvement on the hulks (ships which had reached the end of their useful life) moored in the Thames as holding places for prisoners. It turned out to be worse.

Sarah survived the dismal conditions and on 13 December 1849 she was taken on board the *St Vincent*, in company with 206 other female convicts, bound for Van Diemen's Land.

The voyage took just over three months. For much of it she was sick. We have the ship's surgeon's records (Dr Samuel Donnelly), and they tell us that soon after the ship sailed from London, she was admitted to the infirmary with acute pain and swelling in the shoulder joints – rheumatism. She was also constipated, and had hot spells, and on one occasion she vomited a considerable amount of dark blood.

However, by 1 February 1850, she was said to be 'cured'. This was not her last health problem; she was admitted again with haemorrhoids in February, but again she was recorded as 'cured' when the ship landed in Hobart Town on 4 April 1850. Two women had died on the voyage. Deaths were not uncommon on the voyage to Australia at this time. Life was never a secure thing.

It was in Hobart that Sarah met Edward Lewis, who by then had graduated from being a convict to being a special constable. They were married at the newly built sandstone Roman Catholic Church of St Joseph in Hobart on 7 May 1853. Her conditional pardon was approved in April 1854. It should be noted that during her servitude, Sarah had a few instances of misconduct recorded against her for minor infractions (like disorderly conduct) but there were never any instances of stabbing and wounding.

References

Archer, Thomas, *The Terrible Sights of London and Labours of Love in the Midst of Them*, Stanley Rivers and Co., London, 1870.

Coogan, Tim Pat, *The Famine Plot,* Palgrave, Basingstoke UK, 2012.

Mayhew, Henry, *London Labour and the London Poor*, Volume 1 of 4, Griffin, Bohn & Co., London, 1851.

Image of Asylum for the Houseless Poor: Tufts Digital Library, https://dl.tufts.edu/concern/images/5138jp597

A day at the cemetery

Two of my great great grandparents on my father's side were convicts. They met in Hobart after both had been transported. Sarah Crosby was sentenced to seven years in Van Diemen's Land in 1849 for attacking a police officer after he attempted to "move her on" from a Refuge for the Houseless Poor in London. Edward Lewis was a child pickpocket in London. He had been transported for ten years in 1846.

I gradually pieced together their lives, starting with the reasons they ended up as convicts. Sarah was actually Irish, not English. She had left Ireland during the potato famine. I do not know what happened to her family in Waterford. Edward had been born at Colchester in Essex. It appeared that he had several brothers and sisters, but he was separated from his parents. From the records at his trial for stealing, it appeared that his mother had died and his father had not been able to keep the family together. Edward spent time at the London Orphan Asylum.

After Edward and Sarah married (in 1853), she gave birth to twin girls in Hobart. Edward had a job in the police force. This was not unusual for ex-convicts; it was not a favoured occupation. Then Edward got a job as a detective in Sydney. Now there were two more children, a boy and another girl. But Edward was having a tumultuous time as a detective, having difficulty weathering public opinion about ex-convicts, and the machinations of powerful people who used those opinions to divert attention from their own corrupt schemes.

Edward resigned from his job, sent his family off to Adelaide, perhaps not knowing that Sarah was pregnant. He attempted to survive in Sydney, obtaining help from a dealer in goods. He stole money to survive and was sent to prison. After this episode, Sarah and the children, including the new baby, came back to Sydney, and Edward obtained work as a legal clerk. The children grew up and married.

I learned about their lives from birth and marriage certificates, and newspaper articles, piecing it together to make their lives. I still needed to determine their deaths and burials. I didn't have a date of death for either Edward or Sarah. But, I had reached the stage where

I had all the children – when and where they were born, when they married and the children they had, and lastly, their deaths.

How was I going to find out about the deaths of Sarah and Edward? I didn't have enough clues to identify them in the records of the Registry of Births, Deaths and Marriages. I decided to go and visit the graves of the children. There was no reason to think this would give me any further clues to their parents, but it would fill in the picture a little bit more. Rookwood was the final resting place of most of the children.

I found the grave of Sarah Ann, the elder of the twins. She had married a goldminer, John Alexander Philipson. They had lived at Gulgong for several years, but came back to Sydney to live. Sarah Ann and John are buried in adjoining graves at Rookwood, comfortable, settled. She died in 1931 at the age of seventy-seven.

Sarah Ann's twin sister, Mary Susannah, died young, in 1888, aged thirty-four. She married an Irishman, Timothy Moroney, at the age of sixteen (the minister obviously didn't know that, and didn't ask) and had six children. I don't know the cause of her death. She is buried in the old Roman Catholic section at Rookwood. Her grave is lovely. It is a tall sandstone pedestal with a small, carved angel gazing down solicitously.

Ellen, the next daughter, is not at Rookwood. She is at Woronora Cemetery near Sutherland, to the south of Sydney. I have seen her grave. She married Edwin Eaglestone, a stonemason. She died in 1937. She and Edwin have a carved headstone made of sandstone. They had four children, three of whom lived to adulthood.

Margaret, the youngest daughter, was the last of the children to die – in 1946. She was eighty-five. She was the first in the Lewis family to be cremated. She has a plaque in a wall of remembrance at Rookwood. Leonard is the name of her second husband, Joseph John Henry Leonard, an artist and cartoonist. Her first husband was Louis Jean Baptiste Deleuil, a French chef. Margaret's plaque says "Loved by all".

That left the only son, Edward Lloyd Lewis, or Edmond, or Ted, according to the period of time and the context. Edmond is the name on his birth registration in Tasmania, but he was known as Edward Lloyd when he had grown up. I knew he had a troubled life, or at least, a troubled life as a young man. He had beaten people up, including young women, and robbed people in a gang. He was sent to gaol for four years. And he married Mary Wall, but she left him within twelve months, unhappy with his violence.

I think that he settled down after coming out of gaol. There were no further crimes. He did not marry again. He was a bootmaker by trade. But he died relatively young, at fifty-one. In the Roman Catholic section at Rookwood he was listed, along with the location of the grave. So I set off to see.

It was in the old Roman Catholic section, where Mary Susannah and Timothy Moroney were buried, with the little angel. Through the middle of this section there is a line of vaults, little houses for the dead, all busy with ornaments. The remainder of the section is unkempt, with wild grass over the graves and pathways that were mown only occasionally.

I was expecting to find Edward Lloyd Lewis, not the father, but the son. I had the date for his death, 10 December 1907. I was still without a clue as to the deaths of Edward and Sarah, the parents, so I was content to pursue the lesser duty of viewing the children's graves.

I was walking down the lines of graves, looking for the identifying numbers of the graves, which were only to be seen on one in every twenty or so graves. One had to mentally map the pattern thus revealed or, rather, suggested. The method could be called haphazard. I saw that I was only about thirty metres from where Mary Susannah was buried. It was on the other side of the line of vaults.

Many of the graves were Irish. How could I know this? It was because the gravestones declared their occupants' nativity: "Joseph Marshall, Born at Liverpool, England"; "Patrick Moroney, A Native of Limerick, Ireland"; "Mary Ann, Beloved Wife of the Above, A Native of County Clare, Ireland".

And then I was face to face with the grave of Sarah Anne Lewis. I was reading the words: "Sarah Anne Lewis, Native of County of Waterford, Ireland. Died 4th September 1897, Aged 64 years. R.I.P." I had not known her date of death, but this fitted with what I did know about her. I took a moment. I was taking it all in – the surroundings, the grave, knowing that her daughter Mary Susannah

Moroney lay just nearby, and Margaret Leonard and Sarah Ann Philipson were lying elsewhere in the cemetery. I was looking at the light, the mottled shadows of the jacaranda tree across the gravestone, the pine tree behind the grave.

The gravestone was tall; it stood just taller than me, and certainly taller than Sarah's five feet, one inch height. Slowly, I remembered that I had been looking for her son, not for her, so this was a great gift. But where was her son? And where was Edward, her husband? On that tall gravestone, Sarah's inscription was at the top of the stone, and there was space beneath it for other names, but it was blank. The first inscription is the first according to death's chronology. So, this implied that Edward the father was not dead in September 1897. But where was the inscription for the son, who had died in 1907?

That was not all. It was a large double grave, delimited by a concrete border around the outside, and there was a second gravestone, quite a bit smaller, carved as a decorative cross. The inscription was: "In Loving Memory of Louis Deleuil, died 13th September 1901, aged 51 years. R.I.P." At first I thought, who is this man? What is he doing here? Then I remembered that Margaret had married a French chef. This was the man. But, hadn't they divorced in 1895? Margaret had married again – Mister Leonard.

Why was Louis Deleuil buried here, the divorced son-in-law?

And where was Edward Lewis, the father? He had to have died at some point, and there was space for an inscription for him, and presumably space in the grave for his body. I look at the grave, I read all the words again. You can't expect to talk to a headstone and get answers. But I ask anyway. I get up real close to the headstone, so I am reading the words: "Sarah Anne Lewis, Native of County of Waterford, Ireland", and at that moment a magpie flies up close. He lands on the gravestone at the back of hers, which is taller, so he is just a couple of feet away from my head, and does his magpie performance, singing and nodding and dancing.

I say, "Tell me," but the magpie says it's in the dance, so I just watch the dance. Then it flies away, but not far, and it brings up a worm from another grave. Okay, I say. I still have to work it out, don't I? I still have to figure this out myself.

Where are you, Edward? I wonder if Sarah smiles at this point. I don't think it was always easy for her. But I think there was some sympathy between them, two kindred spirits who had survived a harsh and unkind world as children, and found comfort in each other. To survive, to have a home and a family and a means of livelihood, was a great victory. It was a victory forged only out of defiance, in the face of scorn and derision. It was a victory over the cynicism of the promise of a new life in the colonies. They had indeed found a new life in the colonies, using their own reserves of strength.

I will keep at it, working at new theories, hunting for new sources, until I find Edward. He is the only missing piece among all the great great grandparents. All the others have revealed themselves and I know how they fit into the jigsaw of my life. Their stories are part of me now. And I yearn to honour Edward Lewis in the same way.

Note

I wrote this story in October 2016, before I embarked on a book to investigate Edward Lewis's life in depth. It resulted in the book, *The Search for Edward Lewis* (2018).

Image: Grave of Sarah Anne Lewis, showing gravestone for Louis Deleuil at right; Rookwood Necropolis

Section 9: Great great grandparents, maternal (1)

William Archer (1813-1894) and Ellen Welch (1822-1912)

John Neill (1825-1891) and Alice Wetherell (1821-1867)

Introductory notes

These two sets of great great grandparents are my mother's father's grandparents. They were all born overseas and were immigrants to Australia. William Archer was a convict, and the first one of my direct ancestors to come to Australia, in 1838. He was from Hertfordshire. Ellen Welch came from Scotland in 1841. John and Alice Neil, from Armagh in Ireland, came together in 1855.

There are six stories in this section. The first one, "Tidying up the record", shows how complicated lives could be. Helen Archer (Ellen Welch when she got married) is seeking to guide her son James as to what it would be appropriate to say on her death certificate and on her gravestone.

The second story is about the young Ellen Welch as an unmarried female assisted migrant to Australia. It reveals a secret that Ellen kept all her life (I think it is okay to tell the story).

The next story is called "The romance". It was a story I was told by my mother when I was a child. There was an inexplicable air of whimsy about it. In the same conversation my mother would tell me about her Aunty Dolly, and how she had spent thousands of dollars researching the Archer family's history. Only now do I think I understand the story of the romance.

John and Alice Neil were married in Portadown, Armagh before they emigrated to Australia. I did not know much about them, except for the fact that their daughter, also called Alice, married James Archer, a son of William and Helen Archer. But of course, everyone has a story.

Then there is an addendum to John Neil's story. His wife died young and he married again. I have usually found that there is not much of interest for me in this, because the new spouse is not my direct ancestor. But, in this case, I discovered that the new spouse, Mary Ann Bonham, was indeed interesting.

The last story is about William Archer, the "first ancestor", and his "early life and crimes". I wanted to know what kind of man he was. I believe I have some grasp of it after my delving, and I think there is some scope for admiration of him.

Tidying up the record

This is an imagined conversation between Helen Archer (married as Ellen Welch) and her son, James Archer.

"James, we should talk about what's to go on my gravestone, while I still have my wits."

"But it will say 'Ellen Archer, born in Edinburgh', won't it? Just like dad's says 'Born in Harpenden'."

"No, don't say that. For a start, Helen is my real name."

"But I thought you just adopted Helen when we came back from England in 1874. I thought it was about our higher station in life. I know dad was a convict, but when we came back from those years farming in Kent, he started the hotel."

"I know you thought that, but I was actually baptised Helen. When we came back to Australia, I decided to reclaim it."

For once, James is speechless.

"And on my gravestone, don't say I was born in Edinburgh. I wasn't."

"But that's what was said on my birth certificate!"

"I know. When I came to Australia as an assisted migrant, I actually said I was born in Dublin. Edinburgh is closer to the truth. I am Scottish!"

"But you've told us this story. You said you came out from Glasgow on the *New York Packet,* in 1841."

"And that's true. But it was convenient to have people think I was Irish."

"So, where were you born?"

"It doesn't matter. Edinburgh will do, but not on the gravestone. The truth is complicated."

"What do you mean?"

"There's no need for you to know that. Just, please, say 'Helen Archer, beloved wife of William Archer'. That's enough. It's been a satisfying life."

Image: Gravestone for Helen Archer, Waverley Cemetery

Sources

Birth certificate, James Archer, 12/1/1857, son of William and Ellen Archer, Registry of Births, Deaths and Marriages, New South Wales, 1857/009033.

Birth register, Helen Welsh, 11/10/1822, Markinch, Fife, Scotland, Old Parish Registers, Births 447/ 50 29 Markinch, page 29 of 315, Scotlands People.

Census record for Ellen Welsh, aged 20 and Thomas Welsh aged 1, Millerston, Parish of Barony, in Glasgow City/Lanark 1841 Census, 622/214/1, page 1 of 25, Scotlands People, accessed 26 August 2021.

Death certificate, Helen Archer, 8/6/1912, Cause of death: 'Senile decay', Registry of Births, Deaths and Marriages, New South Wales, 1912/007474.

Death certificate, William Archer, 4/1/1894, Registry of Births, Deaths and Marriages, New South Wales, 12/1894.

Entitlement certificates of persons on bounty ships, Ellen Welch, 23 October 1841, Series: *5314*; Reel: *1334,* State Records Authority of New South Wales.

Grave of Archer family, Waverley Cemetery, Church of England, Section 6, Graves 663B and 664A.

Sands Postal Directory, 1882, Duke of Edinburgh Hotel, 138 Union St Pyrmont, p. 63. City of Sydney Archives & Historical Resources, https://archives.cityofsydney.nsw.gov.au/nodes/view/495003 Accessed 21/6/2021.

Ellen Welch: unmarried female assisted migrant

This story is about Ellen Welch. Initially, there didn't seem to be much to say about her, except that she was William Archer's wife. William was the bad boy of the Archer side of the family (my mother's side), because he had been a convict. He was also a spinner of yarns. I think the story, "There are no convicts in our family", came from him, and my mother believed it to her dying day (in 2017). And he was an entrepreneur: he built a hotel at Pyrmont called the Duke of Edinburgh.

William took the family back to England around 1866 and they had a farm in Kent for a few years before coming back to Sydney to start the pub. They had eight children together, so, a relatively normal family for the time.

But there were odd little things about Ellen. After they came back from England in 1874, she became known as Helen. I thought that that was just pretention. They had re-made themselves (now they could say they had come to the colony as free settlers), and William was now a publican. It says 'Helen' on her gravestone. Fair enough, but then I noticed another little thing: William's inscription says: "Born at Harpenden, Hertfordshire, England". Helen's just says: "Beloved wife of William Archer". Why?

I thought it was a formula for that generation, to say where they had come from. I got curious about Helen's past. What did we know? She came to Australia as an assisted migrant in 1841, at a time when women were scarce, and in England and Scotland they were being encouraged to emigrate. She was a single female, and her passage was paid for under the colonial government's bounty system. She went to the Hunter Valley as a domestic servant, and three years later she married William Archer, convict, at Eldon (Raymond Terrace). Her name was Ellen Welch.[55]

I wondered why she emigrated. She was the fifth of six children; she was the only family member to emigrate. Her father was the

---

[55] Marriage registration of William Archer and Ellen Welch, married 15 July 1844, Registry of Births, Deaths and Marriages, New South Wales, no. 541, vol. 29.

manager of a coalworks at Balgonie Furnace (Markinch) in Fife. She was the boss's daughter. Her death certificate says she was born in Edinburgh, and so do the birth certificates of her children, but she was actually born at Balgonie Furnace. Her birth record checks out.[56] This was odd. Was there something to hide?

I obtained her Unmarried Female Immigrant certificate, signed in Sydney on 23 October 1841.[57] Her character and person are vouched for by two gentlemen in Edinburgh. The statment says she was born in Dublin. There were other Irish women on the ship, but none from Dublin. I think Dublin is not true; I am satisfied she was born in Fife, as Ellen Welch.

Ellen had been in Edinburgh, but also in Glasgow, because the ship departed from nearby Longrock. She turned nineteen during the voyage. As luck would have it, the first British Census was conducted on 6 June 1841, four weeks before the ship left (8 July). In a boarding house in Glasgow was an Ellen Welch, twenty, with a one-year-old boy, Thomas.[58] Ellen would have been eighteen, but the record was credible. I also looked for 'Helen' and 'Welsh' and 'Walsh': there were no competing persons. But we know she boarded the ship as a single woman.

What happened to the child? I have to guess. The Roman Catholic Church had started an orphanage in Glasgow in 1832, after a typhoid outbreak. There was a rise in orphaned children. I think that Ellen took the child there (and for this purpose she is Irish). It is a stunning story. Whose child was it, and why did she feel she had to leave home – irrevocably? And give up the child? And is that all the evidence I have?

---

[56] Birth registration of Helen Welsh, born 20 October 1822, Old Parish Registers Births 447/5029 Markinch (Fife), p. 29, National Records of Scotland.

[57] *Entitlement certificates of persons on bounty ships,* Ellen Welch, 23 October 1841, Series: *5314*; Reel: *1334,* State Records Authority of New South Wales.

[58] Census record for Ellen Welsh, aged 20 and Thomas Welsh aged 1, Millerston, Parish of Barony, in Glasgow City/Lanark 1841 Census, 622/214/1, page 1 of 25, Scotlands People, accessed 26 August 2021. [Note: Welch, Welsh and Walsh were sometimes used alternatively.]

Almost. As I said, William and Ellen had eight children. The first four were named after William and people in his family. Then there was James (my great grandfather, and the informant on Ellen's death certificate), and three more, who were named after people in Ellen's family. Except that, the last one was called Thomas, which did not correspond to names in either family.[59] Ellen/Helen had not forgotten him.

None of this gets us any closer to knowing who the father of the child was, or why she had to leave home. She was probably sixteen when she became pregnant. My only idea is, she was the boss's daughter, as the songs say – a particular source of attraction for men. Was her father one of those severe, religious Scots who would have been outraged at his daughter's pregnancy?

Reflection

Three generations later, my mother believed something (the "no convicts" story) that had the ring of mythology about it, with the ironic inference that it was not true as such. But I could not have contested it with her. I think the statement had humour in it. I imagine William Archer as the raconteur behind the bar in the hotel. But Ellen Archer gets buried in that cheerful bombast.

I wondered what William's attitude would be towards me for writing this story. The family had become socially uplifted. Ellen's story breaches the façade. And what would Ellen's attitude be? Would she want the story known?

In the end, I decided that she did: she left clues. Otherwise, why call her last child Thomas? Why leave the unresolved story about her birthplace, that it may have been in Edinburgh, or somewhere else in Scotland? I think people of this time were used to hardship and adversity, but some hurts remain with you.

---

[59] Death certificate, Helen Archer, 8/6/1912, informant: James Archer, Registry of Births, Deaths and Marriages, New South Wales, 1912/007474.

The romance

A long time ago, an English lad worked in a castle as a groom. A Scottish lass also worked in the castle, as a maid. It was a royal castle. They met and fell in love and decided to get married and go abroad, over the seas to Australia. They saved up all their money, and when they arrived in Sydney they built a hotel at Pyrmont, which was called the Duke of Edinburgh, after the castle.

And of course, they had many children and lived happily ever after.

My mother told me this story when I was a child. She said the two people were ancestors in the Archer family (she was an Archer). She said she was third-generation Australian-born. Where did the story come from, I asked her? She said it came from Aunty Dolly, who was her father's youngest sister.

The couple must be William Archer and Ellen Welch, my mother's great grandparents. William was from England and Ellen was from Scotland. This is the story that serves to negate any suggestion that William was a convict.

An obvious problem with the story is the name of the hotel: it was obviously named after the Duke of Edinburgh, not Edinburgh Castle. There are other questions too. How did a groom and a maid raise enough money to build a hotel? Which castle was it? Was it in Scotland or England? In either case, how did the English lad or the Scottish lass come to be there?

I didn't ask these questions at the time. As a child, I was steeped in the wonder of the story emanating out of the unknown past of our family. Many years later, I was able to consider the story with a more inquisitive mind.

Aunty Dolly, from whom mum learned the story, was christened Alice Lillian but was forever called Dolly. Why? Because she was a tiny baby that lived, and she was so small she was kept in a box, wrapped up warm, and was often sat up on the bar in the hotel, and the regulars said she looked just like a doll.

So, you see, the hotel was real. It was established in 1880-1882 on the corner of Union Street and Harris Street at Pyrmont, and for a hundred years it was called the Duke of Edinburgh Hotel. During the remake of Darling Harbour in the 1980s it survived, and has changed its name to the Harlequin Inn. It is no longer in the Archer family.

However, this story is not about the hotel, it's about the romance. Ah, Aunty Dolly: my mother said she did research into the family's history. She spent thousands of dollars on it. This was in the days before the internet. She even went to England and did research there. So, the story of the romance emanated from Aunty Dolly's research.

My mother said, "There are no convicts in our family." I was left to assume that this statement had the authority of Aunty Dolly's research.

It's easy to know some things. Once you know the Archers have a large grave at Waverley Cemetery (there are twenty people buried in it), you can read the inscriptions on the gravestones. William Archer's inscription tells a story, which I think is what he did in life – tell stories. He was born at Harpenden in Hertfordshire, England on 12 March 1813. He died in Sydney on 4 January 1894. Ellen's inscription simply says she was the beloved wife of William Archer, and she died on 8 June 1912, aged eighty-nine years.

A note: on her gravestone, it says Helen Archer. It seems that in later life she was known as Helen rather than Ellen. She was Ellen on her marriage certificate.

An aside

The crime for which William Archer was transported to Australia was the theft of twenty-eight pairs of 'high shoes' and the basket in which they were being carried. At that time, the 1840s, 'high shoes' were shoes worn by the well-to-do. Often they were made of goats' leather rather than cow-hide. They were made by cordwainers, who made new shoes, rather than cobblers, whose job it was only to repair shoes. William had a cousin who was a cordwainer, so we may assume he knew a little about the items he stole.

I watched a movie, set in Scotland, in which the laird gives a visitor a tour of the estate around the castle. They are passing by a pond, and he comments to her, "This pond dried up once, a long time ago when we were having a rare drought. When all the water was gone, we found a few strange things. We found the skeleton of a sheep, and we found twenty-eight pairs of high shoes."

There was no explanation for why the shoes were there – twenty-eight pairs of them! Or why there were precisely twenty-eight pairs. Presumably someone had stolen them and then had to dump them in a hurry. But, in the vicinity of the castle, one can imagine customers for the shoes. One wonders why it formed part of the script for the movie. There was no explanation for that either.

Back to the story

Yes, William Archer was transported. There was a convict in the family. At least now we have a good reason for the story of the romance. It overrides any suggestion that the first ancestor in Australia was a convict. As time goes by, unto the generations, original memory fades and the sources of dispute steadily leave us, so the myth is allowed to grow. And William was English and Ellen was Scottish, so a romance between them was fertile ground for imagination. There had to be some way they met.

But wait, there are questions about Aunty Dolly. Did she seriously do all that research, to the extent of going back to the mother country to go through historical records, and not discover that William was a convict? You don't believe that, and nor do I.

In fact, I would guess that Aunty Dolly knew the truth from the start. William came to Australia (involuntarily) in 1838. He died in 1894. Aunty Dolly, his grand-daughter, was born in 1899. It's not very distant, is it? Just five years. There would still have been people around who knew, and also a few who would not let the family forget the truth.

In this light, the story of the romance is either a gift to the family, or, it takes an already existing story and gives it the imprimatur of authority. I imagine William telling the story with relish from behind the bar, except for the fact that he was dead by the time Aunty Dolly had done her research and had her story ready. And he would have winked, as if he was happy for us all to share in the lovely joke.

I wonder where the castles came from. Did William have castles in his childhood homeland? Did Ellen? Well, they did, both of them.

I'm not suggesting William and Ellen met in a castle. William was working off his sentence in the Hunter valley in the 1840s, farming, and Ellen turned up as an assisted female immigrant from Britain, unmarried. They met (the real romance) and got married. There were no castles for thousands of kilometres, although their occupations were not a lot different to those in the romance story: a groom, or farm-hand, and a maid, or domestic servant.

Where William came from, Harpenden in Hertfordshire, there were castles. Windsor Castle, one of three official residences of the Queen, is only forty kilometres away. Hertford Castle is situated at Hertford, the county town of Hertfordshire, only twenty kilometres from Harpenden. In 1805 it became the home of the East India Company College.

So, this half of the story is indeed possible: William would have known about these castles, and heard stories about them. He could even have worked as a groom at one of these castles. Did either of the castles have ponds that might disgorge twenty-eight pairs of high shoes during a drought? Scanty as the records of William's trial are, yet it seems that the shoes had been recovered. (And the movie was set in Scotland.)

Off to Scotland

Ellen came from Scotland, but her history was not as simple as that. She seems to have told her family (which could mean, her children, or, William and her children) that she was born in Edinburgh. Of course, that is okay: there is a castle in Edinburgh that is royal. If she lived there, she would certainly have known about it, and its ancient and royal history. Indeed, wherever she lived, she would have known about that castle; it is legendary.

Ellen's story has its complications. Let it be said that she was born as Helen Welsh in the village of Markinch in Fife or, more precisely, at Balgonie Furnace, which was a 'coalworks', that is, a coal-mine. Her father was the manager. Note, now we have an explanation for the 'Helen Archer' on her gravestone. 'Helen' wasn't a new acquisition; it was the reclaiming of something that had been hers initially. And Welsh, not Welch? That story is complicated too; you almost need to know the history of Scotland, but, yes, Welsh, not Welch, at least at birth.

The pertinent question is, would she have known about castles when she was growing up (apart from Edinburgh Castle as a distant, national story)? Were there any nearby? Yes, there is a castle called Balgonie Castle which, you can imagine, is nearby. There are also two other castles in the neighbourhood: MacDuff Castle and Ravenscraig Castle. They have the mystique of being ruins – in the early 1800s when Ellen was around. However, our particular interest is in castles that are habitable and have a need for servants.

On this score, Balgonie Castle qualifies. It does have parts that are in ruins, but it is habitable and it is inhabited, and we know that Ellen was a servant before she emigrated. Yes, it is possible that Ellen worked at a castle.

The story

William and Ellen meet. That in itself is a wonder. William is working in a remote valley near Newcastle, north of Sydney. He is probably thinking to himself – Newcastle, new, castle, Windsor Castle, Hertford Castle, all the while living in a rude bush shelter and doing work to make someone else rich. Not that he minded the work. He loved the smells of crops and cattle, sheep and horses; he loved using his strength. Some men chose to live in misery; he retained his zest.

I don't think he was ever resentful. He had done a lot of young-man things – getting drunk, fighting at the pub – and I think he accepted that sometimes you got caught. Admittedly, the punishment this time was a bit extreme.

I think William also realised there was little benefit in fighting the system. They had the whips and the guns, and they were quite ready, all of the time, to use them. Better to keep your head low, do the time, and look for opportunities. Make friends. Seven years: it wasn't life; it wasn't ten years, or fourteen. He would still be fit and able when he got his Certificate of Freedom. And in fact, he got that certificate in September 1844; he was thirty-one.

But before that, he met Ellen, and in July 1844 they got married. She was twenty-one. Imagine, living in the middle of the bush and a bright young Scottish lass shows up who likes you. It wasn't hard to take a fancy to her. She came with a company of other young women – most of them were Scottish too. Some of the men were even resentful about that, and called them whores, said they made bad servants and worse wives. William couldn't understand that. He thought Ellen was enchanting.

And they had children, eight in all. I imagine that William, when Ellen occasionally got sad about being so distant from her homeland and family, would talk about his life as a lad, and so they would have discovered they were both familiar with castles. And this would have grown into a story, a story they laughed about and which made both of them glad. An English lad worked in a castle as a groom. It was a royal castle. And a Scottish lass worked there too. She was a maid. And they met....

They would have told the story to the children. And in the absence of books, in their imaginations it would have been wonderful. They would have been glad to have their parents, with their two different accents. They would have imbibed his zest and her charm. And they would have told the story to their own children.

Image: Windsor Castle

Emigrants from Ireland: John Neil and Alice Wetherell

One set of my great great grandparents was John Neil and Alice Wetherell. Apart from Sarah Crosby (also a great great grandparent), they are my only direct ancestors to have come from Ireland. But whereas Sarah came from the county of Waterford in the southeast, John and Alice came from the north of Ireland: the town of Portadown in the county of Armagh.

John and Alice were married in Portadown on 2 September 1848. He was twenty-three; she was twenty-seven. They are on my mother's side of the family; their daughter Alice married James Archer, the son of William Archer, the convict from Hertfordshire, England. My mother was an Archer.

John and Alice came to Australia on the ship *Golden Era*, which arrived in Sydney from Liverpool on 16 June 1855. They were assisted migrants, meaning that their voyage was subsidised by colonial government funds. John was an agricultural labourer.

Portadown was a town that went back to the 1600s and to the colonisation of Ireland by Great Britain. Lands were seized and redistributed to English colonists, in what is called the Plantation of Ulster. Irish rebels fought and killed settlers, culminating in what is called the Portadown massacre in 1641, when around 100 captured settlers were shot or drowned. This was followed by the Cromwellian conquest of Ireland.

In the 1800s Portadown became a major town, especially after the establishment of railways. It was a major junction linking Belfast, Dublin and other towns in Ireland. The town became the centre of a thriving linen industry. It also became the focus of strife between the Roman Catholic and Protestant religions, with the foundation of the Orange Order of Protestants in the town. This strife intensified and continued into the twentieth century.

However, in 1855 the dominant influence in Ireland was emigration, which had accelerated in response to the potato famine (from 1846 onwards). It is estimated that between 1850 and 1854, around 200,000 Irish people per year emigrated, after which it began to decline. There were many reasons. Evictions were still occurring in rural areas, conditions were becoming more difficult for agricultural labourers, and participation in the growing industries of Portadown was not evenly shared, because of the religious divisions. The cost of living was also rising, a legacy effect of the famine.

The offer of assisted migration was attractive. Nevertheless, there was still a choice. Ninety percent of emigrants went to the United States of America or Canada. It was only a small percentage that went to Australia. Also, as far as I know, none of John or Alice's close relatives emigrated to Australia, so they were going to a place without having the support of family or friends there.

There was one notable exception: Alice's brother and his wife joined them on in emigrating – Richard and Mary Ann Wetherell. Richard was six years younger than Alice. He was, like John, an agricultural labourer. In the Irish Griffith's Valuation land records of this time, John Neill rented a "house and small garden" in Ballynahinch in the Parish of Kilmore, County of Armagh. It was valued at one pound per year. Richard Wetherall (the spelling varies) rented a house too, in Drumgoose in the Parish of Drumcree in Armagh. It was a house and five acres, land valued at eight pounds, buildings at two pounds ten shillings.

Richard and Alice's father was not an agricultural labourer; he was a grain buyer, sometimes also described as a dealer or merchant. This may have something to do with the fact that Richard's parcel of land was much larger than John's.

Were there children? Richard and Mary Ann Wetherell had two children: Margaret Ann (four years old) and a baby called Alice. John and Alice Neil had one child, called Mary, born in 1854. The arrival of the *Golden Era* in Sydney was reported in the *Maitland Mercury* on 20 June 1855. It said, "The *Golden Era* is a fine clipper ship and has made a splendid run of 85 days from Liverpool. She brings out 13 cabin passengers and 436 government immigrants, all at present enjoying good health. During the passage, however, a few cases of scarlet fever occurred with which five infants died." One of those five infants was Mary Neil, the daughter of John and Alice.

In the great tale of emigration, Mary's death at sea was not to be remarked upon, but it was John and Alice's only child who died. It must have thrown a shadow over their anticipation of a new life in Australia. No doubt it was some comfort to have the presence of Alice's brother and family. Not to despair.

Perhaps it was John and Richard's intention from the outset that they would not be agricultural labourers in Australia. They landed in Sydney and never left. Perhaps their experience of agricultural conditions had been unpleasant, and was part of what they wanted to leave behind them. Or perhaps they wanted to be farmers in Australia, but the avenues did not open up for them.

Richard and Mary Ann had two more children: one was called William John (born in 1859), the other was Edward (born in 1861). John and Allice had four more children: Richard was born in 1856, Hannah was born in 1858, Alice in 1862, and William John (the same name as his cousin) in 1864. Alice is the one who married James Archer. However, there were early deaths – one parent in each family.

Richard Wetherell died in 1864, leaving Margaret Ann with four children. And Alice, his sister, died in 1867, also leaving four children behind her. In her case, her death was related to pregnancy.

The cause of death reported on the death certificate was *phlegmasia alba dolens*, known as milk leg or white leg at the time. Historically, it was often seen during pregnancy and in mothers who had just given birth. It occurred when the left common iliac vein became compressed against the pelvic rim because of the enlarged uterus. It was called milk leg because it was once thought to be caused by the metastasis of the mother's milk. In severe cases of venous obstruction, the arterial pulse could completely disappear, and venous gangrene could ensue. (Information from Wikipedia)

Alice had had the condition for seven weeks. She was buried at Devonshire Street Cemetery, in the Presbyterian section, not the Roman Catholic or Church of England sections. Her death must have been accompanied by the death of the child she was carrying, but that is not mentioned in the records of the Registry of Births, Deaths and Marriages.

In her death certificate, it is mentioned that Alice had had several children who had died, apart from the four who were living. There had been three boys and one girl, deceased. The girl was Mary, the one who died at sea. Perhaps the other deaths were back in Ireland. I suspect that these deaths were not recorded officially.

The family lived in Exeter Place in Surry Hills, a place which no longer exists, swallowed up by the city's frequent reconfigurations of roads. John Neil's four children were eleven, nine, five and three. John's occupation was labourer. How did one survive in that situation? Only with compromises between work, money and time. John was forty-two.

I don't know how that worked, but the family remained at Exeter Place. And as often happened with people who lost their spouse, John got married again. The woman was Mary Ann Bennett. The marriage certificate says there was three years' difference between them (she was older), but she may have been ten years older than that, if the English records I have perused make sense. They were already living together. Mary Ann had no children of her own. Was it an arrangement of convenience for them both?

That may have been what people said. But then there are connections between people, and they can start with the oddest things. They had both arrived in Sydney in 1855 as assisted migrants. While John had landed in June on the *Golden Era*, Mary Ann had arrived in April, on a ship called the *Speedy*. They might have talked about why they came to Australia, and what had been going on in the places they left. Mary Ann had come from Hertfordshire in England, and yes, she had been married at the time she emigrated.

Mary Ann's husband, William Henry Bennett, died in 1867, the same year as John's wife, Alice. Another connection. They both needed to survive. How was Mary Ann with the children? They were 14, 12, 8, 6; boy, girl, girl, boy. Perhaps she was a veritable Mary Poppins, slipping into the role with ease and panache. And beyond all the incidental connections, there may well have been warmth between John and Mary Ann. To be sure, they spent almost the next twenty years together.

John was still a labourer. On the marriage certificate he named his father as Charles Neil, boot manufacturer, of Portadown, and his mother as Mary Colter. It must have seemed a long way back. Mary Ann named her father as John Bonham, miller, of Bushey, Hertfordshire, and her mother as Elizabeth Woodruff.

The marriage took place at the Congregational Church in Albion Street, Surry Hills, on 15 October 1870. Given John's background, I wondered about his religion – well, in Portadown, it seemed more a case of allegiances. When he got married to Alice, it was in the office for civil registrations, not any church. And Alice was buried as a Presbyterian; she was not a Roman Catholic and she did not identify with the Church of England. One gets the sense that it was easier to live in Australia where the choices were not quite like choosing sides in a war.

John and Mary Ann may have also liked their differences. He was Irish, she was English. When he had come to Australia, he had settled down in one area of Sydney and stayed there. Mary Ann, on the other hand, with William Bennett had travelled widely – Victoria, New Zealand and Queensland – for about ten years.

By 1875 John and Mary Ann had moved, although not far. It is recorded in the Sands Directory of Sydney for that year that they lived at 7 Samuel Street, Surry Hills, near Campbell Street. It was a substantial, two-storey house of brick, still standing in 2022, with two arches of brick at the front.

By 1880 they had moved again, to 21 Little Elizabeth Street – again, still in Surry Hills, but another street that no longer exists. It was near the current Central Railway Station and the markets. Sydney was growing rapidly then, as it continued to do so during the twentieth century. 1880 was the year that daughter Alice, aged eighteen, married James Archer. They got married at St David's Church of England at Arthur Street, Surry Hills. John Neil was fifty-five.

The next Sands Directory I have is for 1890. At this point, John Neil is sixty-five years old. I had wondered what happened to him in later life. Indeed, he is listed in the directory, but this time there is a remarkable change. He is not living in Surry Hills. He is living at 4 Paddington Lane, Paddington. Also, for the first time, John is listed with an occupation apart from labourer: he is a lamplighter. In Sydney at this time, lamps at night were still lit manually. Electric street lights did not exist until 1904.

Paddington Lane is still there; it runs parallel to Paddington Street. It is a long lane, running from Cascade Street through to Point Piper Lane, about half a kilometre. At that time there were only ten houses in the lane. Nowadays Paddington is a crowded inner-city suburb, where a two-storey house might cost over three million dollars.

How did John Neil afford to move from Surry Hills? Had he bought this house, or was he renting it? These questions do become clear. But Mary Ann was not there; she had died in June 1889. As I suspected, she was much older than John – the death certificate confirms that she was seventy-eight years old when she died. The cause of death was 'senile decay'. The death certificate confirms that she had had no children. It also tells us that she was born in Watford, Hertfordshire; and, that the house in Paddington Lane was named 'Watford Cottage'. Mary Ann must have died soon after they moved there.

Mary Ann's birthplace was commemorated through the naming of the house, but it is also interesting that John did not name the house after Portadown, where he was born. I suspect Portadown was a place he felt little nostalgia for. And also, Watford was probably a connection between his daughter Alice's husband, James Archer, and Mary Ann: they had both come from Hertfordshire.

Later, when I see John's will, I realise that James Archer must have helped John to buy the house, because the first item in the will is the repayment of ten pounds to James. There is no debt on the house. Ten pounds looks like a deposit.

However, I realise there is a more radical possibility: that James Archer gave the house to John Neil for the token sum of ten pounds. I am willing to confess that I am still just touching the fringes of their lives, and they could well have done things far more extraordinary than I am able to find evidence for. But I do wonder how John Neil would have paid off a house, particularly in only a couple of short years.

Then, one wonders how much houses cost at that time. Obviously not three million dollars. The advertisements in the newspapers of 1890 (say, the *Sydney Morning Herald*) indicate that you could buy an average house in Sydney for 250 pounds – some were cheaper, and the high end was up around one thousand pounds. (You could also buy a cheap hotel for 250 pounds.)

Of course, there is the other indication, which is that, in the probate of John Neil's will, his real estate was valued at 250 pounds.

John died on 18 November 1891, aged sixty-eight according to his death certificate (I make it sixty-six according to the Irish birth record I have seen). He had had cardiac disease for twelve months (that is, from soon after when his wife died). The informant for the death certificate was his son Richard Neil (yes, named after Alice's brother and father).

The son did not know his grandfather's occupation (boot manufacturer). However, he was clear about John's children (his siblings): three were living. And one was dead: somewhere between 1867 and 1891, Hannah died. I have not found a record for this. Understandably, Richard did not know about the other deaths of babies that his mother had experienced.

Richard knew Mary Ann's maiden name (Bonham) as well as her previous married name (Bennett). I think that is a respectable effort in describing his step-mother; he was fourteen years old when his father married her. He got the details about his father's marriage to Alice correct as well, and knew his father had been born in Portadown.

John Neil's estate was divided equally among the three living children. He specified that all his goods were to be sold and the money distributed to them. As noted, there was no debt on the house. The executors of the will were Richard Neil (the son) and James Archer (the son-in-law, husband of his daughter Alice).

John and Mary Ann are buried at Waverley Cemetery, in the Church of England section. I think this indicates, more than anything, an absence of commitment to the Presbyterian or Congregational institutions rather than an affiliation with the Church of England.

I wonder about the influence of James Archer in the choice of Waverley Cemetery, but then I realise that the first Archer to be buried there was not until 1894: William Archer, James's father and the one who came to Australia in 1838 as a convict. In latter days, William became a publican, establishing the Duke of Edinburgh Hotel in Harris Street, Pyrmont. It was John Neil's wife, Mary Ann, who was buried at Waverley Cemetery first, so the influence was probably the other way round – John Neil gave the idea to James Archer. Now there are around twenty people buried in the large William Archer grave.

It was customary for people around the 1890s to state on their gravestones where they had come from. John Neil's gravestone says:

"John Neil, native of Portadown, County Armagh, Ireland, died 18th November 1891, aged 68 years".

Above it, because it was first, is the inscription for Mary Ann, which even gives her parents' names: "Sacred to the memory of Mary Ann, dearly beloved wife of John Neil, and only daughter of John and Elizabeth Bonham, born at Bushy, Hertfordshire, England, July 11th 1811, and departed this life June 30th 1889."

John's first preference as a resting place for Mary Ann and himself may have been the Devonshire Street Cemetery, because this was where Alice, his first wife, was buried. However, she would have been one of the last people to be buried there, as it was virtually closed after 1868. This became a matter of interest around 1900, because it was decided to extend the railway line from Redfern into the city, and all the graves in the cemetery had to be removed to make room for Central Railway Station.

In the process, the grave of Alice Neil has been lost. Many of the graves were moved to Botany, some to Rookwood, and some to other cemeteries around Sydney. But this depended on families responding to the authorities' request to let them know what their wishes were. Who would the authorities have contacted? John was dead. Would any of his children have known or have been in a position to respond?

I think not. The records for the graves of people who responded seem to be good. If someone had responded, it would been recorded where the grave was sent to. But Alice Neil is not in these lists. I suppose it is no surprise that some things get lost. And it is okay. Enough is known to see the part that Alice played in the family ancestry. She and John made the bold move as a young couple to come to New South Wales and make a new place for themselves in the colony. They added their own flavour to the family.

Addendum to John Neil's story

Mary Ann Bonham was John Neil's second wife. As such, in terms of the family tree, she could be just an afterthought. They married when John was forty-five, and they did not have any children together. However, from what I can deduce, they were affectionate towards one another, and John's four children got on well with her.

I went looking for Mary's beginnings, at least for the sake of being tidy and complete. It took some while to unravel, but I think her story is worthy of attention. It is not 'ordinary'. There were already some surprises about Mary: she was fourteen years older than John, and she had had no children. At first, I thought she had a relatively simple story – she had been married, had emigrated with her husband, and after a few years, he had died. After that, she teamed up with John.

I started out by seeking to confirm her age. However, her gravestone tells the story truthfully – she was born on 11 July 1811; she was seventy-eight when she died in Sydney, indeed, fourteen years older than John. Her place of birth was Watford in Hertfordshire. The christening record I found says it was Bushey, but the two towns are in the same vicinity, and I suspect that it was a question of how the parishes were structured at that time. The name Watford is carved on her gravestone. I think she is a reliable witness.

The name Watford would have been of interest to John's daughter Alice, or at least, to the man she married, James Archer, because James's father, William Archer, came from Harpenden, only around fifteen miles north of Watford, in the same county.

The most remarkable fact about Mary is her marital status. When she came to Australia, she was ostensibly married to William Henry Bennett, and they probably spent over thirty years together. He died in 1867. On her death certificate (1889), it says she married William in Birmingham in 1833, and this must have been what she said to John Neil.

I have searched for the marriage of William Henry Bennett and Mary Ann Bonham. There are plenty of records for marriages in the 1830s in England, from the churches. (Civil records started in 1837.)

The only marriage involving William Bennett in Birmingham has him marrying Sophia Smith on 4 May 1833 at St Phillip's Cathedral. In other words, there is no marriage for William Bennett and MaryAnn Bonham. So, why would they say such a bizarre thing, that they both travelled to Birmingham and got married there, given that they both lived in Hertfordshire?

Well, Mary says this on her death certificate, nearly sixty years later and in another country. There is no fear of contradiction. However, what became crystal clear in my search of the marriage records was that Mary Ann Bonham married a man called Samuel Gravestock on 27 August 1832 at Bushey. It shows up in three different record collections.

Subsequent to the 'marriage' to William Henry Bennett, Mary Ann and William lived together. In the 1851 Census, they were living in the town of Hertford, about twenty-five miles to the northeast of Bushey. William is a labourer. What happened to Samuel Gravestock?

There were many persons called Samuel Gravestock in Hertfordshire. If I am right, his father's name was the same. He may have got married again, to someone else. In the records, there are a few possible candidates. I don't think there was any rigorous enforcement of bigamy laws in the rural society of the time. And perhaps everyone was trying to forget about his marriage to Mary Ann.

So, what happened to the marriage between Mary Ann and Samuel? Who knows? I suspect Mary died alone in that knowledge. Sometimes people do a thing, and they realise, almost immediately, that it is a disaster; it is the worst possible thing they could have done, and there would never be any coming back from it. It is irredeemably catastrophic, and you must do whatever you need to, immediately, if you are ever to save yourself. If you have never been brave in your life before, you must be brave now, even if you never have to do anything so brave ever again.

I can only imagine that this was Mary's response to the marriage. In modern movies, it would be like having been drunk, and waking up in the morning in a city hotel with a strange man in your room and a wedding ring on your finger. How else can you explain what happened? There is no doubt the marriage took place, and there is no doubt it ended, and quickly, in whatever untidy way was possible. I assume Mary fled.

My only recourse from this story is to reverse it. What if Samuel Gravestock was the one who lost his senses and fled? What if he ran off, say, back to the farm, and deemed the experience too disturbing? I admit this is possible. I abide in the proposition that there is no doubt the marriage ended, and quickly.

Mary and William seem to get together only about a year later. Was William a rescuer? Perhaps. And perhaps Hertford was far enough away from Bushey for safety and comfort. But, there is another theory. Given that they travelled a lot when they were in Australia – Victoria, Queensland, New Zealand – could they have done the same in England? William, and Mary Ann, could have picked up casual work in various places – two itinerants.

Then, perhaps they did go to Birmingham and get married. No one would have questioned them too severely about whether either of them had been married before. The only problem with this theory is that I found no record of a marriage.

It is not just prominent people who live extraordinary lives. Everyone has something at stake. Some people crush it, sadly, for want of bravery or misconstrued conviction about duty. But for people who do not live in the spotlight, you might never know what they have done in their lives.

The early life and crimes of William Archer

William Archer was born on 12 March 1813 in Harpenden, Hertfordshire. He is a great great grandfather on my mother's side.

Of all the items I have collected concerning William Archer's crimes, most of them belong to other persons called William Archer. It was not my William Archer who stole the duck; the man who did it was tried at Hertford, true, but he was given his sentence of seven years' transportation in 1830, and he left on the *Lady Harewood* for New South Wales in October 1830. He was probably a few years older than my William Archer.

Another William Archer had also left for New South Wales in 1830, on the *York*, and only a month earlier: September 1830. He had also been tried at Hertford, and had also been given seven years. His crime? Not known, but he was born in 1809, which rules him out. My William Archer was born in 1813.

The other William Archer persons who show up in the convict records came from somewhere other than Hertford: Warwick, Buckinghamshire, Northampton, Norfolk, Oxford, Dublin.

The other persons in Hertford called William Archer may well have been related. My William Archer was the second of seven children. His grandparents had had six children, three of whom were males. And my Archer ancestors had lived in Hertfordshire back to at least the 1600s. However, my William Archer did not commit all those crimes – burglary, larceny, or sheep-stealing.

I believe that my William Archer first came to the attention of the courts in February 1836, aged twenty-two, when he was charged with unlawful and malicious wounding with intent to kill and murder, in collaboration with William Jennings. It was a serious charge; in retrospect, an extravagant charge. They were defended in court by Mister Moore. It related to an incident the previous July. They were charged that they wounded Daniel Olney and his brother William Olney. It was Daniel Olney who brought the charges.

The men had all met up between nine and ten o'clock one evening in July 1835 at a beer shop run by John Stretton in Harpenden. They all knew one another. "Some words passed between them; the words ended with a blow" – William Olney struck

William Archer. Soon after, Archer and Jennings left the beer-shop. A man named Thomas Luck went with them. The two Olney brothers left soon after. Everyone was walking towards their homes. Then Daniel Olney met Archer and Jennings, and Jennings threw a stone that struck Olney in the eye.

Daniel Olney told the court he was brought down by a stick or stone, and when his brother interfered to take his part, Archer and Jennings knocked him about. At this point he was cross-examined by Mister Moore. Did he hit anyone? "I never hit any man; my brother did." "Archer and Jennings came to meet us. Thomas Luck hit me with a stick."

Mister Davies, the surgeon at Hertford, had seen the two Olney brothers soon after the incident, and he said one of them had a blow on the eye but it was not dangerous, nor of such a nature as to do him grievous bodily harm.

The Learned Judge here interposed, and addressing the jury, directed them to acquit the prisoners, the evidence not being sufficient to sustain the indictment. The Jury returned a verdict of "Not guilty".

The case was reported in the *Hertford Mercury and Reformer*, on 2 March 1836. It seems that Daniel Olney was not represented, and for a person bringing serious charges, he seemed to have all his facts confused. Mister Moore had done his homework, and presumably arranged for the doctor to be present. It wasn't long before the judge had heard enough; there were many other cases waiting to be heard. So, William Archer was charged, but he was never cross-examined, and the charges were quickly dropped.

However, this was not the last time William Archer appeared in court. He was brought up on charges of stealing in June 1837, at the Hertfordshire Midsummer Sessions; the Honourable Captain Hotham took the chair. There was a considerable muster of Magistrates, and the Grand Jury was sworn in.

Edward Peacock, nineteen, labourer, was indicted for feloniously stealing a gallon of beer, to the value of one shilling. He pleaded guilty and was sentenced to fourteen days' hard labour.

Francis Gentle, labourer, was convicted of stealing a quantity of fowls, the property of William Bacon. He had previously been imprisoned for stealing apples. He was sentenced to seven years' transportation. (He was sent out on the *Moffatt*, arriving in Van Diemen's Land on 1 April 1838.)

When it came to it, William's case was dealt with peremptorily. He was sentenced to transportation with barely an intake of breath in the court. Perhaps it was his misfortune to come directly after the most extravagant theft imaginable. Joseph Anderson and John Kalmier had broken into the house of John Brown in the day-time and stolen eighty-five pounds in Bank of England notes, six sovereigns, six pairs of trousers, nine waistcoats, two coats, one Mackintosh cape, one pair of Wellington boots, several shirts, nine silk handkerchiefs, one silver watch guard, and several other articles. It was comprehensive! Anderson was transported for the term of his natural life, and Kalmier for fourteen years.

After that, William Archer's theft of a basket at Harpenden containing twenty-eight pairs of high shoes and other articles did not seem so worthy of attention. With no comment, he was sentenced to transportation for life. Even the journalist for the *Hertford Mercury and Reformer* (4 July 1837) could find nothing with which to elaborate, except to say the goods were the property of William Bufton Plummer, and the Judge was J.F. Mason, Esquire.

Yet, it was a preposterous crime. How could anybody in a small town hope to get away with stealing a basket full of 'high shoes'? What was the idea? And what were high shoes?

I think the best description for high shoes is 'dainty boots'. They ran high up the ankle, were generally laced, and were made out of the finest leather. They were probably women's boots, although men's fashion boots of the time were not very different, just a little different in styling. They were made by cordwainers, who had their own guild in London, quite separate from cobblers, who mostly mended shoes rather than making them.

Cordwainers had a long and noble history, going back to around 1066, when the Normans invaded England. So, why would a hawker be in Harpenden wanting to sell high shoes? Wasn't it a rural area, populated by poor people with necessarily modest tastes? Well, that is true, but, at the same time, there were estates in the area, and castles. And such places had visitors – people who had money and who at least considered themselves to have good taste.

Hertford Castle was situated at Hertford, and Windsor Castle, the current Queen's official residence, was only twenty-five miles away. It would be feasible for a hawker to be along the side of the road as visitors headed for a castle or an estate, offering an unparalleled variety of high shoes for bargain prices. And if the prospective purchasers wanted a convincing yarn about the quality of the shoes, William could probably summon it up for them.

William's crime could therefore be described as entrepreneurial rather than preposterous. There was a certain irony in the fact that, on this very day, 20 June 1837, King William IV died at Windsor Castle, ushering in the reign of Queen Victoria. William never did get to make those sales to royalty's courtiers and sycophants. Instead, he headed to prison until the authorities had made ready a vessel to transport him over the seas.

William Archer formed part of a company of 224 convicts on the *Waterloo*, which left Sheerness (on the south point of the Thames) on 2 October 1837 for New South Wales. It arrived in Sydney on 8 February 1838, having taken four months for the voyage.

William was five feet seven inches tall, with light-coloured hair and light grey eyes. His complexion was ruddy. He had two small moles on the right side of his neck. He had a tattoo on his back of a woman, and another on his inside lower right arm. On his inside lower left arm was a tattoo of a man and woman.

Somewhere between the courtroom judgement and boarding the ship, his sentence became seven years rather than life. The justice system was characterised by many letters of petition whereby someone would plead on behalf of a prisoner for mercy from a judgement, and William may have prevailed upon an intermediary to write such a letter, bearing in mind that he had had legal representation on his first encounter with the justice system.

William was sent to the Hunter Valley to serve out his sentence. The Australian Agricultural Company had been set up by an Act of British Parliament in 1824 and granted one million acres of land in the Port Stephens area. A group of around four hundred prominent British gentlemen invested an initial one million pounds in the venture. The idea was to grow flocks of Merino sheep to supply wool to Britain, and to use cheap convict labour to run the enterprise.

William may have had aspirations to be an entrepreneur, but these people had experience at it – you could say, a wealth of experience.

William Archer was granted a Ticket of Freedom on 24 September 1842. He was still residing in the Hunter Valley. He married Ellen Welch on 15 July 1844. He and Ellen had eight children. He lived an adventurous, and entrepreneurial, life, and died on 4 January 1894 at 1 Paternoster Row, Pyrmont, aged eighty, as a gentleman and retired hotel-keeper.

Image: Wiliam Archer, Certificate of Freedom, 1842

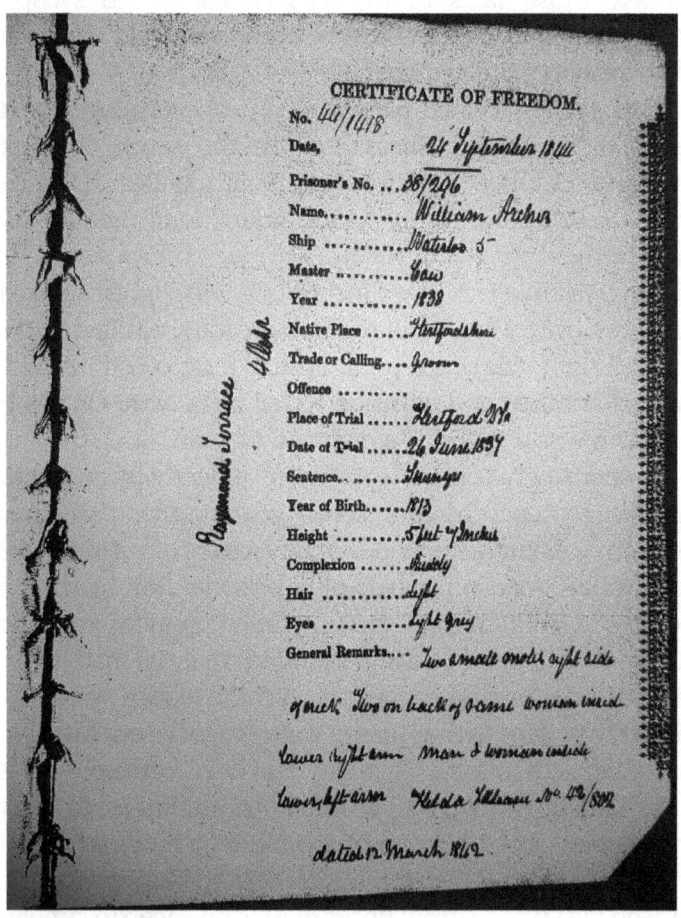

Section 10: Great great grandparents, maternal (2)

Robert Mackie (1832-1863) and Catherine Hood (1832-1900)

Thomas Bulling (1834-1909) and Frances Maria Jones (1832-1890)

Introductory notes

These two couples are the grandparents of my mother's mother. My mother knew a little about her Scottish heritage, the Mackie family, but apparently nothing about the Bulling family.

In the first story, Alexander Mackie is selling the stonemason's workshop he set up and worked in for twenty years in the heart of Melbourne. It provokes a reverie about all the people he has encountered over that time, and the shocking event of his son's death at a young age – Robert Mackie.

"The girl at the wedding" is about the fact that Robert Mackie married Catherine Hood in Melbourne in 1856, but Catherine already had a child. Robert and Catherine were both Scottish and both from Fife, and they or may not have known each other in Fife. The child, Margaret, was born soon after Catherine arrived in Australia. Margaret was obviously accepted as part of the family, and she became part of Robert and Catherine's family, the eldest child with four younger brothers. And she lived a remarkable life.

The Bulling family was another branch of the family tree about whom I knew little, but I have learned. They were a counterpoint to Robert Mackie, because Thomas Bulling was a carpenter and he worked in the goldfields at Ballarat for over twenty years. Robert was the one who was killed in a mineshaft early on, working as a carpenter.

Alexander Mackie in the workshop, 1872

Alexander Mackie (1807-1884) was Robert Mackie's father, so he is my great great great grandfather (on my mother's side). He was a stonemason, and he was the one who brought his whole family out from Scotland to Australia in 1852.

"So, you're looking to sell up?" Mick shook my hand, the firm handshake of another stonemason. It was mid-morning, early spring and a bit windy and chilly, that southern wind from the Antarctic. It was time for a cuppa. I put the kettle on.

"Yes," I said. "I've been here nineteen years. I set up the workshop just after I arrived in Melbourne. I was on the *Wanata*." It was funny; we all tended to say that automatically – what ship we came out here on, just like the convicts did.

"I've got to ask the obvious question," said Mick: "why are you selling?"

"It's simple enough," I replied. "I've just lost my best hand, and I'm thinking it's time to do something a bit lighter. Stones are heavy, and I'm sixty-three. You seem a bit younger."

"That I am. Forty-two. I've been working for someone for a while, but I want my own workshop. This is quite central; two blocks from the Melbourne Town Hall. You must have got this place in the early days."

"Well, the city grew up around me. It was all dust and mud in the beginning. And the houses weren't much better than this shed."

I made the tea. In the end, there didn't seem to be much that needed to be said. Mick seemed to like the place, and I was going to be a grocer. He left soon after, said he had to talk to someone about a loan. He was happy to take the whole thing as it was. We shook hands again, remaining formal. There was no pressure on either side: I had time, and he seemed to be keen.

Later, George came in, as he often did. He seems to like it here, and I like him coming. He was nine years old now, the youngest of four boys. It had been nearly ten years since his father died. My son Robert; he was only thirty-one at the time, and George only six months old. A stupid accident, working for a ridiculous company – a goldmine in Collingwood. It certainly sounds ridiculous now. They never did find gold.

Well, people thought there was gold everywhere then. You just had a to dig a hole and it would be there for the taking. Then the madness set in. There's nothing there in the dirt, so you dig a bit deeper. You even throw a few specks in the bucket to show other people, to convince them – "You see, it's starting to show! If we just keep going, a few feet further, it'll be there. We'll all be rich."

I'm not saying Robert was like that. He was a good Scot, careful with his money, not a big spender or a gambler. He was working for a wage, just as he'd done at Ballarat for nearly ten years. He was a carpenter for one of those big concerns. They had machinery, they had capital, they had a workforce. I suppose Robert wanted to come back to Melbourne and be closer to Rachel and me. And sure, we grandparents wanted them here. So the job came up and he took it.

The problem was, the people running the company were all amateurs. They were shopkeepers, not miners. They'd all thrown a bit of money in – it was a gamble that might pay off for them. So, you wouldn't say the mine was run properly, like Robert had been used to.

He'd only been there two months when he was down in the shaft trying to clear a blockage out of the pump. He was about forty-five feet down. He had to lift the piping. It was heavy, and the equipment wasn't right, and the pipe fell on his hand and crushed it. Before you know it, he was at the hospital and his arm was amputated. But I saw him in hospital and the life had gone out of him. His spirit was broken. They sent him home. Catherine, that's his wife, is a lively person, but the shock of it was too much even for her. There she was with five young kids, devastated. And Robert got worse, not better.

When they took him back to hospital, they said it was his heart, something wrong there, and he died in a couple of days. The whole situation was a wreck, a shambles, a disaster. They called me in to the inquest, two days later. I don't really know what I was doing there. All I said was, I am Robert's father. He had a wife and five young kids at home. In the end, they all decided it was nobody's fault. And that was an end to that. It left a bitter taste.

George said, "Hi, grandad. What are you doing?"

I came back from my reverie. I said, "I'm just working on the plinth for a monument. The city has some famous people now, and some other people want to make statues of them for everyone to see."

"Was it like this in Fife?"

"No, it was quite the opposite. Some of the buildings are a thousand years old – castles, churches, and we would do work on them to fix them up."

"Would I like it?"

"Yes, it's in your blood, but I doubt if you will ever see it. We're in Australia now."

There is gain and there is loss.

I've told the story about George's father many times before, but if I'm leaving the workshop, it seems an appropriate time to go over it again. After things died down, Catherine and the kids moved into a house just down the lane from here, so they were close to us. That's when the boys got into the habit of dropping into the workshop, after they'd been to school.

I meant to tell the story of the workshop, but I started off by getting ahead of myself by about ten years. Well, Robert's death was a major shock, so when I look back, that's the first thing I think of. But there were other things that happened before that.

I set up the workshop, like I said, just after I arrived in Melbourne, in 1852. We were from Fife, in Scotland. I'd never been anywhere where you had to explain that Fife was a place in Scotland. I was forty-five. Still, ready to make a new start. The first thing was the temptation to join the goldrush. Melbourne was only a new place, a few streets of dirt, and a port where ships arrived frequently, and it was being abandoned by hordes of people. It was eerie.

I thought about it for half a day, but I saw the lines of people heading out of town and it looked crazy. Sure, there was the promise of gold. You might stumble into a dragon's cave and find its treasure. But why had I come to Melbourne? I came here to set up a new place for my family, through profitable work, and I knew how to work. And I wasn't young; I couldn't go acting like a young man, racing off on an affair that was based entirely on luck. I decided to stick to the plan.

I made a start, ignoring all the talk around me about gold. I set up my workshop in what is now a laneway in the middle of Melbourne city, Latrobe Parade. I thought, well, if people get rich, they're going to want to build stone houses. The next year another Scot, James McDonald Hood, came to see me. He told me he'd just arrived. I asked him what ship he'd been on.

It was the *Wanderer*. We laughed. "You've wandered a long way," I said. James said another Scot had told him about me. James was a stonemason.

I told him I had also been a weaver in Fife. He laughed, and said he had also been a brewer. You do what you have to; sometimes you get to do what you want to. But James wanted to work with me. It seemed like a good idea. It's always useful to have two people in a mason's workshop.

Once we talked a bit further, we discovered that we had lived only six miles apart in Fife. It seemed a long way to travel to meet one another. But it was comfortable. It meant there were lots of things we wouldn't need to explain to each other. James had a wife, Margaret, and children, seven living. Out of these, two of them had preceded him to Australia. They were already working and moving around Victoria.

I had five children living. They had all come with Rachel and me to Australia, although, as you would have guessed, Robert was grown up.

James's daughter Catherine was close in age to Robert. Inevitably they met, even though Robert had taken himself off to Ballarat. He came back to visit. They took a liking to each other. The odd thing was, Catherine had a baby. What was that about? Apparently, the baby was born sometime after the *Wanderer* landed in Melbourne, father unknown.

There didn't seem to be any baggage attached to this fact. There was no suitor about to arrive, no sorrow over a dead lover or husband. Just Margaret, this cheerful baby who delighted all of us. Robert didn't seem to mind that there was a baby involved. James was interested in Robert too. He pressed him for details about the goldfields. I wondered why, but it soon became obvious. James was interested in being a brewer once again.

This was funny. James and I were alike. He wasn't tempted by being a gold-digger either. He had his eyes on being a liquor merchant. Good money to be made, and it avoided the disappointment that a big proportion of the gold-diggers experienced. Not everybody got rich, no, no; mostly they went home empty-handed, or went back to the city, or took up farming, starting again from nothing.

Sure enough, after Robert and Catherine, inevitably, it seemed, got married, James announced he was leaving the workshop. He started his liquor business in Melbourne first, but soon moved to Ballarat, and I was looking for another hand in the workshop. That was when John Skelly came along.

When was it? 1857. It was an interesting time to be a stonemason. There was lots of agitation for a minimum wage for men working on wages. They had already won the eight-hour day the year before. Revolutionary, some people thought, but many of the stonemasons just thought: it's about time. Companies were getting bigger; there had to be some kind of balance.

Some people hated stonemasons because of the campaigns. They thought it was a violation of the laws of supply and demand. And yes, it's true: Adam Smith was Scottish, with all his wisdom about political economy: supply and demand and so on. But aren't the stonemasons just another instance of market forces? They simply had the good sense to band together. Maybe solidarity is the very thing the big companies fear. And all we are doing is keeping some room for charity. You don't have to turn livelihood into a war. We'll see what comes of it.

The contention didn't impinge on my advertisement for help, because this is a private workshop. John Skelly had a bit of the trade unionist in him. He did, after all, come from the north of England, from Northumberland. Lots of manufacturing going on there. But he was looking for a small workshop to be part of. I've found people from the north of England tend to be amenable.

John was somewhat vague about his past. He said he was thirty-four, so he was half a generation younger than me. I had just turned fifty. He was ten years older than my son Robert. He'd come to Australia ten years before me and my family. What had he been doing?

He said he'd been nineteen when he emigrated. Came out by himself. He didn't give me the name of the ship he came out on. I even wondered for a while whether he had been a convict. He said he'd been gold-mining, done some stone work, and other odd jobs here and there, sometimes farm labouring. Most men in Australia could probably say the same.

It didn't matter. Could he work stone? Would he stick with the job? There were plenty of men around who were bone-lazy and who would steal your money when your back was turned the other way. I blame gold-fever. It bred the idea that you could take whatever you could get hold of, by any means, as if life was a chancer's game in a bar. I don't abide that. I don't care if it loses me some friends. You can call it Scottish; it's definitely Alexander Mackie.

John worked out well. He could get the work done, and it was always decent. The contracts were piling up. Gold money was pouring into Melbourne, and just as I thought, suddenly people wanted 'respectable' buildings. Often, they wanted fancy buildings. We could do that too. It wouldn't be cheap, but they didn't seem to care.

The years piled up too. Robert and Catherine sometimes paid a visit from Ballarat. By 1861 they had three children together, all boys. Plus little Margaret, of course, now aged eight. The big companies were taking over from prospectors. Robert was in his element, qualified, experienced, and respected. The returns were steady for the companies, driven by method rather than luck. Occasionally a big nugget was still found, giving another charge to the excitement, but the main people getting rich were the owners and managers. But Robert was doing alright.

We heard occasional stories about James Hood. He was still doing well from beer and spirits. He had definitely left stonemasonry behind him. You do what you have to do, and sometimes you get to do what you want to do.

Robert and Catherine came to the workshop to have a look. It hadn't changed much. The boys were a bit young at that point to appreciate it, I suppose. Alexander was five, James was three, and Robert had only been born this year. And Margaret. John stopped working and said hello. He was polite and friendly, not bad with the young kids for a man who was single.

It was two years later when Robert got the job at Collingwood, mid-1863. He left Ballarat and brought the whole family back to Melbourne. George had just been born. Catherine's father, meanwhile, seemed quite content to stay on at Ballarat. Having work or a business can tie a man to a place.

I won't go over what happened to Robert again, except to say that it occasioned Rachel and I to buy two graves in the new Melbourne Cemetery. We hadn't even thought about that for ourselves yet, and we ended up having to do it for our eldest son. It shouldn't be like that.

As I said, the grandchildren were living closer to us now, and starting to grow up. I felt the need to remain steady. The expected shape of life had been shaken up. Sure, we had had shocks in our lives. Before Rachel and I left Fife, we lost two sons – one year old, two years old. However, it is not surprising to lose children to illness. It's a kind of sadness you can bear.

1870 came, and Catherine got married again. That was fine; it was to be expected that she would want to do that one day. She had only been thirty-one when Robert died, the same age as him. But the marriage was preceded by the birth of a child in 1868. The child, called William, died at six weeks. Who was the father? I could guess, but I can't say for sure. I found out that she put Robert down on the birth certificate as the father. That was a bit cheeky; he'd been dead five years.

Does it matter? A woman is entitled to a life, and she has been a good mother, first with Margaret, and then with the four boys. Maybe the name William is a clue, because it didn't come from either Rachel's family or mine. No matter. Then she met John Nuson, and they seemed to click. John Nuson – or was it Newson or Newsom? – was an odd sort, a wool sorter, not your everyday occupation. He was Irish, but he had spent time in the north of England.

I would like to say that I warmed to him, but I didn't. I found him a bit too cavalier; a bit too much bravado. He said that he'd worked in Yorkshire in wool-sorting, and he'd only come to Australia in recent years, and obviously he purported to be single. He was supposedly the same age as Catherine. I suppose I'd had the same thoughts about John Skelly – was there a wife or a crime somewhere else that he was hiding from? But in Skelly's case we had worked together for thirteen years now, and he had shown himself to be true.

I suspect that Margaret is having a hard time with her new father. She is seventeen. She's been without a father for seven years. She's even old enough to leave home if she wanted to, if there was a suitable man in the offing.

John Nuson had a different circle of friends. He'd been the manager of a hotel at Fitzroy for a couple of years, but he'd been taken on at one of the wool scouring works on the Yarra River at Collingwood. He sorted wool for export to England. Peter Nettleton's factory alone was cleaning and sorting three thousand sheepskins a week. It was a rapidly growing industry. So, John Nuson was a success, and he was a great talker. And people loved his Irish accent, flavoured with a dash of Yorkshire.

I couldn't imagine anything more different from my workshop. This is a peaceful place, even when it's busy. We work on individual pieces, and we make things that are both functional and beautiful. Sometimes people come around just to spend time, like Catherine's boys and Margaret. They talk, sure, but sometimes they are content to just sit and watch.

I was getting older. In 1870 I was sixty-three, old for a stonemason, and I was having trouble with my lungs. The dust in the workshop doesn't help. I should do something easier. I could run a shop, like a grocery shop, or even a liquor shop, like James Hood. But I wondered what John Skelly would do. I didn't think he'd want to take over the workshop by himself. We talked about it, casually, off and on.

I wasn't in a hurry. The next year, our son George died. No, not George my grandson; George my own son. He'd been born in Fife. He worked as a storeman in a factory; he wasn't married. But he got tuberculosis and didn't recover. It happens. He was twenty-nine, younger than Robert had been when he died. This is the fourth of our children we will have buried. It shouldn't be this way.

His gravestone said: "Erected by Alexander and Rachel Mackie, late of Fifeshire, Scotland, in memory of their youngest and beloved son, George, who departed this life on the 1st June 1871 aged 29 years.

> My dear relations pray agree
> Obey the Lord and follow me
> Prepare for death, make no delay
> You see God soon took me away."

You see? You try to do the right thing, but it's hard to understand death and who it takes and when.

I am sure it has affected Robert and Catherine's boys. I don't think any of those boys will grow up to be a carpenter or a gold-digger.

Where was I? The workshop; selling the workshop; becoming a grocer. I was thinking it over, getting serious about it, when something happened: John Skelly left. But that's only half the story. John Skelly left the workshop, but he also left Melbourne, and he's gone off with young Margaret, together, as a couple. He's nearly fifty, and she has only turned nineteen. And he was single all those years!

I am stunned. I didn't see this coming. I keep going over the facts of it. He has worked with me for fifteen years. He's a good man. But he's known Margaret since she was four. What has changed? I feel the anger building up, whirling around like thunder. I stop myself and ask, what am I getting angry about? I'm going to close the workshop. And Margaret is not a baby anymore. They both have the right to make this choice, if that's what it is. And he's a good man; I know that.

Then I go through it again, getting angry and fuming. Again I have to talk myself down. She wasn't enjoying John Nuson being her father. Why wouldn't she want to get away? And I was going to have to give John Skelly the sack when I closed the workshop or sold it. Why wouldn't he take a chance to go?

He's been a faithful employee all these years, but maybe there were other things he wanted to do. He worked hard, he did good work, he never stole from me. Maybe it's just the loss that's disturbing me. I'm losing my best hand, and I'm losing a granddaughter too. She was a bit special, coming into our lives the way she did, like a mermaid that was sitting on a rock, then she slipped into the water and swam ashore, and came out as a little girl.

I heard the news about them from James Hood in Ballarat. John and Margaret had dropped in to see him, wanted him to let us know they were alright. Thanks and love and all that. I had to accept it. Obey the Lord. Rachel and Catherine were shaken up. It's a confusing time. I am still reeling. I suppose it settles my plans for the workshop. It will have to be sold now.

I think of all the times Margaret and the boys used to come and sit, especially the quiet days after Robert died. They would just sit, and I would chip away at the stones, making shapes that people would tell me were beautiful, but I just thought they were sad. For a long time it became the same thing: beautiful, sad, a monument to Robert's life.

Catherine got a message from Margaret to say that she and John Skelly had got married at Ballarat. It was March 1873. Strangely, James Hood didn't send me any message to say they'd been at the wedding. Had there really been a wedding? But it suggested that John intended to stick with her, and not abandon her in a rough-house gold-mining town. I wondered what John was doing. Had he been infected with gold fever?

I sold the workshop. That was a wrench, separating myself from that life. However, setting up a grocery business is not simple, so I was busy, and that helped. Business was good, and growing. Here I was, talking to people all day. I had to laugh, after nearly twenty years of talking very little, just working with my hands. I said to Rachel, "This is good, and I like it, but this is not my final occupation. Before I die, I am going to become a gentleman."

"And you will deserve it," she smiled.

I needn't have worried about Margaret. Within a year she and John returned to Melbourne and she was having a child. I was still a little awkward with John, I suppose. I had to get over the age difference between them. I had been twenty-five when my first son Robert was born; John was fifty. Here was a man who was living his life backwards!

Still, you could say that about me too, leaving Scotland at the age of forty-five when most men were thinking about retiring, or dying. I hope it works out for them both. I am planning to die of old age. Rachel and I.

Notes

This story is based on a framework of facts, using certificates of births, deaths and marriages, other documents, and newspaper reports. The only invention is Mick, the purchaser of the workshop, although there had to have been a purchaser. Many of the elements of this story, such as the death of Robert Mackie in 1863, are dealt with at more length in my book, *No Gold in Melbourne* (2021).

John Skelly was not a convict. There was a convict of that name who was transported in 1838, but he was from Ireland, and served his time at Camden in New South Wales. John and Margaret Skelly did not get married in 1873; they just led people to believe they did. Astoundingly, they got married over thirty years later, in 1906, towards the end of their lives, and well after they had had eight children. And John was indeed thirty years older than Margaret. Sometimes people live rich and happy lives outside of accepted conventions and expectations.

John Skelly must have been exercising the urge to wander and explore. After Ballarat, he and Margaret spent time at Gulgong, a goldrush town in New South Wales in the 1870s. Margaret had a child there in 1876. But by 1878 they were back in Collingwood, and they stayed there for the rest of their lives, close to Catherine, and Alexander and Rachel

Alexander Mackie died in 1884, aged seventy-seven. His death certificate said he died of 'old age' and 'disease of the lungs'. His occupation? Gentleman. His wife Rachel died five months later.

Regarding the four sons of Robert and Catherine Mackie, it is true that none of them grew up to be a carpenter. Two of them became painters, and one became the proprietor of a furniture shop. The fourth son went off to South Africa in the 1890s, presumably to join the goldrush in Johannesburg. He was not married. He died there; I do not know the cause.

The girl at the wedding

Robert Mackie came from Scotland, from Earlesferry, on the southeast coast of Fife. Both his grandfathers had been fishermen, but his father was a weaver and a stonemason. Robert is my great great grandfather.

Catherine Hood also came from Fife, from Lundin Mill. It is also on the southeast coast, in the parish of Largo. Her father was a brewer, but also a stonemason. Catherine is my great great grandmother, the wife of Robert Mackie.

Robert came to Australia with his parents and siblings in 1852, on the *Wanata*. He was already grown up; he turned twenty soon after landing in Melbourne. He was a carpenter.

Catherine came to Australia with her parents and some of her siblings in early 1853, on the *Wanderer*. She had turned twenty. Two of her older siblings had already come to Australia, Elizabeth in 1848, and Thomas in 1849. Elizabeth was married to a man from Fife. By the time Catherine arrived in Melbourne, Elizabeth already had three children.

There were many Scottish people in Melbourne, because it was seen as a place of opportunity for people who had found that life in Scotland was becoming tough. The timing of the two families was exquisite. Their plans to emigrate were made before the discovery of gold, but the two families landed in Melbourne, seven months apart, in the midst of gold fever. Hordes of people were taking to the roads to go to Ballarat and other places in the hope of striking it rich. Businesses, houses and ships were being left abandoned. It was bedlam. Some men just took off hurriedly and left their families behind them.

Despite the rush, both of the Scottish families stayed in Melbourne. Robert's parents, Alexander and Rachel Mackie, had five children, the youngest being five years old. Alexander set up a stonemason's workshop not far from the present Melbourne Town Hall.

Catherine's older brother, Thomas, got married in 1855, and his marriage certificate tells us that his father's occupation was stonemason. So, if James Hood and Alexander Mackie were both from Fife, and they were two stonemasons in the fledgling city of

Melbourne, did they work together? Did they know each other from Fife or was it Melbourne that led to them meeting?

There was a great deal of camaraderie among the Scots. They considered themselves to be a distinctive people who had an obligation to look out for each other's welfare. There was an active network among them. I think Alexander and James did work together. But, with the goldrush, people were thinking about opportunity, not only as gold-seekers, but also as merchants who could earn a profitable living selling goods to the prospectors.

James Hood, being also a brewer, decided there was an opportunity as a merchant, selling liquor to the thirsty diggers. He began in Melbourne in 1855, probably as a way of establishing his methods, his equipment and his sources of goods and materials. It would be easier to go to the goldfields with these things in place.

Meanwhile, Robert went to Ballarat. Again, there are many things that need to be done in a goldfield; one did not have to be a prospector. Robert was a carpenter, and when mining turned to looking for gold deep in the ground rather than on the surface, carpenters were needed to shore up the shafts.

In all this flurry, how did Robert and Catherine meet? Or, did they in fact know each other from Fife?

It is ten kilometres from Earlesferry (Robert Mackie's family) to Largo (Catherine Hood's family). Not at all far. But could the two families have existed in Fife and not known each other? You would have to think so. There is still open space today between Largo and Earlesferry, and villages have their own lives. When I look at Robert's parents, Alexander was born in Kilconquar and his wife Rachel was born in St Monans, just down the road from Earlesferry. They got married in St Monans. Robert's grandparents came from around St Monans on his mother's side, and from Aberdeen on his father's side.

Looking at Catherine's parents, her father James was born in Dundee, about fifty kilometres to the north. Her mother Margaret came from Largo, and the couple got married in Largo. Margaret had grandparents who had both lived in Largo. It looks quite possible that the two families, Mackie and Hood, could have lived their lives close to each other in Fife but not ever made contact. Between generations, some of their ancestors had moved, but the two circles of people never overlapped.

Emigration can open new doors. My conclusion is that the two families went all the way from Fife to Melbourne, having lived only ten kilometres apart and never met, and finally encountered one another in the colony.

The question remains, how did Robert and Catherine meet? Catherine was in Melbourne, Robert was in Ballarat. But people working at a goldfields often travelled to and fro. We have the image of desperate people who have sold everything and plodded their way to a goldfield and have no family in the country. They stay put in the goldfield, doggedly, until either they make their find or they give up. Yet there were many people who might spend two or three months at the goldfield and then come back to Melbourne to visit family, replenish supplies and sometimes, celebrate the winning of a bagful of nuggets from the ground.

I imagine that Robert came back to Melbourne regularly to see his family, and on a visit to his father's masonry workshop he met James Hood, the new colleague of his father's, and his daughter, Catherine. Robert and Catherine were close in age. Robert was born on 21 October 1832. Catherine was born on 24 December 1832.

Catherine would have been holding a baby. He would have been surprised to see a young woman at the workshop, then a little interested, given that they were close in age and once he learned that she had been born so near in Fife. "So close to home", he would have thought. But the baby would have implied a husband, so his interest would have been dampened.

Later, he would have learned that there was no husband. So what was the story?

The story may have taken several visits before it was able to surface. Perhaps the time between visits became progressively shorter, occasioned by the ostensible desire to check in on his parents, and to update them on developments in the goldfield. Perhaps, too, James Hood was listening carefully to these updates, for he was making his own plans. And occasionally, James would touch the baby's cheek, for the baby was his granddaughter.

The story of the baby could have taken many forms, depending on the felt need for lies, fantasy or justification. But there is no mistaking the fact of a baby, once it has decided to form. At what point did Catherine's parents learn that she was carrying a baby? There is no birth certificate, although the baby was born sometime in 1853 after their arrival in Melbourne at the end of April. Given the tumult that Melbourne was in, it is no surprise that the birth certificate is lacking, but it leaves the month of birth indeterminate.

The baby could have been conceived on board the ship, or beforehand, back in Fife. I think it was the latter. How did Catherine explain it to Robert? It could have been "an unfortunate affair". The lover could have learned of the pregnancy and failed to make a commitment to marry her. Was he a local boy from Largo, someone from the same village? Probably he did not want to join her if she was intent on going with her family to Australia. He only wanted to stay in the village.

Perhaps. My view is that the clue surfaced nearly fifty years later. Catherine died in 1900, and it was Margaret, this baby, who completed the details on her mother's death certificate. The salient item of information is this: Margaret states that her mother was born in Airlie, Scotland. This makes no sense at all, although all the other information on the certificate is accurate.

Catherine was born in Fife. There is no question about this. There are a pile of other certificates and documents that confirm it. The whole family was from Fife, apart from James. So, was Margaret trying to tell us that there is a connection to Airlie, in fact, one that pertained to Margaret herself? That is, that her mystery father came from there?

Sometimes there is a pattern in events. Catherine's mother came from Largo; her father came from Dundee. He travelled down to Largo, fell in love with her, married her and stayed. Did Catherine's mystery lover travel down from Airlie (north of Dundee) and have an affair with her? It is the romance of the lover from the north, played out again. Did he disappoint her? I suspect so, but merely because she was committed to going abroad with her family and he was not.

I also think that Catherine was able to hold onto her secret until after they were aboard the ship to Australia. With wry humour, we can imagine that her morning sickness was initially mistaken for seasickness. And in the midst of the ocean, there was no possibility of the baby's father being forced to proceed with a marriage, and perhaps this was the confrontation that Catherine wanted to avoid. She understood that he was not prepared to emigrate.

Her family was thus more easily resigned to the situation, given that there were no alternatives at sea. They were bound for Melbourne. So, the baby arrived in the new country and was accepted by the family. And in time, Robert came to accept that baby Margaret was simply there, and part of things. She belonged.

When Robert and Catherine got married on 19 January 1856, Margaret was there, tagging along as a three-year-old. They were married according to the rites of the Church of Scotland (the Presbyterian Church). The witnesses were Christine Hood and Robert Keddie, not either of the couple's parents. Interesting. Christine was Catherine's younger sister, aged only seventeen at the time. She was to get married the following year, at Specimen Hill, Ballarat, to John Wilson: occupation, goldminer.

The other witness was also family. Robert Keddie was Catherine's brother-in-law, the husband of her sister Elizabeth. Robert and Elizabeth had been the first ones to emigrate, in 1848 (as noted earlier). At the time of Robert and Catherine's wedding, Robert and Elizabeth Keddie had four children, and Elizabeth was pregnant with the fifth. (The child was a son, and he died soon after birth.)

You might wonder why one of the witnesses was not from Robert Mackie's family. Where were they on the day? I think that both Robert's parents (Alexander and Rachel) and Catherine's parents (James and Margaret) were around – they all lived in Melbourne. I think the feeling was that everyone was now living in a new land, and it belonged to the young, not the old. So, it was time for the young to step up and have their day. Let the witnesses not be the old guard, but represent the new, the future, the life that they would make. So young Christine signed her name on the marriage certificate, along with Robert Keddie.

On the certificate, Robert's 'Rank or Profession' is 'Carpenter'; Catherine is described as a 'Lady'. Marriage certificates of this time usually said nothing for the female. Sometimes, they were a domestic servant, or a dressmaker. Catherine was a lady. Perhaps it was a spin-off from having a father who was now a brewer. Perhaps it was an answer for those who tended to remark on the anomalous presence of an unaccounted-for three-year-old at the wedding.

After the marriage, Robert and Catherine must have gone to Ballarat (in Robert's case, *back* to Ballarat), because in the coming years their children were all born there – well, there is a question about George, the youngest (who is my great grandfather). James Hood and his family also went to Ballarat, to brew beer. James died in 1886, aged eighty-one, and his occupation on his death certificate is "Maltster" (a person who prepares malt for brewing beer). And Margaret became the eldest sister of four younger brothers.

Image: The ship, the *Wanderer*, which brought Catherine Hood, her parents and siblings to Australia in 1853

(Artist: John Ward; Ferens Art Gallery; artuk.org)

Thomas and Frances Bulling come to Victoria

Thomas Bulling and Frances Maria Jones are one set of my great great grandparents. They married at St Pancras, London on 3 September 1854. Their daughter Frances Emily, born in Australia, married George Briggs Mackie (whose parents were Scottish), and their daughter Margaret Florence Mackie married Thomas Richard Archer (grandson of an English convict), and their daughter, Alma Helen Archer, is my mother.

Thomas Bulling was a carpenter. His father had been a carpenter, as had his father before him. That had been in Deptford, Kent. It was Thomas's father, James Bulling, who moved to Kensington, London. Thomas's mother was Hannah Durnford; she had been born in Wiltshire and she moved to London. During the nineteenth century the population of London increased from one million to 6.7 million, much of that growth coming from the movement of rural people to the city (Wikipedia, History of London).

James and Hannah got married at St Martin-in-the-Fields Church, London, on 14 October 1821. They must have still spent some time moving between London and Surrey and Kent, I assume for work, because Thomas was born in Battersea, Surrey, while all his siblings were born in London.

At the time of the 1851 British Census, James and Hannah Bulling and family lived at 2 Jasmine Terrace, St Paul's Hammersmith, London. The Thames forms a pleasant fringe to the area on the south, and the Australian expatriates' haunt, Earls Court, is adjacent to the east. Frances Maria Jones (wife of Thomas) had also moved to London from the country. She was born in Rickmansworth, Hertfordshire, the daughter of a coach-builder. So often it seems that the young folk meet through their parents' occupations, either directly or through some kind of natural sympathy.

Thomas had four siblings, both older and younger, but none of them left England. However, in 1854, plenty of people were leaving England. Between 1840 and 1872, six and a half million people left the British Isles for various colonies.[60] Now that transportation was

---

[60] Greenwood, Martin, *The Promised Land*, Robert Boyd, 2020, p. 56.

drawing to a close, Australia had become a more attractive destination for migrants. On top of this, suddenly there was the excitement of gold having been discovered.

People were starting to believe there was gold everywhere in the Australian colonies – you just had to go there. Sometimes the gold was just sprinkled on the surface of the earth; sometimes nuggets glinted among the pebbles in creeks, and all you had to do was put your hand down and pick them up. By 1854, gold had been announced both in New South Wales and Victoria. There was much excitement.

Thomas was twenty, Frances was twenty-two. Frances had parted ways with her family. She was the second of eleven or twelve children. They all seem to have stayed in Hertfordshire. It looks as if she fled; her older sister was still at home, twenty and unmarried, and one imagines she spent her time helping out with the younger children. (At the 1841 Census there was a nurse living there as well, but not in 1851.)

Thomas and Frances had the spirit of adventure. On 10 January 1855, just four months after their marriage, they boarded the *Essex*, bound for Australia. The *Essex* was described in advertisements as "Magnificent: a fine armed clipper ship of 1,000 tons, commanded by Captain John B. Martin" (he is no relative of mine, but it is amusing). (*Sydney Morning Herald*, 21 April 1855)

What they may not have known at the time they decided to emigrate was that Frances was pregnant. Moreover, they were not travelling as cabin passengers (there were only twenty-three of them), but in intermediate and steerage (there were fifty-six such passengers) – certainly not so comfortable. The ship also carried general cargo. Their voyage took eighty-nine days, arriving at Melbourne on 9 April. What was the voyage like? From the perspective of the shipping line, it was smooth. There were no mishaps, and the voyage was swift, according to the standards of the time. The *Essex* landed in Port Phillip Bay, Captain Martin unloaded passengers and cargo, replenished the stores, organised the passengers and cargo for the return voyage to London, and left again on 31 May.

For the passengers, the voyage would have been either a wonder or a shock, perhaps both – the winds, the waves, the storms and rain, the rolling of the ship, the sheer distance over the open ocean. And the voyage meant travelling from London's winter, through the tropics and then into the southern hemisphere's autumn. And for a pregnant woman – who knows? One hopes Frances and Thomas were both able to muster some enjoyment of the wonder of it all.

The baby was born soon after arrival, on 25 April. She was given the name Hannah Frances, after Thomas's mother and Frances herself. It happened in Bellerine Street, only half a kilometre from the Geelong jetty where they had landed. But it was to be a sad event, for the baby died on 2 May, of jaundice.

There seems no question that their destination was Ballarat. They must have embarked on the journey quite soon, and having got to Ballarat, they stayed there for the longest time – around twenty years. More cautious people might have looked for other destinations: the Eureka rebellion had happened at Ballarat in December 1854. If you were looking for gold, it was also being discovered in other places in Victoria – Bendigo, Mount Alexander, Castlemaine, Kyneton, for example.

However, despite the vociferous public debate about the activist miners, their sense of injustice and their ambitious political goals, and the reactions of the police, with twenty-two miners dead, Ballarat had its evident attraction. It was a thriving goldfield where there was plenty of opportunity – not only for gold-diggers but for all sorts of businesses and trades people. The population peaked at almost 60,000 in 1858. When the easily accessed alluvial gold waned, many people left for other goldfields. By 1859 the population was more like 23,000. (History of Ballarat, Wikipedia)

It didn't matter that many people left, because by now there was a solid economy based on underground mining run by companies, generating, as they say, good returns. They had steady and reliable systems of mining, involving heavy machinery and a workforce. Carpenters were among the skilled people required. Certainly, after Thomas arrived, he would have been buoyed by the confidence of the town's leaders. The early public buildings were generous in scale and respectable in form, both solid (stone) and ornate.

A newspaper had already been established before Thomas and Frances arrived: *The Banner*, in 1853, and a railway was built to Geelong in 1862. It was a town that was rapidly developing a sense of permanency. The composition of the population would also have generated some wonder and excitement for the Bullings, despite their familiarity with the melting pot of London. Apart from fellow English folk, there were Scottish, Irish, Chinese, Germans, and people from many other parts of the world, some of whom came to Australia after having gone to the Californian goldrush.

Thomas and Frances had eight more children between 1856 and 1870, all born in Ballarat. There were more deaths as well. William Percy, born in 1856, died in 1861. Arthur John, born in 1859, died in 1860. But the next three children lived to adulthood and married: Herbert James (1860), Florence Clara Elizabeth (1862) and Frances Emily (1865).

Two more children were born who died young – Tom Oswald (born and died 1867), and Emma Gertrude, born 1868. Emma's death occurred in 1875, marked by a newspaper notice that said she had had a "painful affliction since birth" (*Leader* (Melbourne), 18 December 1875).

The young Emma died at Fitzroy in Melbourne. One suspects that Frances Bulling took her to Melbourne because of her sickness. Perhaps the family moved to Melbourne at this time. They are included in the Melbourne Directory for 1881 at Kerr Street, Fitzroy, and it was in Fitzroy that daughter Frances Emily married the Scotsman, George Briggs Mackie, in 1882. (They are my great grandparents.)

Thomas and Frances had an abundance of grandchildren: twenty-eight. Frances died in the autumn of 1890, of dilatation of the heart, diarrhoea, and exhaustion. She was fifty-eight. Thomas was fifty-six. All the children had grown up. Alice Maud, the youngest, had married the year before, and that had been in Ballarat. And she stayed in Ballarat for life. Children form bonds with place, unless it has been a bad experience.

What about Thomas and Frances's other children who married? Did they stay in Melbourne or live in Ballarat? Herbert James got married in Ballarat, but they came back to Melbourne to live.

Florence Clara Elizabeth did the reverse: they got married in Fitzroy but went to Ballarat to live.

The exception was Frances Emily and George Briggs Mackie. They went to Sydney. Why? George had three brothers in Sydney.

This should be the end of the story of Thomas and Frances Bulling. I don't know about Thomas's work life more specifically than that he was a carpenter. There were two major options that would account for his work: either he worked for one of the mining companies on carpentry associated with the mines, or he worked on constructing houses and other buildings in what was a rapidly growing city.

There is, however, another chapter to his story. Frances died in 1890. Thomas married again in 1891. His new partner was Ellen Ann Desnoy, twenty years younger than him. Ellen had been born in London and emigrated to Australia. She married Henry Bourne in 1873 in Ballarat. He had emigrated from London as a boy, with his family. Ellen and Henry had six children, all born in Ballarat. Henry was a miner with one of the companies.

How did Thomas and Ellen come to marry? Thomas and Frances Bulling had been living in Melbourne. Thomas and Ellen each had established families, with a spouse and numerous children. But Ellen's life was disrupted when her husband was suddenly killed on 20 February 1885. He was forty-one and she was thirty-one.

The death was an immediate newspaper story:

"Friday Evening (by telegraph from our correspondent). A miner named Henry Bourne was killed this afternoon in the Sulieman Pasha mine, Ballarat East, by a fall of earth. He had been working by himself in a stope, and was conversing with a fellow workman a few minutes before he was found dead in the bottom of the drive, with a mass of earth alongside his body." (*Argus*, Melbourne, 21 February 1885) [Stope: an excavation in a mine in the form of a step or notch]

A report in a Tasmanian paper provided some more detail: "At Ballarat, February 20, 1885: A fatal mining accident occurred to-day at the Sulieman Pasha claim, by which a man named Henry Bourne, aged 50 years [he was 41], was killed. He was working in a stope at the 450-feet level, when a large piece of reef gave way, and striking him on the head and shoulders killed him. Bourne, who leaves a wife and five children, had only been working in the claim for three weeks. An inquest will be held tomorrow." (*Mercury* (Hobart), 23 February 1885) [Note: I have recorded six children, and no deaths to 1885, but the newspaper reports consistently say five children, and I have left it as stated.]

On Saturday 21 February, the Funeral Notice was posted in *The Ballarat Star* by the Ballarat Miners' Association: "The funeral procession will move from his late residence, 42 Sebastopol street, To-morrow (Sunday), at half past 3 o'clock."

The jury in the inquest, which was held on Saturday, returned a verdict that death was the result of an accident, but there was no evidence to show how the large piece of reef had fallen upon the deceased. Mister Stewart, the Inspector of Mines, said the underground workings were all in good order, and in accordance with mining regulations. (*Ballarat Star*, 23 February 1885 and *The Age*, 23 February 1885)

However, the incident was soon given an air of mystery and suspicion. On Thursday 26 February, the *Geelong Advertiser* reported that the Inspector of Mines at Ballarat had provided a report on the incident, in which he said that a "*post-mortem* examination of the corpse showed that several ribs were broken, and that the spine was also fractured, as if by a blow from a pointed instrument." The fall of the large piece of slate "might account for the broken ribs, but the injury to the back completely puzzled the medical men". Later, the suggestion was made that the injury to the spine was consistent with a blow from an instrument like a pick.

In the meantime, an appeal was started to assist Mrs Bourne and family. It commenced with a letter to the *Ballarat Star*. The letter said that Mrs Bourne "is left with five little children. The eldest is but 11 years of age, and she herself is in a critical state; and as she stated to us, she had but one shilling in the house when her husband was brought home to be buried." The paper agreed to be the recipient of donations.

The *Ballarat Star* followed up on 3 March with a longer report, addressing the "various rumours in circulation through the press touching the death of the unfortunate miner Henry Bourne." An acquaintance of the mining manager, Mr John Watson, asserted that he had been a mining manager for over fifteen years and "there is not a more careful or trustworthy manager in the district, nor one more worthy of the respect of all classes."

Mr Watson was "deeply pained that a rumour of foul play should have arisen in connection with the case, and the workmen in this mine are also grieved at the unfounded report.... as they were all working together in the most friendly manner with no cause of ill-feeling among them."

Mr Watson's explanation of the accident was that Bourne, when the reef began falling, threw himself with great force in between two props standing close by, and a sharp piece of the reef entered his back, causing the internal injuries.

On 3 March, *The Age* reported that the Mining Department had decided "to have a strict inquiry into the mysterious circumstances attending the death of a miner named Henry Bourne." It was a puzzle that Bourne had been found on top of the earth rather than underneath it. The police were also inquiring into the matter.

On 5 March, the *Mount Alexander Mail* reported that Police Sergeant Hall had completed his enquiries. He had descended the mine and visited the scene of the accident, "but has come to the conclusion that there is nothing whatever to support the belief that foul play took place; and in fact, it is ridiculous to suppose that such did take place." He concluded that it was not the falling slate that killed Bourne, but upon hearing it, he "made a rush towards the legs of the cap-piece, and injured himself in falling among the projecting quartz and slate."

Among the different newspapers, the above reports circulated in overlapping ways. Some reports simply drew from an earlier report in another paper. Accordingly, the impression that a person got of this episode would have depended on which town they lived in, and whether they missed any of the reports. No more reports appear on the matter in 1885 in the Trove newspaper database.

The mining inspector's report is succeeded by the conclusions of Sergeant Hall. At no stage was anyone accused of wielding an alleged pick. There were other men working in proximity, and it seemed well established that one worker, Richard Reardon, had spoken to Bourne a few minutes beforehand when he came to get a drink of water, and it was when he went to check on him again that he found him dead.

Nevertheless, the questions floating around must have added to Ellen Bourne's distress. On 12 March the *Ballarat Star* reported that the South Street Debating Society was organising a concert on 23 March in aid of the Bourne family, to take place in All Saints' schoolroom in Drummond Street. Tickets were already issued. Subsequently the society made a donation to Mrs Bourne of twenty-five pounds, ten shillings.

The Ballarat Miners' Association also made a payment to Mrs Bourne out of its Fatal Accident Levy: nine pounds, eleven shillings, three pence.

This turned out to be a long story. I could have just said, "Ellen Bourne's husband was killed in a mining accident in Ballarat." But the Ellen that Thomas married was the Ellen who had been through all of this drama – not only the death, but the mystery of exactly how he died, and the rumours that he may have been killed deliberately. I don't believe that foul play was committed. Real life is weird and frequently puzzling. But I do understand the doctors and the mining inspector being flummoxed by the circumstances.

In following the story, we also got to see how straitened some people's circumstances were, living week to week (and without credit), and how people's sense of charity was immediate and personal, demonstrated through the debating society's rapid organisation of a successful concert in aid of Ellen.

It was six years later that Thomas and Ellen married. Frances died in March 1890 in South Melbourne. When Thomas and Ellen got married, it was in Ballarat. From the marriage certificate, it is evident that Thomas had moved to Ballarat. The wedding was held "at the bridegroom's residence" in Dana Street. The marriage was conducted according to the rites of the "Ballarat United Town Mission" by Martin Hosking. It was 24 December 1891, the day before Christmas.

Did Thomas forget his first wife? I think not. In March 1891 he had inserted an In Memoriam in *The Age* in Melbourne. It said, "In sad and loving remembrance of my dear wife, who departed this life the 21st day of March, 1890. No last farewell, no lingering look, To treasure up alway; But like a weary child in sleep, Her spirit passed away."

There can be sorrow, even as one embraces the new that comes. One can be cynical about such gestures, focusing on the external effect (what other people think) rather than a person's internal state, but I believe it is more fitting to treat the gesture at face value. I think Thomas was putting her to rest; this was the woman he had migrated to Australia with, as two young adults setting out to face the unknown – excited, hopeful.

How did Thomas get to Ballarat? He had been living in Melbourne, maybe for about fifteen years. One might have expected him to retire there. But then, he had children living in Ballarat, and they had families too. Among them was Thomas's youngest child, Alice Maud, who was twenty-one in 1891; she had got married in Ballarat in 1889. and they had their first child in 1890.

And perhaps Thomas did indeed like Ballarat and did not want to live in a big city! So, that leaves the question of how Thomas and Ellen might have met. You see, it starts to make sense that I told the long story about Henry Bourne's death. Ellen would have been known to many people because of that whole sad episode and its coverage in the newspapers, as well as the fact that it came up in the proceedings of many groups and associations.

Thomas also had the social networks of his children in Ballarat. And then there is the question of occupation. Yes, Henry Bourne had been a miner, but it was mainly Cornish people who were miners from birth. English people who ended up in mining had generally come from other occupations. So, what had been Henry Bourne's background? His marriage certificate for when he married Ellen Desnoy in Ballarat in 1873 states that he was a waggoner (or carrier), but his father had been a carpenter. Moreover, Ellen's father, over the course of his life, had been a carpenter as well as a painter.

Ellen's father was a witness to her marriage to Henry Bourne. In other words her father had also been an immigrant. And Henry married a girl whose father was a carpenter. Life often moves in small circles.

When Thomas Bulling married Ellen, later in life, he was marrying into the old brotherhood of woodworkers, not miners. For all that the miners looked after each other, they still worked in dark holes in the ground.

The Cornish had made peace with their mode of existence aeons ago, just as the mythical dwarves had, but the man-made hollows below the ground are still fearful. Perhaps this was what killed Henry Bourne – not the fall of stone itself, but his total panic in reaction to it, slamming himself against a jagged stone wall and piercing his spine. He had only been on the job three weeks, and it is not clear what work he had been doing before that.

Thomas was also marrying back into a busy family household: the oldest of Ellen's children was still only eighteen, and the youngest was only six. One can imagine that this was part of her attraction. He married because of this, not in spite of it. And one more child added to the throng: in 1893, Ellen bore a son, called Oswald Charles Claud. The 'Oswald' came from a child that Thomas and Frances had had in 1867, who had died. People do not forget. I think the naming of children is part of (or ought to be) the give-and-take of marriage.

Finally, Thomas Bulling died, on 2 April 1909, at the age of seventy-five. His death certificate says (correctly) he had been in the colony of Victoria for fifty-four years. He is buried in Melbourne Cemetery. He and Ellen must have had an agreement that they would each be buried with their first partner: Thomas is buried with Frances Maria, while Ellen, who died in 1923, is buried at Ballarat with Henry Bourne.

At Ellen's grave there are two stones bearing a family name: BOURNE and BULLING. To one who does not know the whole story, this would be inexplicable.

In April 1910, Frances Emily Mackie, the daughter of Thomas and Frances Bulling, who became Mrs Mackie and went to Sydney, published an In Memoriam in *The Age*. I imagine that it was considerably more inconvenient to do this from interstate in 1910 than it would be now. She acknowledged that she had now lost both her parents: "In loving memory of my dear father, Thomas Bulling, who died 2nd April 1909; also my dear mother, who died 21st March 1890."

Also in this issue of *The Age* is an item from Ellen and son Oswald, that gives us an insight into Thomas's last days:

> The weary months and weeks of pain,
> The troubled, sleepless nights are past;
> The ever-patient, worn-out frame
> Has gained eternal rest, at last.
> When alone, in my sorrow, the bitter tears flow,
> There stealeth a vision of the dead long ago:
> And unknown to the cruel world he stands by my side,
> And whispers those sweet words: Death cannot divide.

Thomas's last days had been hard. His death certificate records the cause of death as old age, and gangrene. Yet his death should not overshadow the stature of his life. It is a life that evokes admiration, even in our imperfect knowledge. Without lapsing into unwarranted veneration, one can feel that Thomas, Frances and the other ancestors here strove to be worthy.

Thomas and Frances did not seem to have any grand scheme other than to make a life for a family in a newly forming place, and they did not mind that it was far away from London. It is quite a conviction to leave everything familiar in your early twenties, not minding that you are cutting yourself off from family and the multitude of structures and possibilities that made up an urban life at that time in London. And they showed no wavering in this enterprise.

The label 'colonist' seems a little grand as well. I don't think they were setting out to build a new country. They were simply trying to make their own way, from a past in London they must have seen as an unseemly, filthy and desperate scramble. Their parents had been rural folk. But did they play a part in building a new country (leaving aside the conflicts with this country's original inhabitants)? Only in the sense that much of the whole consists of the aggregate of ordinary people like Thomas and Frances, along with their modest and decent aspirations.

Family tree chart for Thomas Bulling
(Birth dates shown, plus dates married (m.), plus number of children)

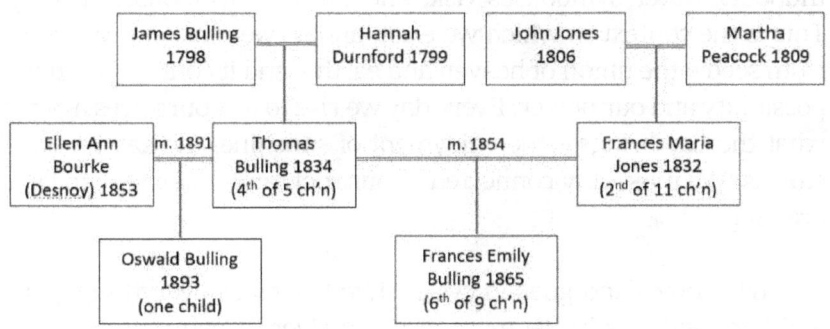

Afterword

All life arises amid difficulty and resistance. It is like water and thunder. Water symbolises risk, and thunder symbolises activity. This is the context in which we exist, and so we must act. We come from seed – the union of heaven and earth – and it contains both our possibility and our power. Every day we rise to test ourselves against what the day brings – the enjoyment of sunshine, the harshness of storms. We must stay connected to our root, and find a way to keep growing.

Life comes and goes in cycles. Life brings us everything, good and bad, and finally we must ford the river. When one cycle has reached an end, disorder will ensue. We have realised all the benefits of the cycle, and we must begin again to be reinvigorated. We must continue on to the farther shore.

END MATTER

Contents

Poem: Family history

Family tree chart – five generations

Profiles of direct ancestors: five generations

Other books by Glenn Martin

Family history (poem)

Beneath the silence, secrets,
things deemed too hard to say.
(Don't go out into the woods to play;
I can't tell you why, just obey.)

As children we could take this to be protection –
from danger, or sadness perhaps,
but we grew older and were never made wiser,
just at home with a false set of facts.

And the keepers of the secrets died,
carrying with them the comfort
that we were safe.
But I say we would have been better
in possession of the truth,
however grave.
There is something ground-worthy about truth,
you can stand on it,
as hard as it may be.
The first thing is having a place to stand
so I can learn how to stand up straight.

But again – soften, think –
this is how dark the woods were to them,
full of hungry souls and angry ghosts.
In dying they hoped to kill the secrets,
for us, to save us,
from danger, from sadness.

But I have dug up the bones
and cried all the tears that were necessary.
The monsters have departed.
It is okay. It is okay to go out and play.

(published in *Volume 4: I in the Stream*, 2017)

Family tree chart – five generations

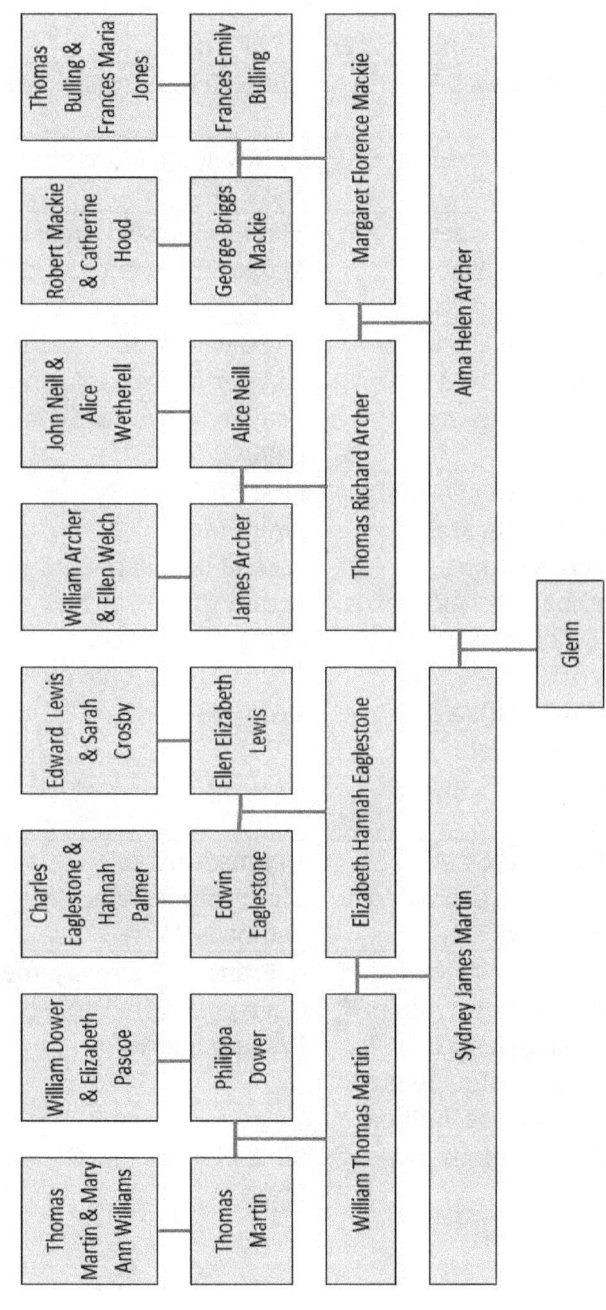

Profiles of direct ancestors: five generations

Section 1: Parents

In the tables, '(dec.)' means deceased as a child.

Names	Sydney James Martin (Sid)	Alma Helen Archer (Nell)
Born	5 Dec 1913, Banksia NSW	15 Nov 1923, Marrickville NSW
Parents	William Thomas Martin & Elizabeth Hannah Eaglestone	Thomas Richard Archer & Margaret Florence Mackie
Places lived	Lived with Uncle Paul and Aunt Maud from age seven. Sydney.	Lived with sister Frances and her husband Norm Gray from age 12. Sydney; Ballina.
Married	First wife: Olive Coates, 11 May 1935 at St Fiacre's (Roman Catholic) at Leichhardt. Olive died 5 Oct 1943. Second wife: Alma Helen (Nell), 4 July 1947 at St John's Church of England, Campsie.	First husband: Sydney James Martin Second husband: George Arthur Crowe, 21 May 1977 at Baptist Church, Greenacre. George died 2 Dec 1998.
Death	4 March 1967 at Greenacre. Cremated at Rookwood.	19 June 2017 at Cherrybrook. Ashes at Ballina NSW.
Siblings	6: Norman William, Albert (dec.), William Thomas, George Edwin, Thelma Ellen May, Frances Phillipa	5: Frances, Thomas James George, Pearl, Victor William, Jackie
Children	Sid & Olive: Jimmy, Patricia	Sid & Nell: Helen, Glenn, Brian

Section 2: Grandparents

Paternal grandparents

Names	William Thomas Martin	Elizabeth Hannah Eaglestone
Born	19 June 1883, Bethanga Vic.	4 June 1882, Balmain NSW
Parents	Thomas Martin & Philippa Dower	Edwin Eaglestone & Ellen Elizabeth Lewis
Places lived	Bethanga; Manager of Lady Rose goldmine at Chiltern Vic; moved to Sydney after 1900.	Balmain; Banksia; Callan Park Mental Asylum; Bloomfield Hospital, Orange
Married	22 July 1908, Methodist Church, St Peters NSW	
Death	16 Dec 1955, Annandale NSW. Buried at Woronora Cemetery.	1 Aug 1957, Orange. Cremated at Orange Cemetery.
Siblings	10: Mary Ann, Frances Matilda, Martha, Thomas, Elizabeth, Stella May, Norman, Paul, Olive Myrtle, Egbert Albert	Charles Edward (dec.), Sarah Ellen, Blanche Ellen
Children	8: Norman William, Albert (dec.), William Thomas, Sydney James, George Edwin, Thelma, Ellen May, Frances Phillipa	

Section 2: Grandparents

Maternal grandparents

Names	Thomas Richard Archer	Margaret Florence Mackie
Born	29 Nov 1886, Pyrmont NSW	18 Aug 1887, Richmond Vic
Parents	James Archer & Alice Neill	George Briggs Mackie & Frances Emily Bulling
Places lived	Pyrmont, Marrickville	Richmond Vic; moved to Sydney (Arncliffe) before 1910
Married	1 Oct 1910, St David's Church of England, Arncliffe	
Death	11 June 1936, Marrickville NSW. Buried at Woronora Cemetery.	20 March 1941, Leichhardt NSW. Buried at Woronora Cemetery.
Siblings	8: William John, James, twins (dec.), Frederick, Mary (dec.), Hellen, George Henry, Charles Victor Reign, Alice Lillian	8: Thomas Robert (dec.), Jessie, Frances May, George Herbert, William Percy, Florence Alice, Robert, Vera Lillian
Children	6: Alice Frances, Thomas James George, Florence Pearl, Victor William, Alma Helen, John Donald	

Section 3: Great grandparents, paternal (1)

Names	Thomas Martin	Philippa Dower
Born	13 May 1856, St Ives, Cornwall	30 Oct 1857, Kooringa, Burra SA
Parents	Thomas Martin & Mary Ann Williams	William Dower & Elizabeth Pascoe
Places lived	Migration to South Australia, 1857; to Bethanga ~1874; to Sydney ~1905	Burra SA; Broken Hill; Bethanga ~1874; to Sydney ~1905
Married	18 Jan 1879, Bethanga Vic	
Death	27 Dec 1945, Sutherland NSW. Buried at Woronora Cemetery	12 Jan 1931, Arncliffe NSW. Buried at Woronora Cemetery
Siblings	Martha Ann. Half-siblings (5): John William, Paul James, Eliza Jane Matilda, Mary Isabella, Theresa Elvira	10: John Donald, Matilda Pascoe, Elizabeth, Phillipa (dec.), Mary Ann Wiley, Thurza, William (dec.), Francis, William, Joseph, Frances Ann, James
Children	11: Mary Ann, Frances Matilda, William Thomas, Martha, Thomas, Elizabeth, Stella May, Norman, Paul, Olive Myrtle, Egbert Albert	

Section 4: Great grandparents, paternal (2)

Names	Edwin Eaglestone	Ellen Elizabeth Lewis
Born	19 Jan 1858, Bletchington, Oxfordshire	24 Oct 1857, Launceston, Tas.
Parents	Charles Eaglestone & Hannah Palmer	Edward Lloyd Lewis & Sarah Ann Crosby
Places lived	Migration to Auckland, 1860, then Melbourne. Lithgow ~1876; Sydney, 1878	To Sydney, 1859. Adelaide 1860-62. Sydney: Balmain, Penshurst
Married	30 Dec 1878, 'Friendville', Paddington (Presbyterian)	
Death	7 Jan 1916, Rockdale. Buried at Woronora Cemetery	6 Jun 1937, Penshurst NSW. Buried at Woronora Cemetery
Siblings	7: Elizabeth, Thomas, Mary Ann (dec.), Emmanuel (dec.), Albert, Frances Emma, Charles (dec.)	Mary Ann (half-sibling, dec.). 6: Mary Susannah, Sarah Ann, Edmond, Margaret, John Sydney (dec.), Emily (dec.)
Children	With Ellen: Charles Edward (dec.), Elizabeth Hannah, Sarah Ellen, Blanche Ellen	Edward George (father unknown; dec.).

Section 5: Great grandparents, maternal (1)

Names	James Archer	Alice Neill
Born	12 Jan 1857, Fullerton Cove (Hunter valley)	6 July 1862, Sydney
Parents	William Archer & Ellen Welch	John Neill & Alice Wetherell
Places lived	Hunter valley; Wilmington, Kent (~1871-1874); Sydney (Duke of Edinburgh Hotel, Pyrmont); Petersham	Surry Hills, Pyrmont, Petersham
Married	Alice Neill: 17 July 1880, St David's Church of England, Surry Hills. Margaret Storey: 15 Aug 1905, St Bartholomew's, Pyrmont	
Death	25 Aug 1917, Petersham. Buried at Waverley Cemetery	19 Oct 1903, Ultimo NSW. Buried at Waverley Cemetery
Siblings	7: William, Hannah, Edward, John, Ellen, George, Thomas	Mary (dec.), Richard, Hannah, William John
Children	With Alice (11): William John, James, twins (dec.), Thomas Richard, Frederick, Mary, Hellen, George Henry, Charles Victor Reign, Alice Lillian	

Section 6: Great grandparents, maternal (2)

Names	George Briggs Mackie	Frances Emily Bulling
Born	May 1863, Ballarat, Vic	15 March 1865, Ballarat West, Vic
Parents	Robert Mackie & Catherine Hood	Thomas Bulling & Frances Maria Jones
Places lived	Collingwood, Melbourne. Moved to Sydney in ~1892	Ballarat, Melbourne. Moved to Sydney in ~1892
Married	2 May 1882, Fitzroy Vic	
Death	5 April 1926, Arncliffe NSW. Buried at Woronora Cemetery	19 Oct 1934, Auburn NSW. Buried at Woronora Cemetery
Siblings	Margaret (half-sister), Alexander, James Hood, Robert, William (half-brother; dec.)	8: Hannah Frances (dec.), William Percy (dec.), Arthur John (dec.), Herbert James, Florence Clara Elizabeth, Tom Oswald (dec.), Emma Gertrude (dec.), Alice Maud
Children	9: Thomas Robert (dec.), Jessie, Margaret Florence, Frances May, George Herbert, William Percy, Florence Alice, Robert, Vera Lillian	

Section 7: Great great grandparents, paternal (1)

Names	Thomas Martins (later Martin)	Mary Ann Williams
Born	27 April 1834, Towednack, Cornwall	19 Oct 1832, St Ives, Cornwall
Parents	Paul Martins & Martha Chellew	Thomas Williams & Mary Ann Morcom
Places lived	Towednack, St Ives (Cornwall), Adelaide, Chapel Hill (Vic), Albury (NSW), Germonton (NSW), Bethanga (Vic), Chiltern (Vic)	St Ives (Cornwall), Adelaide, Chapel Hill (Vic)
Married	Mary Ann: 13 May 1854, St Ives, Cornwall. Jane Elvira McCartin: 4 April 1863, Beechworth Vic	
Death	28 April 1904, Chiltern Vic. Buried at New Cemetery, Chiltern Vic	8 May 1860, Chapel Hill Vic. Buried at Castlemaine Vic
Siblings	6: Paul, John, Matilda, Elizabeth, Jane, William	Elizabeth (dec.), Thomas Henry, John
Children	With Mary Ann: Thomas, Martha Ann. With Jane Elvira (5): John William, Paul James, Eliza Jane Matilda, Mary Isabella, Theresa Elvira	

Section 7: Great great grandparents, paternal (1)

Names	William Dower	Elizabeth Pascoe
Born	14 May 1825, Crowan, Cornwall	6 Sep 1826, Mullion, Cornwall
Parents	William Dower & Phillipa Walters	Francis Pascoe & Elizabeth Willey
Places lived	Crowan, Adelaide, Burra (SA), Thakarinka (Broken Hill), Bethanga	Mullion, Crowan, Adelaide, Burra, Bethanga
Emigration	On *Abberton* to Adelaide; arrived 3/8/1848	Emigrated as couple with one child (John Donald); Matilda born 4 weeks before arrival
Married	10 Feb 1846, Crowan, Cornwall	
Death	17 Sep 1907, Bethanga Vic. Buried at Bethanga (82)	1 Feb 1920, Bethanga Vic. Buried at Bethanga (94)
Siblings	9: William (dec.), Elizabeth Hannah, Joseph, Samuel William, Phillipa, James, Mary, Sampson, John	8: Francis, Thomas, Jane Carne, Matilda, Joseph Willey, William Henry, Ethelinda, John Willey
Children	14: John Donald, Matilda Pascoe, Elizabeth, Phillipa (dec.), Mary Ann Wiley, Thurza, Philippa, William (dec.), Francis, William, Joseph, Frances Ann, James (dec.), James (dec.)	

Section 8: Great great grandparents, paternal (2)

Names	Charles Eaglestone	Hannah Palmer
Born	3 Oct 1819 (baptism), Kirthlington, Oxfordshire	28 Feb 1830, Bletchington, Oxfordshire
Parents	Thomas Eaglestone & Mary Rogers	William Palmer & Elizabeth Smallbrook
Places lived	Oxfordshire, Auckland (NZ), Geelong Vic	Oxfordshire, Auckland (NZ), Geelong Vic
Married	To Elizabeth Eaglestone (cousin): 30 Oct 1847, Bletchington, Oxfordshire. She died 11 March 1851, Bletchington. No children. To Hannah: 23 June 1853, Oxford	
Death	4 Feb 1911, Geelong Vic. Buried at Geelong Cemetery	5 Feb 1890, Geelong Vic. Buried at Geelong Cemetery
Siblings	Martha, Joshua, Caroline	Elizabeth: 7: Edward (dec.), Caroline, Sarah (dec.), Sarah, Eliza, Edward (dec.), Lewis (dec.) Hannah: 9: George, Mary, Eliza, Ann, Maria, William, Charles, John, James
Children	8: Elizabeth, Thomas, Edwin, Mary Ann (dec.), Emmanuel (dec.), Albert, Frances Emma, Charles (dec.)	

Section 8: Great great grandparents, paternal (2)

Names	Edward Lloyd Lewis	Sarah Ann Crosby
Born	18 Oct 1829, Colchester, Essex	May 1833, County Waterford, Ireland
Parents	William Lloyd Lewis & Mary Everitt	Martin Crosby & Sarah Fitzgibbon
Places lived	Colchester, London, Hobart (convict), Point Puer (convict), Launceston, Sydney	Waterford, Bath, London, Hobart (convict), Launceston, Sydney, Adelaide (1860-1862), Sydney
Married	1 March 1853, Hobart Tas	
Death	Nov 1897? Sydney?	4 Sep 1897, Annandale NSW. Buried at Rookwood (Roman Catholic)
Siblings	6: William, Samuel, Sarah Mariah, George Henry, Louisa, Richard	James +?
Children	7: Sarah Ann, Mary Susannah, Edmond, Ellen Elizabeth, Margaret, John Sydney (dec.), Emily (dec.)	To unknown father: Mary Ann (dec.)

Section 9: Great great grandparents, maternal (1)

Names	William Archer	Ellen Welch
Born	12 March 1813, Harpenden, Hertfordshire	11 Oct 1822, Markinch, Fife, Scotland
Parents	Edward Archer & Mary Clifton	Alexander Welch & Helen Forbes
Places lived	Harpenden, Parish of Eldon (convict), Fullerton Cove, Wilmington (Kent) (~1871-1874), Sydney	Markinch, Glasgow, Fullerton Cove, Wilmington (Kent), Sydney
Married	15 July 1844, Parish of Eldon, Port Stephens NSW	
Death	4 Jan 1894, Pyrmont NSW. Buried at Waverley Cemetery	8 June 1912, Petersham NSW. Buried at Waverley Cemetery
Siblings	6: Elizabeth (dec.), Charlotte, Milly, Hannah, John, Frederick	Elspeth, George, Alexander, Margaret, Archibald
Children	8: William, Hannah, Edward, John, Ellen, James, George, Thomas	To unknown father: Thomas (left with St Mary's orphanage, Glasgow)

Section 9: Great great grandparents, maternal (1)

Names	John Neill (later Neil)	Alice Wetherell
Born	1825, Portadown, Co. Armagh, Ireland	23 Dec 1821, Birr, Co. Offaly, Ireland
Parents	Charles Neill & Mary Colter	Richard Wetherell & Mary Wilson
Places lived	Portadown, Sydney	Birr, Portadown, Sydney
Married	To Alice: 3 Sep 1848, Presbyterian Church, Portadown, Co. Armagh, Ireland. To Mary Ann Bonham: 13 Oct 1870, Sydney	
Death	18 Nov 1891, Paddington NSW. Buried at Waverley Cemetery	13 Jan 1867, Sydney NSW. Buried at Devonshire Street Cemetery, Presbyterian. (Grave moved 1901 to ?)
Siblings	None known	Richard
Children	To Alice: Mary (dec.), Richard, Hannah, Alice, William John. No children with Mary Ann.	

Section 10: Great great grandparents, maternal (2)

Names	Robert Mackie	Catherine Hood
Born	21 Oct 1832, Earlesferry, Fife, Scotland	24 Dec 1832, Lundin Mill, Fife
Parents	Alexander Mackie & Rachel Bridges	James McDonald Hood & Margaret Bell
Places lived	Earlesferry, Fife; Melbourne, Ballarat, Collingwood	Lundin Mill, Melbourne, Ballarat, Collingwood
Married	19 Jan 1856, Melbourne	To John Newsom: 28 Feb 1870, Fitzroy
Death	2 Nov 1863, Melbourne (mining accident). Buried at Melbourne General Cemetery	13 Nov 1900, Collingwood Vic. Buried at Melbourne General Cemetery
Siblings	George (dec.), Janet Jessie, David (dec.), George, Elizabeth, Annie	Thomas, Elizabeth, David, Ann Adamson, James, John (dec.), Christine Bell, Margaret
Children	Robert & Catherine: Alexander, James Hood, Robert, George Briggs	Margaret (at 21; father unknown). William (father unknown, after Robert died; dec.)

Section 10: Great great grandparents, maternal (2)

Names	Thomas Bulling	Frances Maria Jones
Born	1834, Battersea, Surrey	22 Jan 1832, Rickmansworth, Hertfordshire
Parents	James Bulling & Hannah Durnford	John Jones & Martha Peacock
Places lived	Battersea, London, Geelong, Ballarat, Fitzroy Vic	Rickmansworth, London, Geelong, Ballarat, Fitzroy Vic
Married	To Frances: 3 Sep 1854, St Pancras, London. To Ellen Ann Desnoy: 1891, Ballarat Vic	
Death	2 April 1909, Fitzroy Vic	21 March 1890, Melbourne
Siblings	James Frederick, John, Emma, William	10: Martha, John Frederick, William, Robert, George, Clara, Thomas, Ann, Henry, Emily
Children	With Frances (9): Hannah Frances, William Percy, Arthur John, Herbert James, Florence Clara Elizabeth, Frances Emily, Tom Oswald, Emma Gertrude, Alice Maud. With Ellen: Oswald Charles Claude	

Other books by Glenn Martin

Stories/Reflections on experience
The Ten Thousand Things (2010)
Sustenance (2011)
To the Bush and Back to Business (2012)
The Big Story Falls Apart (2014)
The Quilt Approach: A Tasmanian Patchwork (2020)

Books on ethics and life
Human Values and Ethics in the Workplace (2010)
The Little Book of Ethics: A Human Values Approach (2011)
The Concise Book of Ethics (2012)
A Foundation for Living Ethically (2020)
Future: The Spiritual Story of Humanity (2020)

Books on family history
A Modest Quest (2017)
The Search for Edward Lewis (2018)
They Went to Australia (2019)
No Gold in Melbourne: A Scottish Family in Australia (2021)

Poetry collections
Flames in the Open (2007)
Love and Armour (2007)
Volume 4: I in the Stream (2017)
Volume 3: That Was Then: The Early Poems Project (2019)
The Way Is Open (2020)

Local histories
Places in the Bush: A History of Kyogle Shire (1988)
The Kyogle Public School Centenary Book (1995)

Quotations
Hua-Ching Ni, *I Ching: The Book of Changes and the Unchanging Truth*, Seven Star Communications, Santa Monica CA, 1994, p. 427.
Strenger, Carlo, *The Fear of Insignificance*, Palgrave, 2011, p. 2.